SMART FINANCIAL MANAGEMENT

SMART
FINANCIAL
MANAGEMENT

The Essential Reference for
the Successful Small Business

WILLIAM W. SIHLER

Ronald E. Trzcinski Professor of Business Administration
Darden Graduate School of Business Administration
University of Virginia

RICHARD D. CRAWFORD

Visiting Lecturer
Darden Graduate School of Business Administration
University of Virginia

HENRY A. DAVIS

Henry A. Davis Associates

ᴀMACOM

AMERICAN MANAGEMENT ASSOCIATION

New York | Atlanta | Brussels | Buenos Aires | Chicago
Mexico City | San Francisco | Shanghai | Tokyo
Toronto | Washington D.C.

This publication is designed to provide accurate and authoritative information in regard to the subject matter covered. It is sold with the understanding that the publisher is not engaged in rendering legal, accounting, or other professional service. If legal advice or other expert assistance is required, the services of a competent professional person should be sought.

Library of Congress Cataloging-in-Publication Data

Sihler, William W.

    Smart financial management : the essential reference for the successful small business / William W. Sihler, Richard D. Crawford, and Henry A. Davis.

    p. cm.

    Includes index.

    ISBN 0-8144-0789-7

1. Small business—Finance I. Crawford, Richard II. Davis, Henry A. III. Title.

    HG4027.7.S5 2004

    658.15—dc22   2004006537

Printing number

10 9 8 7 6 5 4 3 2 1

Contents

Contents
vi

PREFACE

Smart *Financial Management* is designed to help the chief executive of a smaller enterprise, and particularly of a rapidly growing business, ensure that the company's financial management is in harmony with the company's strategy. It will also help ensure the reverse, that the company's strategy is feasible given the company's financial environment and situation.

To achieve these goals, we bring together the essentials of financial management and the basics of the legal framework within which your company's finances must be arranged. The book is not intended, however, to substitute for legal counsel or to turn the chief executive into a chief financial officer or controller. It will help you deal intelligently and effectively with these specialists and others, such as commercial bankers. Because specialists focus on their own narrow areas, it is important that you be able to put their insights into a broader business context.

Smart Financial Management addresses the three major concerns of the small business owner:

1. Not running out of money
2. Wisely allocating the firm's financial resources
3. Exiting from the business with the value created

The first two topics are common to all businesses but are of particular concern to the entrepreneur because of the small business's limited access to funds. The third is a special concern to the owner of a closely held company.

The book's structure is straightforward. Part I first provides a framework for thinking about a company's financial condition and policy and, second, a similar framework for considering the company's legal structure.

Because of the importance of cash management, Part II begins with a chapter on ratio analysis (with the use of ratios in assessing performance) and a chapter on forecasting and cash management. Individual chapters then deal with a business's three major assets: accounts receivable, inventory, and capital equipment investment (including valuation).

Part III turns to the right-hand side of the balance sheet, beginning with a chapter on the conceptual approach to the debt-equity decision. The following two chapters discuss the nonequity and equity financing alternatives available to the enterprise.

Finally, Part IV reviews the ways of exiting a business under both favorable and unfavorable conditions. Part V summarizes the principles presented throughout the book.

Because it is impossible to cover all topics in full detail, we have included a list of further readings suggestions at the end of the book.

Many of these chapters were developed from material prepared for use in the financial-management courses of the M.B.A. program at the Darden Graduate Business School, University of Virginia. Although they were extensively revised and rewritten for the entrepreneur and small business owner, the support given by the Darden School Foundation and its permission to use this material is gratefully acknowledged. Support was also provided by the Batten Institute for Leadership at The Darden School. Professor Laurence C. Pettit, Jr., of the McIntire School of Commerce at the University of Virginia, provided thoughtful insights on the corporate life cycle and its relationship to financial management. C. Ray Smith, Tipton R. Snavely Professor of Business Administration, Emeritus, was helpful in preparing the chapter on ratios. Material on legal issues was drawn from a variety of sources, but special thanks is due Professor Ronald J. Gilson, Stanford University Law School, who shared material from his course, "The Economic Structure of Venture Capital Contracting." Charles O. Meiburg, J. Harvey Wilkinson, Jr., Professor of Business Administration, Emeritus, provided insights on nonequity financial sources. John May, Batten Fellow at The Darden School, made useful contributions to the chapter on equity sources. The bankruptcy material was developed with the assistance of David A. Harrison while he was a student in the Darden M.B.A. Program, Paul H. Hunn, Visiting Lecturer at The Darden School and formerly Senior Vice President at Manufacturers Hanover Bank, Andrew DeNatale, Esq., of Stroock & Stroock & Lavan, and J. C. McCoid, II, O.M. Vickers Professor of Law, Emeritus, University of Virginia Law School. Frank Genovese offered suggestions for the section on exiting successful businesses. The authors are delighted to thank these individuals for their help but remain responsible for any errors and omissions that may remain despite the helpful efforts of the editors at AMACOM, whose support was most valuable.

PART I
OVERVIEW

CHAPTER 1

BASIC FRAMEWORKS FOR FINANCIAL MANAGEMENT

Acompany's financial management is an integral part of its business strategy and not a separate set of decisions made without regard to the company's other characteristics. Marketing and production strategies, allied with the company's location on the growth curve, will largely determine suitable financial policies. If you recognize these relationships, then managing your company's financial requirements will be much simpler and more effective. You'll make better decisions about investments in assets and better decisions about financing those assets.

Although analytical frameworks for finance can be complex and elaborate, a few simple techniques provide most of the significant insights and relate a company's operating situation to its financial policy. The techniques can usually be applied without the use of anything more complicated than a four-function calculator. This chapter describes these four basic frameworks and how you can use them most productively.

The first topic is the effect of a company's life cycle on its financial management. A brief set of ratios will provide quick insight into your company's performance. Then, an approach to analyzing your company's financial structure will be outlined. Finally, a way of estimating your company's economic worth will be sketched.

Examining the Life Cycle of a Company

Companies, like living organisms, have life cycles, although they are not as actuarially predictable. Companies of all sizes experience the same life-cycle patterns, but all firms are not in the same stage for the same length of time. The main phases are (1) startup, (2) initial growth, (3) rapid growth, (4) maturity, and (5) decline (see Exhibit 1-1). Each of these stages challenges a firm with significantly different financial requirements.

❯ **SMART FINANCIAL MANAGEMENT: Your first step in analyzing your company is to figure out what the sales' long-run, secular trend has been, and what it might be in the future. Are the sales volatile? How are**

EXHIBIT 1-1

Company Life Cycle

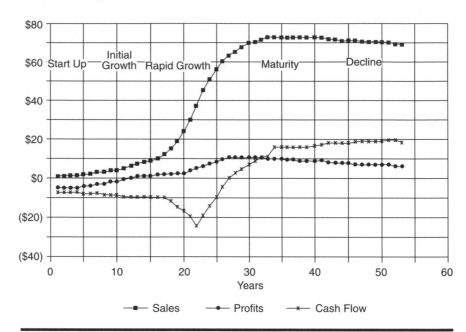

they affected by the business cycle? By commodity prices? Because sales
volume is the locomotive that pulls along the rest of the business, understanding sales characteristics is central to understanding your firm's situation. It is also central to forecasting the company's future performance.

The descriptions that follow are generalized—a company may simultaneously have products that are growing rapidly, are mature, and are in
decline. Companies may skip phases or pass through them very rapidly.
Nevertheless, the concepts have use as general analytical frameworks.

PHASE 1: STARTUP

During this initial stage of a venture's life, the firm is often little more than
an idea. Sources of funding are few, but much expenditure is typically
required to prove your idea, develop your plans, and get the resources
needed to begin operations. You probably provide the funding for your
idea during this phase, along with others you can persuade to provide
equity funds.

PHASE 2: INITIAL GROWTH

This phase occurs after your enterprise has begun to deliver its product or
service. Losses characterize this period of a company's life, often because
the initial sales volume does not generate sufficient profits to cover the
overhead and fixed costs of initial operations. During this phase, the com-

pany absorbs funds to cover the money it is losing and to build the assets necessary to meet the growing demand of its customers.

▶ **WATCH THIS: This is a difficult phase in a company's life cycle. Your enterprise needs funds to show it can survive, but until you show it can survive, you will have a difficult time getting financing. Funds are still provided by equity or near-equity financing in this stage, so they must be allocated with care to the assets most important to the company's survival and growth. Unnecessary investment can seriously damage the firm's chance to survive.**

As the owner of an initial-growth company, you may decide to subcontract the low value-added portions of the business, foregoing some profit to avoid committing assets to plant and equipment. The subcontractors also may help finance the venture by granting generous terms on accounts payable, more generous financing than a bank would be able to provide. You also should avoid excessive investments in raw materials—a firm can easily fail by investing so much of its funds in raw material that it does not have the resources to complete the conversion to saleable merchandise.

Once demand for your product or service has been established, life becomes much easier in many respects. If demand then stabilizes at a profitable level without continuing growth, the company enters a mature phase of its business without going through the rapid-growth phase. The reliance on new financing is reduced—or even eliminated.

PHASE 3: RAPID GROWTH

A period of rapid growth can be challenging, but it is still easier than the initial growth phase. In addition, it is potentially more rewarding for you and any other founders. The company becomes profitable, marginally at first and then handsomely. Demand, however, grows more rapidly than internally generated sources (including sources spontaneously provided by accounts payable and accruals) can support.

▶ **SMART FINANCIAL MANAGEMENT: During this phase, you must plan periodic forays into the financial markets. To raise long-term capital in sufficient amounts, you'll often have to obtain more short-term *bridge financing* than needed only for seasonal short-term needs.**

If growth is expected to be higher than the *sustainable growth rate* (SGR) (discussed later in this chapter and in Chapter 3), financing should be planned as a sequence, so a complete picture of risks and rewards can be created and assessed. A *fund-needs profile* should be forecast, and a plan developed to finance these needs. A fund-needs profile is simply a balance-sheet projection, allowing for all existing financial sources, that shows a balancing "plug figure" on the right-hand side representing an additional need for funds.

PHASE 4: MATURITY

Trees do not grow to the sky, however, and the period of rapid growth will end when the consumers' demands have been fulfilled and the market enters its mature phase. With services and disposable products, the company's sales may stabilize at a high level—subject, of course, to your competitors' inevitable introduction of alternatives and substitutes. When the market for a durable item becomes mature, the demand may fall dramatically to a replacement level. This situation can be very dangerous, particularly if you are caught with finished goods that might become obsolete before they can be sold. Many events in the audio, video, and computer businesses provide clear illustrations of this danger.

In an ideal situation, the mature phase allows you to enjoy the fruits of your innovation. Profit margins will have been eroded by competition but will remain satisfactory. Cash flows will be positive and strong because funds are not required for new assets to support growth. Without inflation, the accounting allocations for depreciation may even exceed the new investment in plant and equipment. Without growth, the firm will have the cash to increase the proportion of earnings paid its owners as dividends or other compensation. Debt may also be repaid, which can unbalance the capital structure unless common stock is bought back. Alternatively, remember that a high proportion of earnings must be paid as dividends.

> WARNING: The temptation at this phase is to use the spare cash from one business to enter another. This is a dangerous route, however. The new business may be one you do not fully understand, it may not be as similar to the original business as you thought it was, and your skills from the original business may not transfer easily to the new business. If problems arise in the new business, it will divert your attention from the existing business, which can then easily go awry. Furthermore, having been successful in the first business, you may be reluctant to admit the skill transfer is not successful. As a result, you may take too long to decide to get out of the venture.

PHASE 5: DECLINE

The decline phase is a difficult one for you, your company, and your external sources of capital. Profit margins gradually degenerate and ultimately turn into losses. Adverse developments—which could be absorbed by a company in its growth or mature phases—become life-threatening events.

During the initial stages of decline, the firm is often generating greater funds than needed to support assets. These funds find their way out of the firm as distributions to the owners or as reductions of debt.

As the losses become more serious, however, the company can no longer generate sufficient internal funds. You'll turn to the capital markets, often to the commercial banks, for funds to tide the situation over until the problems can be corrected. This approach is particularly likely if there has been a sudden event—loss of a major customer or a strike—that has created the need for funds. The problem appears a temporary one rather than a symptom of a long-run decline. "Just help us over this hurdle," you'll plead, "and the company's health will be restored. After all these years, you owe it to us to help. Think of the effect on the community if the company fails."

> **IMPORTANT: The skill of getting out gracefully is an important characteristic for the management of a declining company. This is a rare talent, often one that the growth-company or mature-company managers do not have. The company's operations must be reduced, assets with more value to others must be sold, and the remainder may have to be shut down.**

As this brief exposition demonstrates, by identifying the phase in which your company is operating, you gain insight into the way the company's assets are likely to develop, into your company's financial needs, and into appropriate ways to fund them.

Understanding Critical Financial Ratios

In the early 1900s, the management of the DuPont company, which was running the first conglomerate, developed the most famous and useful financial ratios. Not only did management have to rethink the way the organization was structured, but it also had to find a way to measure the performance of businesses with a variety of operating characteristics. For example, some divisions had a large amount of fixed assets, others had few.

> **SMART FINANCIAL MANAGEMENT: DuPont's solution was to create a set of numerical tools that provide quick insight into a company's financial characteristics and performance, once the basic sales situation and life-cycle phase have been identified. The core set of ratios was designed to measure the central functions of the business—marketing, operations, and finance—as well as its general performance.**

Because of their use as a basic financial framework, the summary DuPont ratios will be briefly introduced here. In using these ratios to judge performance, however, it is critical to make the comparison with companies in similar businesses.

DUPONT RATIOS

1. Operating Efficiency: *Sales ÷ Assets*

The volume of sales a dollar of assets can generate shows the asset intensity of a business. An electric power company may generate only 20 cents of sales per dollar of assets. A retail chain may generate several dollars in sales for each dollar of assets. The more sales per dollar of assets, the more efficiently the business is being run.

2. Marketing Efficiency: *Profits ÷ Sales*

The profit margin suggests how well the marketing function can position the product and deliver it to the consumer. The ratio is also indicative of the intensity of competition, as greater competition pushes prices down and lowers the profit-to-sales ratio.

3. Return on Assets: *Profits ÷ Assets*

This ratio shows the efficiency with which assets are being used. It is the product of the first two ratios: the sales component cancels, leaving profit and assets. The relationship shows why the first two ratios are usually inversely related. To generate sufficient profitability to attract capital, a business with a low profit margin must do a high sales volume on the capital invested. A business with a low volume of sales on assets must have high profits on the sales it does make. A high profit on assets, however, attracts competition and new entrants; a low profit on assets drives out marginal players. The profit margins of an asset-intensive business are protected, to a degree, by the high cost of entry. The asset-light business has no such protection. Its margins will erode quickly without assets such as protected intellectual property.

> **WATCH THIS: You should carefully consider the characteristics of your firm's business to make sure these relationships are understood. Attempting to position your business against what the ratios suggest is the way that industry works can present serious problems.**

These first three ratios provide insight into marketing and production, but not into the financial dimension. Less risky businesses should operate with less equity; businesses with higher risks usually require more equity. A key financial task is to balance the debt and equity of the capital structure to provide a return to the equity investor that is suitable for the risk involved. If the returns are too low, investors will withhold or withdraw funds. The wise entrepreneur knows when it is efficient to redeploy assets. The gross measure of financial structure is the next ratio.

4. Financial Efficiency: *Assets ÷ Equity*

This ratio (also called *financial leverage*) measures the quantity of assets a dollar of equity can command. In a safe business, such as banking, a dollar of equity can support 12 dollars of assets. In a highly risky business in a startup phase, equity might command less than two dollars of assets.

The return on equity (ROE) is the product of Ratios 3 and 4, return on assets and financial efficiency. When Ratios 3 and 4 are multiplied, the asset term drops out, leaving the return on equity.

5. Return on Equity: *Profits ÷ Equity*

This ratio measures equity's efficiency. The ROE is arguably a better measure of capital attraction than the return on assets, assuming a capital structure that enhances value rather than destroying it with excessive risk. ROE can show the positive effect of appropriate leverage. Return on assets may appear low when debt can be efficiently used in comparison with cases when a high proportion of equity is required.

Analysts expect much less variation in the ROE than in other components of the DuPont ratios. The ROE ratio, therefore, can be used to make comparisons across types of companies because the special characteristics of each type should be "washed out" of the ratio analysis. If the ROE is low, you should contract the business or perhaps sell it to someone who can better use its assets. This extracts your capital so it can be redeployed in higher ROE investments.

MAKING A RATIO ANALYSIS

The five basic DuPont ratios can be elaborated depending on the analytical depth required. Ratios 1, 2, and 4 have many components, such as the turnover of accounts receivable and inventories, the ratios of cost of goods sold and other components of the income statement to sales, the days of purchases outstanding, and the long-term debt-to-equity ratios. A review of the initial set of five ratios, however, and of *their trends over time,* will identify those ratios for which further analysis is likely to be a productive activity.

Two major problems in ratio analysis are the variations in accounting among companies and between the income statement and the balance sheet for a given firm. The use of last-in–first-out (LIFO) inventory accounting, for instance, creates serious distortions in all ratios for which the inventory is a component. Although this technique helps provide more realistic income statements in inflationary times, it creates an unrealistically low inventory figure. The asset efficiency of a steel company may therefore look as good as that of a grocery chain, because the steel company has been on LIFO since 1956 and carries its inventory at a fraction of current cost. The return on assets figure is also distorted. These distortions are reduced, however, when calculating the return on equity because the asset component of the fraction cancels.

CALCULATING SUSTAINABLE GROWTH RATE

The SGR has again become a popular analytical tool because it shows the sales growth rate that can be sustained without recourse to external equity. Internally generated funds include retained earnings supported by spontaneously created liabilities, such as accounts payable and short-term debt, and by the target proportion of long-term debt, an external source.

A precise computation of the SGR is complex, but a reasonable approximation can quickly be derived by calculating the rate of increase in the equity account from newly retained earnings, that is, earnings retained in a year divided by total equity at the beginning of the year. If the DuPont ratios have been calculated, this ratio is the ROE (Ratio 5) multiplied by the proportion of the earnings *not* being paid out as dividends. For many smaller enterprises, which do not pay dividends, the SGR is the same as the ROE.

6. Sustainable Rate of Growth:

Return on Equity = (Profits – Dividends) ÷ Profits

This ratio, like any other calculation of the sustainable growth rate, must be carefully interpreted to allow for volatile returns. Another complication occurs when a company decides to use excess debt capacity or has too much debt and wishes to reduce it. In the first instance, the SGR is temporarily higher than the calculation would indicate. For the moment, debt can be added in greater than the optimal proportion as provided by Ratio 4. In the second instance, growth is temporarily hampered because internally generated funds must be devoted to reducing the company's debt rather than to investing in new assets. In this case, new equity may be needed to lessen the problem.

The logic behind Ratio 6 as an estimate of the SGR relies on the relatively stable relationships in Ratios 1, 2, and 4 that exist for most businesses. Given a stable relationship between assets and equity (and without spare or excess debt), assets can grow no faster than equity.

In a mature or declining business, sales often grow at a slower rate than equity. This condition permits retirement of debt, payment of higher dividends, and perhaps repurchase of shares to keep the proper relationship between debt and equity.

> **WATCH THIS: A greater challenge occurs when sales are growing faster than equity. Because management, and particularly owners of smaller**

enterprises, avoid issuing equity, the leverage ratio (Ratio 4, asset to equity) is allowed to move upward. The locomotive of sales pulls the train of assets along faster than the equity and proportional debt can provide the sources needed to fuel the speed of expansion. To keep the train from slowing, debt is added to the fuel mix in a higher proportion than the target. The solution can only be temporary. If it continues, the capital markets will shortly force the company to raise new external equity. For a smaller enterprise, this occurs when the bank or the trade refuses to provide additional credit until the company adds more equity.

Identifying Your Capital Position

In reviewing your company's strategic and financial situation, it is useful to identify the "capital position" in which the company is operating. This is particularly useful when preparing sensitivity analyses that will identify the conditions that might move the company from one position to the next. The four positions or states are:

1. Paying net debt
2. Maintaining the existing dollar amount of debt
3. Increasing the dollar amount of debt, but not the leverage ratio
4. Increasing the leverage ratio

CAPITAL POSITION #1

Net repayment of debt, as already noted, is characteristic of a mature or declining company. Such a company no longer needs resources to support growth and does not yet need them to stave off decline. This company is not a very good customer for loans from a financial institution. It may be a customer of the bank's money-market desk or syndication department as management looks for assets in which to invest the company's liquidity. This is often a safe company for a financial institution to have as a customer as long as it is careful to avoid being drawn into financing a company in an irreversible downward spiral to costly liquidation.

CAPITAL POSITION #2

It is rare for a company to *maintain a level amount of debt;* debt tends to decline or increase. Nevertheless, this state is a "corner point" that a company may turn during its life cycle. This position implies that the company's cash flows are in balance. The firm does not need additional long-term capital, but it is not yet able to start repaying it.

Such a company is an enviable customer for a financial institution because it requires funds yet should be lowering its risk level with additions to retained earnings. The leverage ratios should be declining. You may even consider increasing its dividend payout to slow the decline in the ratio. Furthermore, if the funding institution needs to reduce the relationship to rebalance its own portfolio, other institutions are likely to find dealing with the customer an attractive opportunity. A company with this characteristic can probably strike a very good deal with its lenders.

CAPITAL POSITION #3

The third stage, *increasing debt but declining debt ratios,* is characteristic of a company in the late stages of its growth phase or perhaps in the early part of its maturity. The firm still requires additional outside financing but is not exceeding its sustainable rate of growth. The financial markets are still called on for additional long-term debt, and profits are retained in the company to support these requirements. The financial risk is declining as the proportion of debt declines despite its increase in dollar amount. Possibly the nature of the company's operating risks is also declining as the enterprise attains its natural maturity. Additional financial institutions would probably be willing to help provide funding if an existing source believed it was getting overexposed to one customer.

A firm of this type will typically show a saw-tooth pattern of short-term debt. Short-term debt will gradually increase until it has become large enough to be refunded efficiently with a mortgage or a private placement of long-term debt, probably with an insurance company. At that point, the short-term debt will suddenly drop.

CAPITAL POSITION #4

A company requiring *additional debt that increases its debt ratios* is either in a strong growth stage or is in a very serious decline. Companies in either of these conditions are challenges for a financial institution because the firm must go to the external equity market to set the ratios right. Other institutions may not be enthusiastic about helping the existing funding sources reduce their position. Even equity investors prefer putting money into new assets rather than toward debt reduction. These preferences require careful planning of a fund-raising sequence for the growing firm. The options for a declining firm are less attractive—sell assets to repay debt.

❯ SMART FINANCIAL MANAGEMENT: Knowing where your company is with respect to its capital requirements is important in dealing with external financial sources. Should you plan for additional debt or plan to repay existing debt? Should you curtail expansion to a level that external sources can support? If you have thought through these issues, you'll find it much easier to deal effectively with the bank or, if necessary, with sources of additional equity.

Analyzing Long-Term Capital Structure

The preceding discussion has occasionally referred to an ideal, or appropriate, capital structure. Building a capital structure that adds value to your company's operating performance is challenging because of the large number of judgments that must be made based on intangible evidence. On the one hand, noted economists have proved conceptually that in a perfect capital market, in which the effect of taxes is uniform, the capital structure does not contribute to value. As debt is added, levering up the return to the equity, the additional risk pushes down the equity valuation. This leaves the firm's total value unchanged. However, when different capital sources are taxed differently, the formulation specifies a capital structure with as much of the tax-advantaged, low-cost capital as possible.

The capital markets are seldom perfect, at least in the short term, and a variety of frictions (such as taxes and bankruptcy regulations) spread costs unevenly among the capital sources. Therefore, theories generally agree an appropriate capital structure can add value and an inappropriate one can destroy it. In analyzing an appropriate capital structure, the following six dimensions (known as FRICTO) can be considered: **F**lexibility, **R**isk, **I**ncome, **C**ontrol, **T**iming, and **O**ther. Thanks to the "other" category, the FRICTO components are mutually exclusive and collectively exhaustive.

Note: This discussion takes the perspective of the equity investor, such as you and whoever else has invested in your company. Without an equity foundation, no enterprise will get started. Chapter 8, "Basic Capital Structure Decisions," will provide a more thorough discussion of capital structure. This brief discussion provides a conceptual overview.

INCOME

The income factor is usually an investor's first consideration. If a company can borrow at an interest rate lower than its before-tax return on assets, the difference between the earnings on the assets financed with debt and the cost of the debt goes to the equity owners. The ROE goes up. This positive effect is magnified when interest has a more favorable tax treatment than earnings for the equity holders.

Other factors must also be considered. As an early Baron Rothschild reportedly asked when a person with a recent inheritance sought investment advice, "Do you want to eat well or sleep well?" A high degree of leverage is an eat-well strategy.

> **RISK VERSUS FLEXIBILITY: Sleeping well, or even reasonably soundly, requires consideration of the closely related Risk and Flexibility factors. Risk events for some companies may be flexibility problems for others. In**

this discussion, risk problems are those recurring events whose nature can be predicted but whose occurrence is uncertain. Business cycles are the most common type of risk event. They occur at erratic intervals, but their nature is sufficiently well known so their effects can be anticipated and dealt with. Businesses know inventories must be cut, receivables disciplined, and financial resources maintained to tide them over the trough in the cycle.

RISK

The analysis of risk events concentrates on the event's effect on the *existing capital structure.* A risk event, almost by definition, should not require significant new financing. Risk events are often dealt with by hunkering down, converting assets to cash, and using the cash to service the existing financial obligations rather than rolling them forward. The analysis of a company's exposure to risk events leads to such questions as: How well can the company meet its existing debt? Does it have sufficient resources to handle the situation? How many risk problems can it sustain at once without financial collapse?

Although the debt in the capital structure enhances the ROE, the value of this extra return may be discounted. At the extreme, if the company's risk exposure is excessive, the loss in value from the exposure to financial risk may be greater than the value created from the extra earnings.[1] If this happens, the equity value would actually be increased by a more conservative capital structure.

FLEXIBILITY

Flexibility events require the company to access the capital markets for additional financing. Such events do not allow the company merely to transform its assets into cash to service its external obligations. They require that the company spend more cash to protect its position, to grow, and to survive. "Positive" flexibility events can be created by a highly profitable company that is exceeding its sustainable growth rate. This company usually has little trouble obtaining the necessary financing.

The "negative" flexibility events are the "unknown-unknowns" of the financial world. They are large and life-threatening to the company. Innovation threatens a major product: the pocket calculator made the slide rule, the rotary calculator, and the interest-rate table-book all obso-

---

1. A different way of saying this is that the earning per share will increase as debt is substituted for equity. At some point, the price-earnings ratio begins to fall because of the greater problems the level of debt creates for dealing with a risk event. When the price-earnings ratio falls faster than higher leverage increases the earning per share, the market price will start to fall.

lete. Sometimes a risk event, such as a labor situation, becomes so serious that it turns into a flexibility crisis.

The analytical perspective for flexibility events requires consideration of the types of flexibility problems that might occur for a company and the amount of funds needed to resolve them. Has the company access to these funds? Can the company raise funds at a reasonable price, a cost the new assets can earn with room to spare? Or, will the company have to give away some of the existing equity owners' value to survive? If so, how much?

All-equity financing clearly leaves a firm with the greatest room to deal with flexibility problems. This is too great a sleep-well strategy for most entrepreneurs, who want to enjoy a high return on their equity. On the other hand, too high a level of senior claims can create skepticism about the company's survival. The capitalization rate for debt is raised. The adverse effect on the value of the equity is the same as that described in the risk situation: ROE may be higher, but it is more than offset by a lower valuation multiple.

Unfortunately, it is not easy to identify the precise debt-capital ratio at which the market takes fright nor the point at which the fright turns to panic. Moreover, these points probably change with market conditions. When the market is optimistic and confident about the future and the company appears strong in its position, a greater proportion of debt is not only tolerated but encouraged.

▶ WARNING: The danger for companies pushing too close to the limit is that market fads can change suddenly. Investors become more conservative. Liquidity, not growth or earnings, becomes the touchstone of value. Acceptable capital structures become more conservative and, often in this environment, the value of equity is discounted. The firm at the edge finds the cliff has collapsed beneath its feet. Raising equity funds to restore the foundation is now much more expensive than anticipated.

Considering the difficulty of determining where the edge of the precipice is, the optimal capital structure, balancing eating and sleeping to create the highest value for the equity holder, fortunately lies more on a mesa than a mountain peak. There is reasonable room for capital-structure decisions that enhance stockholder values.

CONTROL

Control matters for the smaller enterprise, for example, often point to debt as the favored financial source because additional equity will dilute the existing control position. Entrepreneurs, however, often overlook the control lenders exercise through the structure of the loan agreements. As the proportion of debt increases, these terms become stricter and circumscribe management's decisions. If these terms become too onerous, issuing equity may actually sacrifice less control than loan covenants would take.

TIMING

Timing considerations become important when the market situation tempts management to vary from the strategic plan laid out. For example, if the plan is to issue short-term debt but long-term interest rates fall to low levels, you may consider raising long-term debt immediately although the plan had been to delay long-term debt.

Timing is also important when you are planning a sequence of issues for a company that is in the "fourth" state of fund needs. The eat-well–sleep-well tradeoff is between issuing debt now (in the hope of raising the market price of the common stock for a subsequent issue of equity) and of issuing equity now (to provide a base for easier future debt financing). An assessment of what type of financing is in current favor in the marketplace, and an estimate of what will be in favor at the time of the next issue are important aspects of judgment in making the decision.

OTHER

The "other" factors can tip the decision either way. For instance, estate planning may incline the entrepreneur to raise debt to replace equity, making it easier to sell the business to another entrepreneur. Occasionally, creating liquidity and a way for investors to exit may require the enterprise to make a limited issue of equity.

> **KEY POINT: Income considerations usually point toward more debt; risk and flexibility considerations usually point toward less debt. The remaining factors can point either way depending on the circumstances.**

APPLYING THE FRICTO FACTORS

Although in this discussion the FRICTO factors have been applied to the capital-structure decision, these factors are also appropriate for assessing capital-investment and dividend decisions. Thus, FRICTO offers a framework in which the effects of most financial decisions can be analyzed.

With respect to capital investments, the major analytical issues are the return (income) the project offers and the rate of return (cost of capital) that should be demanded given the uncertainties (risk and, sometimes, flexibility) associated with it. Timing is often a factor—should the project be undertaken at once or deferred?

Similarly, the dividend policy issue can be evaluated with the FRICTO factors. Does paying a higher dividend mean cutting back on investments (reducing income growth)? Does it mean more debt (increasing risk and flexibility exposure)? Does it mean issuing more equity (cutting future income and diluting control)? Will it create greater value (the sum of the dividend and the stock price)?

Figuring Economic Value Added

One approach to determining whether a business or an investment is economically justified is to figure out how much more the business earns than its cost of capital. Firms that return less are consuming capital value rather than earning an adequate return, even though they may report a profit. Firms and investments that return more are adding economic value.

Many techniques exist for analyzing a company's or a project's economic value, including elaborate proprietary methods marketed by consulting firms. Many companies, however, have developed their own measures suited to their circumstances.

> **SMART FINANCIAL MANAGEMENT: The following basic technique will enable you and your co-owners, if any, to determine whether your company is creating or losing economic value.**

➤ First, recast the income statement to show economic income: deduct operating costs from sales, and then calculate and deduct the income tax that would be due on the resulting net operating profit figure. The result is net operating profit after taxes.

➤ Second, calculate the capital-cost percentage. This is the after-tax weighted average cost of the firm's sources of funds using the book-value proportions on the balance sheet as the weights. The cost of current liabilities is often zero, if the accounts payable terms are met, except for short-term debt. The cost of long-term debt and leases are the stated or implied interest rates, which must be reduced by the tax cover. You can assess the equity cost of capital directly as the return necessary to keep your money in the business.

➤ Finally, deduct the capital cost in dollars from the net operating profit after tax to find the economic value in dollars the business is generating. If this amount is positive, it represents the value the company is creating by earning a return greater than its capital cost. A negative amount represents how much the company is losing you and your fellow owners compared with the returns you could make elsewhere.

The Four Frameworks

The four analytical frameworks reviewed in this chapter offer ways of approaching the most common and most critical financial decisions. They do not offer solutions as such, however. The frameworks point to the *analyses* that need to be made and to the *judgments* required. These are common to both smaller firms and to the biggest of the *Fortune* 500, although the environments in which they are made are very different. The owners of a smaller enterprise can decide precisely what they wish to do in balancing the risks and rewards of their situations. The managers of large, widely held companies must guess what the market will value. In this day of increasingly aggressive financial markets, a serious misjudgment can threaten management's position—and even the company's survival—much more quickly than in the past half century.

CHAPTER 2

LEGAL ASPECTS OF FINANCING STARTUP, EARLY-STAGE, AND EMERGING BUSINESSES

Every business is born as a startup and goes through identifiable stages of development. During the development period, and particularly when the company seeks financing, its owners and managers face a thicket of legal issues and questions involving corporate law, securities law, and contract law. Your decisions on these issues will usually influence potential financing. This chapter discusses the basic law relating to:

- ➤ A business's legal organizational structure.
- ➤ The steps required to maintain a corporation (the most complex of the legal organizational forms that small businesses use).
- ➤ Corporate capital structure including the basic types of corporate securities.
- ➤ Federal and state laws regulating the issuing of securities.
- ➤ Contracts and agreements commonly used in the early financing of a small business.

The Five Financing Stages of a Company's Development

Professional investors typically divide a company's development into five financing stages: (1) startup, (2) development or second-round, (3) expansion or third-round, (4) growth or fourth-round, and (5) public offering. Most small businesses fall into one of the first four categories.

A *startup company* has at least one individual involved, an idea, and possibly a business plan to implement the idea. A business, even one with some capital and employees, is considered a startup until evidence proves that the idea will work. That evidence can be a working prototype or an economic or marketing study that supports the idea.

At this point, a company enters the *development* stage, with the goal of developing and marketing the product or service and generating revenue. Once the company has generated revenue, it is an *expansion-stage* company. A company in the expansion stage has revenue and is usually no more than a year away from breaking even. When a company is above the break-even point and earning a profit, but needs capital to support

Legal
Aspects of
Financing
Startup,
Early-Stage,
and
Emerging
Businesses

19

additional sales and profit, it is classified as a *growth* company. These four stages are subphases of the first three life-cycle phases discussed in Chapter 1, where they are related to cash flow, profit, and financial sources and uses.

> **SMART FINANCIAL MANAGEMENT:** As the company passes through these stages, you face a new set of legal issues and complexities at each stage. At the startup stage, you must plan a legal structure for the company and address the legal issues associated with its initial financing. These range from the type of securities to offer to whether new investors will be entitled to representation on the board of directors. By the time the company has become a growth company, you must deal with legal issues ranging from minimizing taxes on the company's profits to whether to seek additional funding through a venture capital investment.

Legal Structures for the New Company

You can choose from the following legal forms in establishing a new venture: sole proprietorship, partnership, limited-liability corporation (LLC), and regular corporation. Each has advantages, disadvantages, and a variety of subtypes. You should be familiar with the benefits and liabilities of each to select the most suitable structure for your enterprise.

SOLE PROPRIETORSHIPS

Most enterprises start as a sole proprietorship, which is the most common legal structure for small businesses. In a sole proprietorship, one person owns the business. That person alone receives the profits from the business but is also personally responsible for the company's debts. The company's profits are taxed at the personal income tax rate of the proprietor. Nevertheless, a sole proprietorship can become a large business. A sole proprietorship can borrow money, but it cannot raise equity investment from other investors unless it changes its legal form to a partnership, corporation, or LLC.

PARTNERSHIPS

Partnerships allow a business to have multiple owners without assuming a corporate form. A partnership is an unincorporated business owned by two or more entities. A formal filing with state authorities is necessary to form a partnership. The filing will contain certain essential facts about the partnership. Partnerships can be general or limited. Most partnerships are organized as general partnerships, although the limited partnership structure is common in real estate and is also used for large, publicly traded partnerships and in natural-resource projects.

In a *general partnership,* all partners have equal legal rights to manage the business and are liable for the full debts of the partnership.

A *limited* partnership, however, has at least one general partner and one limited partner. The general partners are liable for all the debts of the business, but limited partners are only liable for what each partner has actually invested. To maintain their limited partnership status and the limited liability associated with that status, a limited partner cannot participate in the day-to-day management of the partnership. If a limited partner chooses to participate, that partner automatically becomes a general partner with the full liability of that position.

The most important business document in a partnership is the *partnership agreement,* which sets up the basic business relationship among the partners. Normally the partnership agreement covers the following items:

> The name, location, fiscal year, accounting procedures, and duration of the partnership
> The capital contributions made by and required of the partners
> The duties of a partner and the division of management responsibilities among the partners, including the procedure for electing a managing partner
> The allocation of profits among the partners
> The procedure for admitting new partners and expelling existing partners
> The method of liquidating the partnership interest of a retiring or deceased partner

In smaller partnerships, the departure of a partnership normally results in the creation of a new partnership. This process must be carefully done to avoid legal and tax problems for the partners.

> **TAX STORY: A partnership is not taxed as a separate legal entity. Instead, the income and losses of the business are allocated to the individual partners according to the terms of the partnership agreement. The individual partners are then taxed at their personal tax rates. Although it does not pay taxes, a partnership does have to file a partnership tax return for information purposes.**

CORPORATIONS

Corporations are the legal form that most entrepreneurs chose if they have plans to grow their business to any size and need outside financing. A corporation is a legal entity separate from its owners, who own shares of stock in the company. A corporation generally has a perpetual existence. It must be set up according to the laws of the state in which it is to be

Legal
Aspects of
Financing
Startup,
Early-Stage,
and
Emerging
Businesses

21

legally domiciled—which is usually, but not necessarily, the state in which its business will be conducted. Shareholders elect a board of directors, which manages the corporation.

As a rule, shareholders are not liable for the debts of the company beyond their investment in the corporation's stock. The limited liability of a corporation's owners is the primary reason that many businesses choose the corporate form. In certain circumstances, however, directors may be liable for the corporation's debts. Further, the creditors of a small company often require the key owners to give personal guarantees for the company's debts. This requirement makes the owners personally liable for those debts.

To maintain its status as a separate legal entity, a corporation must comply with the detailed corporate laws of the state in which it is incorporated. Failure to do so can result in the loss of the corporation's corporate status, which would have significant ramifications for the shareholders and the business.

> **TAX STORY: A corporation is taxed directly on its income. Any dividends that a corporation distributes to its shareholders are also subject to taxation as part of the shareholders' personal income.**

Subchapter-S corporations are normally incorporated companies that are taxed differently from other corporations as provided by the Subchapter-S provisions of the federal Internal Revenue Code.

> **TAX STORY: Subchapter-S allows a qualifying corporation to choose to be taxed as a partnership. Thus, the corporation itself pays no income tax. The corporation's shareholders, however, must include their pro-rata share of the corporation's income and losses in their gross income statements, whether or not that income has been distributed to them.**

To qualify to elect for a Subchapter-S tax treatment, a corporation:

➤ Must be a U.S. corporation.
➤ Must not be a member of an affiliated group.
➤ Must not have more than 35 shareholders (all of whom are either individuals or estates).
➤ Must not have shareholders who are nonresident aliens.
➤ Must not have more than one class of outstanding stock.

This structure gives the shareholder limited-liability-status protection as a shareholder of a corporation, but also the tax advantages of a partnership. Thus, an investor can probably write one venture's loss against the profit of another without having the liability of a general partner or the limited partner's inability to participate in the firm's management.

LIMITED-LIABILITY CORPORATIONS

The *limited-liability corporation* (LLC) is a new business form (as opposed to an election under the federal tax laws) established by state legislation in the last 20 years. The LLC is designed to combine the tax benefits of a partnership with the limited-liability benefits of a corporation. Unlike a general partner, an individual shareholder in an LLC is not responsible for the firm's debt. Although an LLC is taxed like a partnership, in the same way a Subchapter-S corporation is, LLCs do not have some of the significant Subchapter-S disadvantages. For example, LLCs can offer several different classes of stock with different rights. They can have an unlimited number of shareholders. The shareholders can be individuals, partnerships, or corporations, and they do not have to be U.S. residents. The disadvantages of an LLC are restrictions that severely limit the transferability of LLC shares.

Choosing a Legal Structure

FOR A NEW BUSINESS

To determine the best legal form for a new company, you and your legal counsel should evaluate your expectations and goals using the following considerations:

> ➤ Your potential liability as the business owner(s)
> ➤ Tax considerations and the distribution of profits and losses
> ➤ The need and ability to raise capital
> ➤ The expense and complexity of organizing the business
> ➤ The amount of government regulation and reporting requirements
> ➤ Management control

FOR AN EXISTING BUSINESS

To determine the best legal form for an existing business, you should answer the following questions:

> ➤ Who are the current owners and investors, and who will be in the future?
> ➤ What will be the cash-flow characteristics and capital requirements of the business over time?
> ➤ How long is the business expected to be in operation?
> ➤ What are the expected profits of the business and the expected tax situation of the owners now and in the future?

The answers to these questions must be evaluated and weighed against each other to figure out the optimal legal form of the business.

For example, a wealthy, early-stage "angel" investor will seldom want to take the risk of serving as a general partner. The angel investor also may want to have more control over the venture than a limited partner is allowed. Finally, the angel may want to write off the venture's losses against other income, which rules out a regular corporation. An LLC or Subchapter-S corporation may be the best alternative. If so many new investors are required that it would violate the Subchapter-S requirement, the LLC might be appropriate. If it is likely that less tax-sensitive investors will be added soon, however, a regular corporate structure might be used from the start, with Subchapter-S status elected temporarily at the beginning. (The tax code restricts how frequently the Subchapter-S election can be changed.)

> **SMART FINANCIAL MANAGEMENT: In practice, businesses often evolve through several legal forms over time, as the importance of different factors change. If the business is expected to remain small with few owners, a partnership, an LLC, or a Subchapter-S corporation may make sense as the legal form. If the business is expected to grow vigorously, have several owners, and raise substantial capital from financial institutions, professional venture capitalists, or a public offering, then it is usually necessary for the business to be a regular corporation.**

The Legal Aspects of Creating and Maintaining a Corporation

In the eyes of the law, a corporation is an entity separate and distinct from its owners. As such, a corporation is born, lives, is taxed, and dies separately from its owners. Consequently, a change in status of one or more of its owners, for example by death or the transfer of an ownership interest from one investor to another, does not affect the status of the corporation. This is different from a partnership, which is normally dissolved by the departure or death of one or more of its partners.

> **KEY POINT: As a creature of law, a corporation owes its creation as a distinct legal entity to the filing of the proper legal documents, the most important of which are its certificate of incorporation and its bylaws. These documents create the corporation as a distinct legal entity and define how it will be governed, its powers, and the relationship among its owners.**

CERTIFICATE OF INCORPORATION

The first step in establishing a corporation is for the incorporator to file a *certificate of incorporation* with the proper authority in the state in which the company is being incorporated. The certificate is the basic document on which the very existence of the corporation depends. A well-drafted certificate is usually simple. It will state:

- ➤ The name of the corporation
- ➤ The corporation's registered office in the state (often its attorney, required for the serving of legal documents)
- ➤ Its purpose (generally very broadly defined)
- ➤ The authorized capital stock
- ➤ The names of the initial directors (if any) and the incorporator(s)

The certificate is written to allow for any planned complexities in the ownership or management arrangements of the corporation. For example, the relative rights and privileges of all classes of stock (present and contemplated) in a corporation are often specified in a certificate. Similarly, if there is a plan to allocate directorships among investors, that plan may be specified in the certificate. Special supermajorities may be specified for certain actions, such as approving a merger.

Although regulations vary from state to state, most states require the certificate to be filed with the Secretary of State. Once the certificate is approved by the proper governmental authority, the corporation comes into being as a distinct separate legal entity. In most states, approval is virtually automatic when all of the legal requirements have been met.

> **IMPORTANT: The certificate of incorporation is normally sufficient to allow a corporation to do business in the state of incorporation, but additional legal documentation is normally required to do business in other states. Specifically, a corporation normally must file the necessary forms with the proper office in each state in which it does business outside of its state of incorporation. It registers to do business in that state as a "foreign corporation." This filing will subject the corporation to taxation and regulation as dictated by that particular state's law.**

BYLAWS

If the certificate of incorporation is the birth certificate for the corporation, the *bylaws* represent the rules by which the corporation will be governed as it matures. Consequently, the bylaws are very important to the company. Founders and corporate management will find themselves

Legal
Aspects of
Financing
Startup,
Early-Stage,
and
Emerging
Businesses

25

checking the bylaws periodically to see how they should act in a variety of corporate legal matters. The initial bylaws of the corporation are normally drafted by the corporation's incorporating counsel while it is preparing the certificate of incorporation. Unlike the certificate of incorporation, however, the bylaws of a corporation need not be filed with the authorities in the state of incorporation. In addition, while changes to the certificate of incorporation typically require the consent of the shareholders, amendments of the bylaws normally only require the consent of the board of directors.

Bylaws generally have provisions covering such matters as:

> How meetings of stockholders are called and conducted
> The size and duties of the board of directors, such as how and when the directors meet, how they are elected, how they can be removed, how vacancies are filled, and what duties of the board can be delegated to committees of the board
> The titles and duties of corporate officers
> How books and records are kept
> How stock shares can be transferred
> Indemnification provisions for officers and directors
> Requirements for amendments

Once a corporation has been legally established the key group is its board of directors. This group manages the corporation for the shareholders.

The board may (and generally does) delegate the management of the corporation to the corporation's officers, such as the president and chief executive officer. It is always the board's ultimate responsibility, however, to oversee the corporation's activities for the shareholders.

How members of the board are selected is a central issue in financing any corporation, particularly in a private company in which investors cannot easily sell their investments. They, in particular, look to the board to safeguard and enhance their investments. A voting arrangement for directors also may be established in a side agreement among investors. A typical clause may provide that any investor owning at least a specified percentage of the common stock will be entitled to nominate a director for whom the other shareholders agree to vote.

While major shareholders typically want to maximize their representation on the board, creditors of the corporation, such as banks, value experienced outside directors on the board. They believe outside directors will more likely protect the creditors' interests. Achieving the proper balance on the board to satisfy the various interested parties can be difficult, particularly when directors have a significant personal liability associated with the position. This condition makes qualified directors (both from shareholder ranks and from outside) difficult to attract.

> **SMART MOVE:** The effort to recruit outsiders and achieve balance can be beneficial. An active, independent board with outside, qualified directors can provide several advantages. Board members can provide complementary skills to the CEO and bring perspective and experience to the enterprise, particularly if directors have been CEOs and entrepreneurs themselves. They can also provide a framework for control and discipline and be both mentors to and checks on the CEO.

MINUTES AND RESOLUTIONS

Once a corporation is operational, the key legal documents for the management of the corporation are the *minutes* of the board of directors' meetings and any *resolutions* the board passes. Specific actions of the board, such as election of officers, the approval of a particular financial contract, an issue of additional stock, and salaries for the corporate officers, are reflected in the minutes. The minutes of board of directors' meetings and its resolutions, the certificate of incorporation, and the corporation's bylaws create the legal framework of the corporation and are required for any financing of the corporation to be completed. Improperly drawn and maintained documents may create problems with the tax authorities, and even threaten the corporation's existence.

OTHER TASKS

As a small business owner, creating and managing the corporation properly is only one task that you must consider when choosing the appropriate form of organization. An additional task is obtaining the licenses required to do business in the states and localities in which the business operates. Most states and local jurisdictions (e.g., cities, towns, counties) require that a wide variety of businesses obtain licenses to begin operations in that jurisdiction. Because licensing requirements vary greatly among local jurisdictions, you should study these requirements before deciding where to open your business.

Corporate Capital Structure and the Basic Types of Corporate Securities

The first issue that must be addressed in raising capital for a corporation is its capital structure. You must decide whether to raise debt, equity, or some combination of the two by analyzing the tradeoffs between them in light of flexibility, risk, income, control, and timing.

> **SMART FINANCIAL MANAGEMENT:** The greater the business risk and the greater the need for financial flexibility, the greater the reliance

Legal
Aspects of
Financing
Startup,
Early-Stage,
and
Emerging
Businesses

27

the corporation must place on equity financing. On the other hand, if the goal is to maximize income (return) to current owners and maintain their control of the corporation, the corporation can rely more on debt as its source of financing.

During startup and early stages, corporations usually rely almost exclusively on equity financing because of the great risk associated with the business and the need to maintain flexibility for the future. Equity provides more flexibility than debt, which usually requires cash interest and principal payments. As corporations develop more stable revenues, they normally increase the use of debt in their capital structure. This policy gives the current owners the best chance of maintaining control of the business and the benefit from the potential income as the business grows.

As a corporation seeks financing, a key issue is whether it will issue a *security* as part of the financing transaction. If a corporation uses a security, it will be subject to federal and state securities laws; if it does not, it will not.

Generally, a financing transaction involves issuing a security whenever one entity supplies money or an item of value to another for the purpose of generating profits or other monetary return *and* if the supplier of the funds has only a passive involvement in the business. However, this broad definition would result in issuing securities for all financing transactions, which would then be subject to federal and state securities laws. In practice, therefore, many common financing transactions, such as bank loans or the provision of trade credit, are not included in the definition of security transactions, and their basic legal documents, such as loan notes and account receivables, are not subject to securities laws.

❯ **KEY POINT: Under federal and state securities laws, the basic types of securities used in financing a corporation fall into two categories: equity or debt. The three basic types of equity securities are common stock, preferred stock (which may be ordinary preferred or convertible into another security such as common stock), and warrants. Debt securities may be straight or convertible debt, secured or unsecured by the corporation's assets.**

These security types are used, sometimes in combination, to finance the private company as it progresses from startup to initial public offering. Therefore, it is important to understand their features and characteristics. To decide which securities are appropriate often includes evaluating significant tradeoffs that affect the company's growth and cost of capital. In addition, different security types can also create significantly different contractual obligations, some of which may not be readily apparent.

EQUITY SECURITIES

Common stock is the most basic form of equity. Every corporation has common stock in its capital structure. All other types of securities are defined in relation to the common stock and its owners. All residual rights of the corporation, after all other corporate obligations have been resolved, belong to the common-stock owners. When only one class of stock exists (that is, common stock), the holders have equal pro-rata rights to any dividend distribution, to the assets of the company upon liquidation, and to vote on certain matters including the election of directors and designated major corporate transactions.

If more than one class of common stock exists, the rights and preferences of each class to participate in profits, dividends, assets, and governance must be defined in corporate documents. For example, one class of stock may have the right to elect more directors than its percentage ownership of the corporation would entitle it to have. On occasion, one class of common stock may be entitled to more dividends than another class. This device may be used when the controlling shareholders think dividends will help the company raise equity at a better price-earnings multiple (that is, less dilution) and the controlling shareholders do not need immediate cash returns from their ownership. In this instance, control considerations are likely to be more important than short-term income.

Preferred stock is equity with preferences and certain superior rights over common stock. Classes of preferred stock can be structured in a variety of ways with preferences over both common stock and other classes of preferred stock. Preferences can relate to dividends, distributions on liquidation, covenants, antidilution protection, redemption, and other characteristics. Preferred stock may be convertible into common stock. Convertible-preferred stock, often issued by a startup business, typically converts into common either at the option of the holder or automatically upon the occurrence of an event such as a public offering.

If preferred stock is sold in an investment transaction, the terms of the preferred stock will be defined in the company's articles, certificate of incorporation, or *Certificate of Designation*. A Certificate of Designation is used when a company's charter allows the board of directors, acting without the need for stockholder approval, to specify the terms of authorized but undesignated and unissued shares of preferred stock. Such a provision is called a "blank check preferred provision." It gives the board a significant amount of flexibility in negotiating issue terms when arranging a merger or venture-capital financing. If the charter of the company does not have a blank check preferred provision, any modification of preferred-stock terms from those specified in the charter requires a charter amendment or a charter restatement.

Warrants are an option to buy a security (debt, preferred, or common stock) of a company at a specific price. A company will typically issue

Legal
Aspects of
Financing
Startup,
Early-Stage,
and
Emerging
Businesses

29

warrants to enhance the appeal of other securities or sell the warrants for a small amount of money. Warrants make an investment more attractive by allowing an investor to delay a purchase while maintaining a fixed purchase price. Warrants give an investor an upside (that is, if the stock appreciates, the investor can purchase it at the original lower price) with no downside (i.e., if the stock price falters, the investor will let the warrant expire unexercised and will not have put any additional funds into the company). Warrants are sometimes attached to subordinated debt and even to senior obligations to make them more attractive. Warrants sweeten the return to a lender without committing the borrower to a contractual cash payment.

DEBT SECURITIES

A company can issue a variety of debt securities. The permutations of the forms debt can take are ultimately limited only by the requirements of the company and the investors and the creativity of the company's attorneys. Debt is classified by its maturity as either long term or short term. *Long-term debt* is usually due more than 12 months from the date of issue; *short-term debt* is due in less than 12 months from the date of issue. The portion of long-term debt due within a year appears on the balance sheet as *current maturities of long-term debt.*

Long-term debt with a maturity of less than seven years is usually termed a *note.* There are two classifications of longer-term debt: *debentures,* which are unsecured by property, and *bonds,* which are secured by property (usually real estate). Debt may be senior or subordinated regardless of its maturity.

Senior debt is the lowest-risk form a lender can use because it has priority on a company's available assets in case of liquidation. Because *subordinated debt* receives payment in liquidation only after the senior debt's claims are satisfied, it is higher risk than senior debt. Subordinated debt therefore normally must offer the lender higher interest rates than senior debt.

Convertible debt can be converted into the common stock of a company under certain predefined terms and conditions. The issuing company usually has the right to call the debt. This provision allows the company to force conversion when the current stock price is higher than the call price. The call price is normally set above the conversion price. This allows the debt owners to enjoy some appreciation of the common stock before they are forced to convert and, for institutional holders, to sell the equity. Without a call feature, the debt owners would have no reason to convert until the cash dividend on the common stock was appreciably greater than the interest on the debt.

> **KEY POINT: Debt is rarely used to finance startup or early-stage companies, particularly if the financing is provided by friends and family**

or angel investors. Professional investors, such as venture capitalists, often prefer securities that combine features of debt and equity. This compound structure helps to increase the certainty of the investment's repayment (a benefit of debt) while also maximizing the investors' control of the business and their participation in the upside of the business (a benefit of equity).

Professional investors normally prefer convertible preferred stock or convertible debt. When convertible debt is used, it typically has a maturity under seven years and is unsecured, because the company seldom has hard assets to pledge as collateral. Although these securities may be more attractive to investors and assist in raising capital for the startup or early-stage corporation, they can leave a corporation with a difficult capital structure to manage as the company matures or needs additional financing.

SOURCES OF CAPITAL

Once you have selected the type of capital structure to finance your corporation's development, you can choose among several sources for that capital, including private investors and angels, venture-capital firms, other corporations, leasing companies, government, commercial banks and finance companies, and public equity markets. Which sources you use depends partly on the type of capital structure you are seeking to develop. Each source comes with its own legal issues that revolve around its effect on flexibility, risk, income, control, and timing. A finance company that specializes in short-term accounts-receivable lending has a different set of issues and approaches than a venture capitalist who focuses on long-term equity investment. An aspect that is often central to selecting a source of capital is whether the planned financing will require the use of a security that must be registered under federal or state securities laws.

Securities Laws

When you are fortunate enough to develop a business with dynamic market appeal, your enterprise will enter a rapid-growth phase. In most situations, this growth cannot be financed from internal sources and debt. You must then turn to the venture-capital market even though this source is now providing less funding than in the peak years. In arranging financing with capital sources, you should be aware of the basics of security laws discussed in this section and with the types of agreements and common provisions discussed in the next section.

Securities laws are either federal or state laws. Federal laws are more broadly applicable to a business because any effort to raise funds across state lines must follow federal laws. Any business seeking financing must also pay attention to state securities laws in those states where funding is being sought, even if the offering is exempt from federal registration as a

Legal
Aspects of
Financing
Startup,
Early-Stage,
and
Emerging
Businesses

31

securities offering. Complying with state regulations is often complicated because state securities laws vary despite efforts to make them uniform.

FEDERAL SECURITIES LAWS

U.S. securities laws assume that full and accurate disclosure—rather than complex governmental intervention—is an effective remedy for the ills affecting the securities market. Consequently, U.S. securities laws focus on requiring that companies selling securities to the public provide adequate information about the company. Furthermore, the information must be publicly available. Trading by those with inside, nonpublic, information is prohibited. This disclosure is expected to provide three benefits:

1. Protection of the unwary public from fraud and risky investments
2. Equal treatment for the small investor compared to insiders and institutions
3. Promotion of a more efficient market by the dispersal of information obtained from the company through full and fair disclosure

The key federal laws are the Securities Act of 1933 (the Securities Act) and the Securities Exchange Act of 1934 (the Exchange Act). Federal securities laws classify offerings as public or private. *Public offerings* require an extensive registration and approval process with the U.S. Securities and Exchange Commission (SEC) that *nonpublic,* or *private, offerings* may avoid. All company offerings before its initial public offering (IPO) are by definition private offerings. All offerings of securities to the public, however, are public offerings that are subject to public securities registration (unless they qualify for a specific exemption). Understanding the exemptions is key to understanding the securities laws surrounding private offerings.

Qualifying for a Private-Offering Exemption

The Securities Act of 1933 is the key federal law defining registration and exempt private offerings. The important sections of the act for nonpublic offerings are sections 3(a)(11), 4(2), and 5. Sections 3(a)(11) and 4(2) deal with avoiding the registration and approval process for public offerings of securities. Section 5 prohibits the use of interstate commerce or the mails to sell any security unless a registration statement is in effect for that security or an exemption from the registration requirements of Section 5 is available.

Section 3(a)(11) provides an exemption from the registration requirements for intrastate offerings. An intrastate offering is "any security which is part of an issue offered and sold only to persons resident within a State or Territory, where the issuer of such security is a person resident and doing business within, or if a corporation, incorporated by and doing business within, such State or Territory." This provision is important to most startup and early stage companies because they usually sell their stock locally to a few private individuals. Nevertheless, a company must still satisfy the appropriate state laws.

> **WATCH THIS: Because qualification for the intrastate exemption limits offers and sales to residents of the state in which the business is incorporated, the company has the obligation to find out the residence of each purchaser. The exemption may be lost if the security is offered or sold to even one out-of-state purchaser. Similarly, if a valid purchaser resells securities to someone outside the state within nine months of the original issue, the entire exemption may be lost. This action has the potential to put the transaction in violation of federal securities laws. Because of the resale provision, there is normally no aftermarket for securities sold under the intrastate exemption.**

Section 4(2) provides an exemption from the federal registration requirements for "transactions by an issuer not involving any public offering." The 1933 act does not directly define a public offering. Therefore, the courts and the SEC, through a series of interpretations of when 4(2) applies, have defined the characteristics of a private offering entitled to the exemption. These interpretations have defined private sales by the number of persons to which the issue is offered (offerees, not purchasers), the sophistication of the offerees, the size and manner of the offering, and the relationship of the offerees to the issuer. Generally, people who have access to information about the company and sufficient knowledge to take care of themselves are considered *sophisticated investors* and are within the scope of the exemption. They are wealthy investors who routinely invest in early-stage ventures and who attest to their ability to evaluate and gauge the risk involved.

Securities qualifying for a private-placement exemption cannot be offered through any form of general solicitation or public advertising The persons to whom the corporation is selling the securities must:

> ➤ Have sufficient knowledge and experience in finance to evaluate the investment or, alternatively, have sufficient net worth to bear the risk of the investment.
> ➤ Have access to the type of information normally provided in a prospectus.
> ➤ Agree not to resell or distribute the securities.

If the offering is made to even one person who does not meet these conditions, then the entire offering may violate the securities law.

Regulation D

Sections 4(2) of the Securities Act of 1933 has been defined and clarified by a series of SEC regulations, of which the most important is Regulation D. Adopted in 1982, Regulation D was intended "to simplify and clarify existing exemptions, to expand their availability, and to achieve uniformity between federal and state exemptions to facilitate capital formation consistent with the protection of investors."

Regulation D provides three exemptions from registration for limited private offerings:

> ➤ Rule 504 exempts offerings of less than $1 million in a 12-month period.
> ➤ Rule 505 exempts offerings of less than $5 million in a 12-month period to an unlimited number of "accredited investors" plus 35 additional persons.
> ➤ Rule 506 exempts offerings of any amount by any issuers to an unlimited number of accredited investors plus 35 sophisticated persons.

A key term under Regulation D is *accredited investors.* Generally, Regulation D allows the issuer of securities to sell as much as it wants without having to register the securities provided that the sale is to accredited investors. Accredited investors are those with the knowledge and resources to invest in private companies without the mandatory disclosure protection provided by the public-company registration process. The Regulation D definition of accredited investors includes:

> ➤ Institutional investors, such as banks, insurance companies, venture-capital companies, registered investment companies, and Small Business Investment Corporations (SBICs)
> ➤ Any person who, together with a spouse, has a net worth of more than $1 million at the time of purchase
> ➤ Any person whose income was more than $200,000, or $300,000 including spouse's income, in each of the last two years, and who expects at least the same income for the current year
> ➤ Directors, executive officers, or general partners of the company or partnership selling the securities

Qualifying a Public Offering for an Exemption

Under Section 3(b) of the Securities Act of 1933, the SEC has the power to exempt certain small-dollar offerings from registration. To carry out this section, the SEC published *Regulation A,* which provides a conditional exemption from the full registration and approval requirements for public offerings not exceeding $5 million in a 12-month period. Although technically an exemption from the registration requirements of the Securities Act, Regulation A is often called the "short form" of registration.

Under Regulation A, no offers to sell the security can be made until the company has filed an offering statement with the SEC. No sales can be completed until the offering statement is qualified by the SEC and an offering circular has been delivered to the prospective buyers. However, a company may obtain *indications of interest* based on a proposed Regulation A offering before the filing of the offering statement, provided it does not solicit or accept money or any commitment to purchase until the offering statement is qualified by the SEC. An offering statement consists of a notification, an offering circular, and exhibits similar to, but less detailed than, a prospectus. The principal advantages of Regulation A offerings are that the required financial statements for the offering circular are simpler and need not be audited. In addition, there are no periodic SEC reporting requirements unless the issuer has more than $5 million in assets and more than 500 shareholders. Finally, unlike an unregistered private intrastate offering, securities issued under Regulation A may be freely traded in the aftermarket.

STATE REGISTRATION

Securities must also be registered (or exempted from registration) according to the laws and regulations of each state in which it will be offered. These laws are known as *blue-sky* laws because their original intent was to prevent abuse by promoters whose promises were as insubstantial as several feet of blue sky.

In most states, securities listed on the New York or American stock exchanges or traded on the NASDAQ national market system are exempt from the registration requirement, but an intrastate offering may still require registration with the state securities administrator. When state registration is required, it is usually registration by coordination, registration by notification, or registration by qualification.

Registration by coordination is available when a registered offering is made under the Securities Act of 1933. Under this method, the issuer files three copies of the current federal prospectus along with any supplemental information required by the state with the state securities administrator.

Registration by notification requires filing a short-form registration statement with the state securities administrator. This alternative is generally available only when the company and its predecessors have a business history of at least five years.

Registration by qualification goes further than mandating full disclosure by authorizing the state securities administrator to engage in *merit regulation.* Under merit regulation, the state securities administrator can stop an offering because it is not "fair, just, and equitable." California regulators have particularly strong powers of merit regulation.

Legal
Aspects of
Financing
Startup,
Early-Stage,
and
Emerging
Businesses

35

> **WATCH THIS: A key element of the private placement of securities is restrictions on resale of those securities. As a rule, the SEC and the**

courts have required that privately placed securities have a legend written on the certificate that states the securities were purchased in a private placement and may not be resold unless they are either registered or sold in a transaction exempt under the 1933 Act. The requirement is intended to restrict resale of these securities to another private placement. Otherwise, securities in a fraudulent venture could be sold privately to a confederate who could then sell them to the unsuspecting public.

PENALTIES

Violation of securities law is potentially a civil rather than a criminal liability. The potential civil liabilities, however, can be serious for the management and controlling shareholders of a corporation, as they may be held liable as the controlling persons. In this situation, the corporation's independent legal status provides no protection against personal liability. It is also relatively easy for damaged investors or others to sue under securities laws.

> **KEY POINT: Because of their complexity and the potential liability of those who violate them, federal and state securities laws are a central issue in any corporate financing. To be sure of proper compliance with securities laws when undertaking financing, it is critical that you retain experienced securities counsel.**

The Stock Purchase Agreement

Most companies in their startup and early-stage phases raise capital by selling common or preferred stock in private placements to friends, family, and angel investors under an exemption allowed by the securities laws. For this type of transaction, the key legal elements revolve around the *stock purchase agreement*. This principal document will range from simple to complex depending on the sophistication of the investor, the maturity of the company, and the complexity of the transaction. It may contain only basic provisions to comply with applicable securities laws' requirements, or it may also include a variety of sale provisions and extensive representations, warranties, and positive and negative covenants by the company issuing the securities and the people associated with the issuer, including the company's founder and management.

> **KEY POINT: You and the company's other owners (if any) will want a simpler document. The investors want a more complex document, with as much protection for them as possible in writing.**

The detailed characteristics of the security (which, for example, might be a complicated convertible preferred stock) are listed in the body of the stock-purchase contract. Key elements of this contract are representations, covenants, closing conditions, and registration rights.

Representations. The beginning of a stock-purchase contract has a long set of representations, a characteristic of a purchase contract, that include details about patents owned or licensed by the company, major real estate and equipment, and key leases and contracts. In addition, general representations will be made on a variety of subjects, including organization and authority, corporate action, capitalization, governmental approval, absence of litigation, employment of key personnel, compliance with other agreements, ownership of assets, insurance, taxes, environmental protection, and insider transactions.

Covenants. Covenants are promises made by the company as part of the stock-purchase contract. Common covenants include commitments to maintain life-insurance policies on key executives, to supply regular financial reports and periodic projections to major investors, and to use management's best efforts to elect persons nominated by the investors to the board.

Closing Conditions. Closing conditions usually fall into two major categories—conditions on the timing of the payment of funds and standard provisions. *Conditions on the timing of the payment of funds* specify whether full payment for the securities being purchased is to be made at closing, or whether payment will be staged over an extended period and conditioned on the company's reaching certain targets. *Standard closing provisions* also include an affirmation that the representations made in the purchase contract were true at closing, the receipt of certain certificates from the officers of the company, and an opinion from counsel to the company that the pertinent agreements are valid, binding, and enforceable.

Registration Provisions. Registration provisions of a stock-purchase agreement establish the circumstances that require the company to register its securities with the SEC. This is usually as soon as the company is eligible to register because unregistered securities cannot be resold to the public. Clearly, investors prefer securities registered with the SEC because investors then have the option to sell their securities privately or publicly. Because registration broadens the market for the company's securities, it also increases their value.

> **WATCH THIS: From the company's standpoint, granting registration rights can be very expensive in money and time. First, there are filing fees and charges by accountants, lawyers, and printers. Then, filing can divert management's time and efforts at critical periods. In addition, the sale of blocks of stocks by existing shareholders limits the ability of the company itself to raise new capital by public sales.**

Legal
Aspects of
Financing
Startup,
Early-Stage,
and
Emerging
Businesses

—

37

The two forms of registration provisions are demand rights and piggy-back rights. *Demand rights* require the company to use its best efforts to register securities when and in the amount desired by investors. *Piggy-back rights* allow investors to require the company to register securities if the company is already registering other securities.

Other Special Contracts and Provisions

Besides the stock purchase agreement, a variety of special contracts and provisions are often used in private securities offerings to protect investors. A selection of the most common is described in this section.

A *stockholders' voting agreement* is primarily intended to provide investors with the ability to elect their own nominees as directors of the company. This agreement gives investors who are minority owners the ability to influence or control the company. It also may address other issues, such as how votes are to be cast on a variety of issues that might be presented to the company's stockholders for approval.

Voting rights determine the rights a particular class of stock has to vote for members of the board of directors and on certain key issues facing the corporation that require shareholder approval. Venture capitalists normally seek special voting rights for their convertible-preferred stock. These rights give them a greater percentage of the votes for the board of directors and on issues requiring shareholder approval than their percentage ownership of the business entitles them to have.

A *right of first refusal and co-sale agreement* provides investors with the ability to increase their ownership in a company, to influence the selection of other stockholders, and to liquidate their investments in the company. Right-of-first-refusal provisions normally prohibit founders and management stockholders from transferring their shares in a company to a third party without first giving existing investors the right to purchase them at the price being offered by the third party. Co-sale provisions usually prohibit management shareholders from transferring their shares in the company to a third party without giving existing investors the right to sell a pro-rata portion of their shares to the third party at the same price. The first-refusal provision is often vigorously opposed by the company, especially if a co-sale term exists, because it may reduce the company's attractiveness to prospective buyers.

A *buy-sell agreement* provides a liquidity option to shareholders, while limiting stock ownership to a small group. They are distinguished by three features. First, shareholders who are party to the agreement cannot transfer their shares except as permitted by the agreement. Second, permitted transfers, such as transfers to family members, are spelled out. And third, the conditions on which the company or other shareholders will buy the shares from the shareholder who wishes to sell the shares are specified.

Because buy-sell agreements are most useful when open-market indices of the stock's value are absent and usually do not require an arms-length, open-market transaction, they usually provide a mechanism for setting the price of the stock to be sold. This mechanism may be a preset price written into the agreement or a formula for valuing the stock at the time of sale, such as a multiple of earnings or a multiple of sales.

A *stock restriction and stock vesting* agreement ensures that stock allocated to employees is held by current employees. To accomplish this, vesting provisions may be required for large blocs of stock held by founders and key employees, under which they earn rights to the stock over time. These provisions also may provide the company with the right to repurchase "unvested" shares from the founder or manager on termination of employment. The purchase price of the stock under a buy-back agreement may be based on book value or on a formula. It is usually below market value. Vesting agreements define how key employees of venture-backed companies actually receive title to their equity ownership in the company. Shares typically "vest" over time; that is, the company's repurchase rights lapse over time as the employee earns the shares by remaining employed by the company.

Preemptive rights allow existing shareholders to purchase enough of any new shares being issued to maintain their existing proportionate ownership.

Antidilution provisions protect existing shareholders against a reduction in the percentage of a company they own. Antidilution provisions may include structural antidilution, full-ratchet antidilution, and pay-to-play. *Structural antidilution* provisions protect preferred stock against the dilutive issuance of securities in a corporate recapitalization that involves such actions as stock dividends, stock splits, and reverse splits. This protection ensures that preferred stockholders maintain their same ownership share after recapitalization. *Full-ratchet antidilution* provisions prevent the percentage of the corporation owned by lead investors from being reduced if shares are sold later at a lower price than the original shares. This provision normally allows the lead investors to receive free additional shares to maintain their percentage ownership. A *pay-to-play provision* provides that preferred stockholders get the benefit of price-protection antidilution only if they buy their share of any subsequent round of financing sold at prices lower than they paid.

Information rights require that the company regularly send information to the investor, including financial statements and budgets. The reporting frequency will be as often as the venture investor monitoring the company believes necessary to anticipate problems and to respond rapidly and appropriately. Usually, at least monthly reports are required.

Inspection rights allow investors to examine and inspect the properties and records of the company, to make copies of the records, and to discuss the affairs of the company with officers, directors, and key employees.

Employment contracts, executed between a company and key employees, usually specify compensation, benefits, the conditions under which the contract can be terminated, and the consequences of termination. Employment contracts normally contain "noncompete" clauses, which limit for a period of time a terminated employee's ability to work for a direct competitor. The restricted period may vary depending on whether the termination was the company's or the employee's decision.

Conversion rights define the conditions under which holders of convertible-preferred stock may convert their shares into common stock. Conversion rights may be optional (giving the holder discretion on when and whether to convert, which theory says should always be just before the rights expire) or automatic (triggered by the occurrence of certain events such as the completion of a public offering).

Dividend preferences define the conditions that will allow the company to pay dividends to the various classes of shareholders.

Liquidation preferences define priority claims that preferred shareholders have to the corporation's assets over other equity investors in case of liquidation.

Redemption rights allow a company to buy back or redeem its securities at a predetermined price at the company's option. This right is used to force a convertible security to convert into common stock rather than having to repurchase the convertible for cash. If a company does not go public, venture investors may be able to force the company to redeem the investment according to a predetermined pricing formula. Redemption rights are also known as *put-and-call rights.* Many venture-capital stock-purchase agreements include put-and-call provisions. Under a *put provision,* venture capitalists can force a company to purchase their shares (common or preferred) at a predetermined price. Under a *call provision,* a company has the option to repurchase a security at a predetermined price and time.

The Importance of Legal Issues in the Financing of Startup, Early-Stage, and Emerging Companies

Often entrepreneurs working 20-hour days to build businesses and realize dreams prefer not to be distracted by the legal details of financing, but dreams can be destroyed if such details are ignored. The legal details of financing can come back to haunt you in many ways, including the failure to maintain the corporation's legal basis through proper board activity, poorly thought through legal capital structure, and securities laws violations that can undermine the most promising business.

KEY POINT: Although dealing properly with the legal details of the corporation can be time consuming for senior management, it is an extremely important investment in the long-term success of the business. The legal aspects of a business should receive the same attention as marketing, financing, and operating decisions. They should not be left strictly to the discretion of the company's attorneys. *Note:* Use of experienced attorneys is nevertheless essential. Attorneys lacking knowledge and experience in these technical areas may not be able to guide the company around dangerous pitfalls.

Legal
Aspects of
Financing
Startup,
Early-Stage,
and
Emerging
Businesses

41

PART II

FINANCIAL PLANNING AND ASSET MANAGEMENT

CHAPTER 3

RATIOS AS ANALYTICAL TOOLS

This chapter first reviews the nature of the major financial reports provided to you and your company by its external auditors. Companies not dependent on the public capital markets do not require externally prepared statements or may prepare them in less detail. Financial institutions, however, may insist on audited statements before making loans of any size.

Next, the purposes and limitations of financial analysis are discussed. Finally, the principal ratios used in financial analysis are defined, along with the methods by which they are calculated and how they are applied.

In the art of financial analysis, ratios can be calculated and used in different ways. Some analysts prefer to divide sales by assets to calculate an asset-turnover ratio, but the same information can be gathered by dividing assets by sales to calculate an asset-efficiency measure. For now, however, the focus will be on the major techniques. Chapter 4 will use the ratios to prepare forecasts and budgets.

Financial Statements

Reports, or statements, based upon financial data are prepared for a variety of users and uses. For most businesses, the audience includes management, creditors, stockholders, trade associations, employees, regulatory and other governmental agencies, and the securities exchanges.

The usual statements prepared for both internal (management) and external (other users) purposes include the Balance Sheet, the Statement of Income (or of Earnings), and the Statement of Stockholders' Equity. In recent years, the Statement of Cash Flows has been added to the list of statements presented externally.

The *Balance Sheet,* or statement of financial position, reflects the financial status of a business according to its accounting records at *one point in time,* such as the close of business at the end of a month, quarter, or year. The balance sheet lists assets, liabilities, and owner's equity.

The *Statement of Income* shows the revenue realized from the sale of goods or services during a *specific period* and the expenses (not expenditures[1]) incurred during the same period to earn this revenue. The difference between revenues and expenses is the net income or profit of the business. The statement of income thus summarizes the firm's activities over a specific period, as opposed to showing the status at a point in time. These periods may be weekly, monthly, quarterly, or annually. Publicly owned companies usually publish income statements quarterly.

The *Statement of Stockholders' Equity,* sometimes combined with the income statement, reflects the changes in various owners' equity accounts. The most significant one is the change in retained earnings. Changes to other equity accounts occur, for instance, because of changes in the number of outstanding shares. A typical statement will show an increase in retained earnings from the addition of net income for the period and a decrease for the dividends declared.[2]

The *Statement of Cash Flows* summarizes all significant changes that occurred between the beginning and end of a company's accounting period. It highlights the financial resources marshaled and the uses to which they have been put.

The first part of the statement adjusts net income to show the "cash provided by operating activities." The second shows the "cash flows from investing activities," such as capital expenditures and acquisitions. The third shows the "cash flows from financing activities," by detailing changes in the capital structure and short-term borrowing. The balance of these segments is the change in the balance in cash and cash equivalents during the period. For the smaller company, the cash flow statement may be the most important management tool.

❯ **IMPORTANT: Traditional financial statements are based on historical data and are not very useful for day-to-day management of a business. Often, they are not available until long after the accounting period involved has passed. As one specialist in rescuing troubled companies has observed, "If you are relying on the financial accounting statements to run your business, it has probably already failed."**

You therefore must depend on a variety of other reports—daily, weekly, monthly, or when requested—for operating purposes. The interpretation

---

1. Expenditures may be made during an earlier period or during a period after the period in which the related revenue is recognized. The accrual system of bookkeeping strives to match the costs with the revenue by expensing them during the proper period. It holds the expenditures on the balance sheet as a prepaid asset if payment was made in advance of the recognition of the expense. Expenses that have been recognized but not yet paid are put on the balance sheet as liabilities.
2. Changes in retained earnings, usually net profit from the income statement less dividends, is basically as an entry to the retained earnings account on the balance sheet.

and timeliness of these reports is critical for successful management. Otherwise variances from planned results will be identified too late to be useful in helping management identify and address problems before they become serious.

> **KEY POINT: Without timely reports, costs, quality, quantity, and other key operating factors cannot be controlled effectively.**

Often, particularly in smaller businesses, a few key factors are critical to determining the company's financial health. In soft-drink bottling, for instance, key performance indicators are the number of cases shipped and whether the bottles are accurately filled. These data can be readily available with a lag of only a few hours. In a retail store, the factors may be the total sales per day and, given the ability to scan bar codes and process the associated data, the gross margin.

Nevertheless, reports based upon historical data may prove helpful in predicting future trends. But remember that not all factors that may affect the future are reflected in historical statements. For example, they may not provide the quantity of unfilled orders, particularly for smaller companies, yet this figure may be critical to estimating a firm's future financial requirements. Thus, traditional statements must be used with care in predicting such items as revenue, income, and cash balances.

Purpose and Limitations of Financial Statement Analysis

The analysis and interpretation of financial statements are basic to the decision-making process for creditors, stockholders, managers, and other groups. The external analyst, such as a bank credit officer, must answer questions related to a company's earnings capacity, ability to meet interest and principal obligations, ability to pay dividends, and general financial strengths and weaknesses.

> **SMART FINANCIAL MANAGEMENT: A comprehensive analysis, presenting data in meaningful terms, is a significant aid to understanding the profitability and financial strength of a company. When properly prepared, financial evaluations can be used in performance appraisal and to highlight similarities and differences among units of the same organization.**

Many limitations are inherent in financial statement analysis, partly because the statements themselves have the following limitations.

1. Many financial statements are prepared only in aggregate form, without a breakdown by such important factors as product line,

geographical area, fixed costs, variable costs, and responsibility centers.

2. Many dollar items included in the statements are estimates. Such items include valuing inventory (and thus cost of sales), computing the annual expense for depreciation,[3] determining doubtful accounts (bad debts), and deciding whether to write off goodwill or carry it on the balance sheet as an intangible asset. Thus, financial statements are not exact, although they often give an impression of preciseness by being shown "to the last penny."

3. Different companies, even in the same industry, may use different accounting methods and techniques. Among the more common alternatives are the last-in–first-out (LIFO) versus first-in–first-out (FIFO) inventory methods and accelerated depreciation versus straight-line depreciation. These differences can materially affect the comparability of statements among companies. Most companies in the steel industry adopted LIFO accounting in the 1950s, as soon as it was allowed. Consequently, a considerable portion of their inventory is still carried at 1950s' prices. This makes their inventory-to-sales relationship look like a food retailer, which turns its inventory eight or more times a year.

4. Financial statements do not show many factors that affect the financial condition and potential profitability of a company. Such factors as order backlog, proposed capital expenditures, and the importance of intangible assets (such as patents and intellectual property) and key personnel are often not revealed.

5. Environmental conditions are constantly changing. Thus, the economic and operational environment is usually different for the same company from one period or year to the next. Also, the environment may be different for companies of the same relative size operating in the same general industry depending on such factors as geographic location and product niches. A chain of nursing homes operating in the Midwest may have significantly different financial characteristics from a similar-sized one operating in the Southeast. The characteristics also will differ depending on whether the chain serves the private-pay or Medicaid market.

6. Financial statements are based on historical accounting data; analysis of these statements depicts past relationships. The analyst and the business owner are more interested in what is going on

3. The tax law may specify the period over which an asset must be depreciated for tax purposes, but good financial accounting practice may require a different period. *Tax rules are not a foundation for sound financial reporting and analysis.*

now and what is probable for the future. Although a business's characteristics seldom change rapidly and analysis relies heavily on past data in predicting the future, the analyst must be aware the future may be different.

Using Ratios as Tools for Financial Analysis

PREPARATION FOR ANALYSIS

To analyze financial statements, you should have an understanding of the process of collecting and presenting accounting data so you will understand the nature and limitations of the statements with which analysts work.

> **KEY POINT: To make a complete appraisal of a company's profitability and financial strength, the analyst should have a grasp of the physical facts that lie behind the numbers presented in dollar statements. The analyst must understand the environment in which the company operates, its production processes, its marketing policies, the nature of its inventories, the accounting practices and policies followed, and the relative competence of management. This last factor is particularly important in evaluating a new company, for which it may be the only factor that can be appraised.**

The presentation of financial statements varies from industry to industry, company to company, and sometimes from period to period for the same company. The analyst should rearrange and condense the statements according to the particular analytical needs and purposes for which the analysis is being made. For many small companies, the detail presented can obscure critical trends.

By rearranging and condensing the statements, the analyst has fewer numbers to work with and will have key numbers available for computing percentages and ratios. For example, in calculating costs as a percentage of sales, the analyst may productively group subcategories of the cost of goods sold and the selling, general, and administrative expenses rather than compute the ratio for each item.

Because the analyst must work with *comparable* statements, current statements may need to be recast so they are comparable with statements of previous periods or previous statements must be recast according to the principles underlying the current statements. If a company has had many significant acquisitions or dispositions of assets, development of comparable information may be almost impossible. Even the U.S. government does not adjust its numbers for many prior years when a series changes.

The more widely used analytical methods and techniques for statement analysis are:

> Comparing financial statements in terms of:
  o Increases and decreases in dollar amounts from one statement to the next.
  o Trend evaluation using percentage changes over time.
  o Component percentages—calculating the parts as a percentage of the sum, such as the cost of goods sold as a percentage of sales.
> Ratio analysis, which is a special form of percentage analysis.

These techniques may be used in analyzing external statements to measure the profitability and financial condition of a company, as well as in analyzing internal management statements to detect trends and variations in actual "happenings" compared with planned events.

> **SMART FINANCIAL MANAGEMENT: The analyst must remember that the purpose of analysis is to present the data in more understandable and meaningful terms. It is always possible to do a more thorough analysis than may be completed in the time available and to tell the reader "more about penguins" than the reader needs to know. The analyst therefore must focus quickly on the important aspects of the analysis and minimize time spent unproductively.**

COMPARATIVE STATEMENT ANALYSIS

Comparative statements are necessary for the analyst to study trends over several periods. For a comparative balance sheet showing increases and decreases in dollar amounts, see Exhibit 3-1.

> **KEY POINT: A comparative statement can highlight major changes that have occurred in the numbers being analyzed. It is easier to grasp changing relationships when the data are presented as increases and decreases rather than as absolute amounts. Increases and decreases can be stated as percentages as well as dollar amounts.**

Comparative Statements: Percentage Changes

In analyzing statements for more than two periods, trends should be explored and interpreted by comparing each line item in a statement with the same line item in a base period. The base period is usually the first period in the series being analyzed.

EXHIBIT 3-1

The Distributing Company
Comparative Balance Sheets as of
December 31, 20X4 and 20X5
(thousands of dollars)

ASSETS	12/31/X4	12/31/X5	INCREASE (DECREASE)
Curret assets			
Cash	$ 1,017	$ 1,141	$ 124
Accounts receivable (net)	2,622	2,557	(65)
Inventories	6,644	6,332	(312)
Prepaid expenses	25	17	(8)
Total current assets	$10,308	$10,047	$(261)
Long-term investments	—	257	257
Property and equipment (net)	580	598	18
Other assets	71	156	85
Total assets	$10,959	$11,058	$ 99

LIABILITIES AND OWNERS' EQUITY

	12/31/X4	12/31/X5	INCREASE (DECREASE)
Current liabilities			
Accounts payable	$ 1,500	$ 1,290	$(210)
Notes payable	514	—	(514)
Income taxes payable	38	155	117
Total current liabilities	$ 2,052	$ 1,445	$(607)
Long-term debt	—	400	400
Total liabilitics	$ 2,052	$ 1,845	$(207)
Owners' equity			
Capital stock	$ 600	$ 785	$ 185
Retained earnings	8,307	8,428	121
Total owners' equity	$ 8,907	$ 9,213	$ 306
Total liabilities and owners' equity	$10,959	$11,058	$ 99

Trend percentages are index numbers showing changes over a period related to the base period. The line-item amounts for the base period are stated as 100-percent figures. If the amount for a succeeding period is more than in the base period, the trend percentage will be more than 100; if the amount is less than in the base period, the trend percentage will be less than 100. A comparative income statement, with trend percentages computed, is illustrated in Exhibit 3-2.

Exhibit 3-2 shows, for example, that although total revenue in 20X2 was only approximately 13 percent above that of 20X1, net income increased more than 65 percent. In 20X4, however, total revenue was approximately the same as 20X2, but net income was only 12 percent of the amount realized in 20X1, the base year.

EXHIBIT 3-2

The Distributing Comany
Comparative Income Statements and Trend Percentages
for the Years Ended December 31, 20X1-20X5

	AMOUNTS					TREND PERCENTAGES				
	20X1	20X2	20X3	20X4	20X5	20X1	20X2	20X3	20X4	20X5
Sales revenue	$58,471	$67,227	$66,922	$65,833	$ 80,793	100.0%	114.9%	114.4%	112.5%	138.1%
Service revenue	15,824	16,704	17,899	17,970	20,427	100.0	105.5	113.1	113.5	129.0
Other revenue	1,722	1,949	2,023	1,773	2,051	100.0	113.1	117.4	102.9	119.1
Total revenue	$76,017	$85,880	$86,844	$85,576	$103,271	100.0	112.9	114.2	112.5	135.8
Costs of goods sold	32,572	35,456	37,036	38,112	42,695	100.0	108.8	113.7	117.0	131.0
Salaries and wages	23,688	26,737	26,954	27,761	32,389	100.0	112.8	113.7	117.1	136.7
Depreciation	920	1,046	1,192	1,266	1,875	100.0	113.6	129.5	137.6	203.8
Interest	—	—	—	18	161	—	—	—	—	n.a.
Income taxes	2,876	3,286	1,757	18	1,980	100.0	114.2	61.0	0.6	68.8
Other operating expenses	14,577	17,060	18,443	18,253	22,302	100.0	117.0	126.5	125.2	152.9
Net income	$ 1,384	$ 2,295	$ 1,462	$ 166	$ 1,869	100.0	165.2	105.7	11.9	134.9

What accounted for this difference? The most significant element is the increase in other operating expenses. At this point, the analyst should ask why operating expenses increased. An analyst is usually not interested in the trend of just one item, but in the trend of one item as it relates to another item, such as the cost of goods sold related to sales revenue.

A disadvantage of trend percentage analysis is that it is impossible to compute a trend percentage for an item if the item did not exist or was negative in the base period. For example, in Exhibit 3-2 does not show a percentage for interest expense.

As with all percentage calculations, trend percentages may not reflect the relative significance of individual items. This is another reason why statements should be presented in both dollar amounts and percentage terms. Exhibit 3-2 shows a much sharper increase in depreciation than in other operating expenses. Other operating expenses, however, are significantly higher in actual dollars than depreciation.

Comparative Statements: Component Percentages

The percentage relationship between a particular financial item and a significant total that includes this item is called a *component percentage*. Exhibit 3-3 presents an illustrative component-percentage income statement. A component percentage depicts the relative importance of the item in question to the total. For example, if labor expense is 82 percent of total expenses, it is obviously a much more significant factor than if it were only 15 percent of total expenses. Exhibit 3-3 shows that sales revenue is the most important element of total revenue—averaging approximately 77 percent during the period covered. Also, the three components of total revenue have been reasonably stable as percentages.

▶ SMART FINANCIAL MANAGEMENT: Component-percentage statements are particularly helpful in identifying items whose amounts are out of line with past periods and future plans. They are also useful in comparing data among companies and industries when you are checking the performance of a company against others in a similar business.

Again, it is important to show and evaluate dollar amounts as well as percentages. It is possible for an item to remain constant in dollars and to vary as a percentage because of changes in other items making up the total.

RATIO ANALYSIS

Ratios, which show relationships between items, are widely used in analyzing financial statements. The computation of ratios is mechanical; ratios do not explain the causes of relationships. The skilled analyst interprets

EXHIBIT 3-3

The Distributing Company
Comparative Income Statements and Component Percentages
for the Years Ended December 31, 20X1-20X5

	AMOUNTS					COMPONENT PERCENTAGES				
	20X1	20X2	20X3	20X4	20X5	20X1	20X2	20X3	20X4	20X5
Sales revenue	$58,471	$67,227	$66,922	$65,833	$ 80,793	76.9%	78.3%	77.1%	76.9%	78.2%
Service revenue	15,824	16,704	17,899	17,970	20,427	20.8	19.4	20.6	21.0	19.8
Other revenue	1,722	1,949	2,023	1,773	2,051	2.3	2.3	2.3	2.1	2.0
Total revenue	$76,071	$85,880	$86,844	$85,576	$103,271	100.0%	100.0%	100.0%	100.0%	100.0%
Costs of goods sold	32,572	35,456	37,036	38,112	42,695	42.8	41.3	42.7	44.5	41.3
Salaries and wages	23,688	26,737	26,954	27,761	32,389	31.2	31.1	31.0	32.5	31.4
Depreciation	920	1,046	1,192	1,266	1,875	1.2	1.2	1.4	1.5	1.8
Interest	—	—	—	—	161	—	—	—	—	0.2
Income taxes	2,876	3,286	1,757	18	1,980	3.8	3.8	2.0	—	1.9
Other operating expenses	14,577	17,060	18,443	18,253	22,302	19.2	19.9	21.2	21.3	21.6
Net income	$ 1,384	$ 2,295	$ 1,462	$ 166	$ 1,869	1.8%	2.7%	1.7%	0.2%	1.8%

the trends and deviations the ratios reflect by getting behind the figures. The analysis must identify the underlying causes and make a judgment on the operating results or financial condition of a business.

Investors, entrepreneurs, managers, credit agencies, security analysts, and other interpreters of financial statements use many ratios. Various trade associations and government agencies collect and publish information in ratio form, thus making averages and trends widely available for many industries. When analyzing a specific organization, you should look at its operation over time and in comparison with industry trends. Some common ratios and their computations are discussed in this section.

> **KEY POINT: Ratios can be grouped into families according to the type of insights the ratio offers. Within each family, each ratios contributes a different facet of the analysis. Because of the large number of ratios that can be calculated, the skillful analyst conserves time by selecting the most significant ratios to study. Each business has its own critical ratios that should be watched carefully.**

The four major ratio families are grouped by the type of information each provides:

1. Profitability: measures that relate earnings to sales or assets
2. Liquidity: measures that suggest ability to pay current bills
3. Asset use: measures that show the volume of business being generated by the investment in assets
4. Capitalization: measures that show how an enterprise finances its business

Profitability is measured in two ways: profits related to revenue and profits related to investment.

PROFITABILITY RELATIVE TO REVENUE The gross measure of profitability on revenue is the ratio of net income to sales:

$$\text{Return on Sales} \ = \ \frac{\text{Net Income}}{\text{Sales}}$$

When this relationship is stable, it can be used to forecast future profits once an estimate of future sales has been made. In most cases, however, the relationship varies because of changes in prices, product mix, and expense components. Thus, a detailed review of the relationships among the expense components of the income statement and sales is useful.

A typical component-percentage income statement is provided in Exhibit 3-3. Revenue is usually the key item in an income statement, and the level of many expense items is related directly to the volume or revenue. In The Distributing Company, the cost of goods sold is the largest single expense. It has varied between 41.3 percent and 44.5 percent of total revenue. After the cost of sales peaked in 20X4, management apparently brought the costs under control in 20X5.

For most companies, changes in gross margin and net profit percentages are important items for analysis. Different ratios would apply to a service operation, such as a taxi company. For the taxi company, salaries and wages, fuel, and maintenance expenses might be the most important items for analysis.

PROFITABILITY RELATIVE TO ASSETS EMPLOYED The continuation of a business hinges on its ability to earn a satisfactory return on the assets employed. Failure to do so may severely limit the firm's access to funds for growth or even for maintenance. A measure of this return is often computed as follows:

$$\text{Return on Assets} \ = \ \frac{\text{Net Income}}{\text{Assets}}$$

From Exhibits 3-1 and 3-2, the *Return on Assets* (ROA) for The Distributing Company for 20X5 is calculated as follows:

$$\text{Return on Assets} \ = \ \frac{\$1,869}{(\$11,058 + \$10,959) \div 2} \ = \ 16.9\%$$

There are several variations used in computing the ROA ratio. These include adjustments for interest expenses, nonoperating assets, and other items that affect the operating income and operating assets. One alternative, for example, measures the earning power of the assets without the distortion created by the amount of debt in the capital structure and by changing tax rates. This ratio, which uses the earnings before interest and taxes (EBIT) in the numerator, is computed as shown below. This measure can be termed the *Before Tax Return on Unlevered Assets* (a variant of the ROA calculation).

$$\text{Return Before Taxes on Unlevered Assets} \ = \ \frac{\text{Earnings Before Interest and Taxes}}{\text{Average Total Assets}}$$

For small businesses in particular, a company's cash-flow-generating capacity is more important than income measures. The ratios described above can easily be changed to substitute a measure of cash flow in the numerator. For instance, *earnings before interest and taxes* (EBIT) may be replaced with *earnings before interest, taxes, depreciation, and amortization* (EBITDA).

These ratios must be interpreted by considering the dollar costs ascribed to the assets and how net income (or cash flow) is calculated. For example, a company with older plant and equipment, purchased when the dollar was less inflated and largely depreciated, may show a higher ROA than a company with newer assets and a higher gross margin. The asset investment of the first company is so small its ROA overwhelms the more efficient performance of the second. The ratio calculated using the EBITDA figure may show the reverse, however. Also, companies with the same assets can report significantly different income depending on the accounting principles they use for such items as depreciation and inventory.

PROFITABILITY RELATIVE TO SHAREHOLDERS' EQUITY This ratio measures earning power from the viewpoint of the equity investor—after payment of interest and taxes. The *Return on Equity* (ROE) is typically computed as follows:

$$\text{Return on Equity} \quad = \quad \frac{\text{Net Income Available for Shareholders}}{\text{Shareholders' Equity}}$$

This measure appropriately uses net income; all claims above the common stockholders' claim on the company's earning have been deducted. If the firm has preferred stock outstanding, the dividends on this form of equity are subtracted from the net income for shareholders to derive the net income available for common shareholders. A *Return on Common Shareholders' Equity* can be calculated by using the adjusted net income in the numerator and the common shareholders' equity in the denominator.[4]

A further variation, for companies with publicly traded equity, is to calculate the ROE measures using the *market value* of the equity in the denominator. This ratio is called *Return on Equity Market Capitalization*. A similar return ratio can be calculated using all of the securities in the company's capital structure at their market value. This ratio is called *Return on Total Market Capitalization*.

It is very common to use the book value of the debt, however, in computing this ratio rather than to obtain market values. First, a market value for most debt is not available because the debt is not traded. Thus, an effort must be made to estimate the value of the debt by extrapolation from value of traded debt of the same risk rating. Second, most corporate debt now has a floating interest rate. The presumption therefore is that the debt would trade close to its book value.

---

4. Typical of the confusing nomenclature in the finance area is the term *Return on Investment* (ROI). Whether it refers to the ROA or the ROE can only be determined by inspection. The ROI can also refer to a measure of return on total capital, such as EBIT Capitalization.

Liquidity Ratios

Liquidity refers to a company's ability to meet its current obligations. These ratios, then, are related to a company's assets and liabilities classified as current (by definition, likely to mature within one year). The most common of these is the *Current Ratio:*

$$\text{Current Ratio} = \frac{\text{Current Assets}}{\text{Current Liabilities}}$$

From Exhibit 3-1, the Current Ratio for The Distributing Company for 20X5 is computed as follows:

$$\text{Current Ratio} = \frac{\$10,047}{\$1,445} = 6.9 \text{ to } 1$$

When interpreting this ratio, the analyst must consider the component items of current assets and current liabilities. For example, a company with most of its current assets in accounts receivable is more liquid than a company with most of its current assets in inventory. The *Acid Test* ratio can highlight these characteristics:

$$\text{Acid Test Ratio} = \frac{\text{Quick Assets}}{\text{Current Liabilities}}$$

Quick Assets include cash, short-term marketable securities, and accounts receivable. The assumption is that these items can be converted into cash quickly and at amounts close to those stated on the balance sheet.

Again, the nature of the underlying figures must be examined carefully. The accounts receivable number for a utility is usually reliable. Those accounts (excepting budget accounts) are due within thirty days. Most of the bills are paid within the time specified because customers do not want to risk an interruption in their power supply. The accounts receivable of an electronic equipment company, however, may be collectible only after the equipment has been tested and may be subject to deductions for rework and other claims.

For The Distributing Company, for 20X5, this ratio is:

$$\text{Acid Test Ratio} = \frac{\$3,698}{\$1,445} = 2.6 \text{ to } 1$$

No universal rule of thumb defines a "good" or "bad" current or acid-test ratio. A high current ratio, such as 3:1, may look good to a creditor. From the business owner's viewpoint, however, maintaining such a high ratio requires large amounts of idle cash. The owner may prefer to use the cash to repay long-term debt, which would lower the company's liquidity ratios, but might reduce its risk exposure. Thus, interpreting these ratios calls for caution and a knowledge of industry characteristics, the seasonal nature of the business, and the quality of assets and liabilities.

Asset Utilization Ratios

Several ratios measure the utilization or turnover of a company's assets or liabilities. The most widely used is called the *Receivables Collection Period* or *Days Sales Outstanding*. The ratio is computed (in days) as follows:

$$\text{Receivables Collection Period (Days Sales Outstanding)} = \frac{\text{Accounts Receivable}}{\text{Credit Sales}} \times 365$$

The collection period (DSO[5]) can be compared to the company's credit terms to get an indication of the quality of the receivables. If the for-credit sales figures are not available, a usable ratio can be made using total sales. If the proportion of credit sales to total sales remains stable over time, the trend may be analyzed even if the ratio is inaccurate. It will be consistently inaccurate, but the trend will correctly show whether collections are accelerating or stretching out. Note also that the number of days in the sales period must match the number of days in the calculation. If a quarter's sales are used, 90 rather than 365 days should be in the calculation.

On total revenue, the collection periods for The Distributing Company in 20X4 and 20X5 were 11.2 days and 9.0 days respectively. Even based solely on sales revenues, the numbers are 14.5 and 11.6 days. These suggest the company probably has short credit terms and perhaps many cash transactions. Furthermore, although sales went up in 20X5, receivables dropped.

Another measure of asset turnover is *Inventory Turnover*, which is computed as follows:

$$\text{Inventory Turnover} = \frac{\text{Cost of Goods Sold}}{(\text{Inventory Beginning of Year} = \text{End of Years}) \div 2}$$

This ratio expresses the number of times inventory was sold and replaced during a particular period. Again, no universal standard determines good

---

5. The designation "Day's Sales Outstanding" (DSO) is becoming more common, perhaps because "collection period" is a confusing term for what is actually the "non-collection" period. The term "collection period" also refers to a method of calculating the collection experience by determining the proportion of sales made in any given month that is collected in any subsequent month. For example, for sales made in any given month, the collection period may be 50 percent between 30 and 60 days later, 40 percent between 60 and 90 days, and 9 percent between 90 and 120 days with a 1 percent write-off. This approach is discussed in Chapter 5, Managing Accounts Receivable

or bad. Also, different methods of computing inventory cost (LIFO versus FIFO) distort comparisons among companies. The ratio can be useful, however, in identifying changes in the way a company is managing its inventory. The Distributing Company's inventory turnover was 6.9 times in 20X5, a high figure reflecting its nonmanufacturing nature.

It is sometimes possible to apply a measure to accounts payable similar to the collection period for accounts receivable. The *Days' Purchases Outstanding* or *Accounts Payable Period* ratio is computed as follows:

$$\text{Accounts Payable Period} = \frac{\text{Accounts Payable}}{\text{Purchases}} \times 365$$

The result can be compared to credit terms extended by suppliers to see if the company is riding creditors or if accounts are paid promptly. The information needed to compute this ratio accurately may not be available to the outside analyst. The purchases figure is, however, often provided for smaller companies as part of deriving the closing inventory figure. For larger companies, the analyst must resort to using the cost of sales rather than purchases. This approximation usually will show a shorter payable period than the true period because nonpurchased items (such as labor and overhead) are included in cost of sales. Nevertheless, the trend in the payables period can suggest whether payment practices have changed.

A company with cash-flow problems will typically stretch its payables to gain a source of funds from its suppliers. This practice may be more expensive than negotiating a bank loan, but it can raise funds more quickly and with less explanation.

Capitalization Ratios

Capitalization refers to a company's long-term financing—the investment made in the company by long-term creditors and owners. Ratios can show the relationship of debt to equity, to total capitalization, and to total assets. The ratios may be calculated on book value or on the market value of the securities, if this information is available. These ratios suggest the extent to which a company is leveraged or "trading on the equity." The higher the percentage of debt, the more a company is using borrowed money compared with equity supplied by stockholders.

Common capitalization ratios include:

$$\text{Leverage on Capital} = \frac{\text{Assets}}{\text{Long-Term Debt} + \text{Equity}}$$

which shows how many dollars of assets have been (and, if optimal, can in the future be) acquired by each dollar of capital invested. The higher this ratio is, the more the company is relying on current liabilities to finance its operations.

The definition of long-term debt, unfortunately, is imprecise. Ratios calculated on the same balance sheet may therefore differ depending on how intermediate-term and short-term bank debt perpetually on the books are classified. Ratios included in loan covenants should be clearly specified if costly misunderstandings are to be avoided.

$$\text{Leverage on Equity} \ = \ \frac{\text{Long-Term Debt}}{\text{Equity}}$$

which suggests the ability of the owners to obtain long-term debt for each dollar they contribute as equity. Higher ratios usually belong to safer ventures, but startup situations may rely heavily on senior debt (which may have a contingent claim on the equity if all goes well). Troubled companies may inadvertently find themselves with a high leverage on equity because of operating losses that erode the equity balance.

An alternate method of calculating leverage is:

$$\text{Long-Term Debt to Capital} \ = \ \frac{\text{Long-Term Debt}}{\text{Long-Term Debt} + \text{Equity}}$$

One advantage of this ratio is that its limits are 0 percent and 100 percent, whereas the leverage-on-equity ratio is unbounded at the top.

A third useful ratio is the simple *debt-equity ratio*. These ratios may be derived from each other because both involve long-term debt and equity. For instance, if the long-term debt-to-equity ratio is 40 percent, then:

$$\frac{\text{Debt}}{\text{Equity}} \ = \ \frac{40}{100}$$

and the long-term debt-to-capital ratio will be:

$$\frac{\text{Debt}}{\text{Debt} + \text{Equity}} \ = \ \frac{40}{40 + 100} \ = \ 29\%$$

Alternatively, if the debt-to-capital ratio is 25 percent, then:

$$\frac{\text{Debt}}{\text{Debt} + \text{Equity}} \ = \ \frac{25}{100}$$

If debt equals 25 of the 100, then equity must be 75. Therefore, debt to equity is 25:75 or 33.3 percent.

The Distributing Company had only $400,000 in long-term debt, which was approximately 4 percent of the total capitalization in 20X5.

Return Ratios

Return on total assets (ROA), a significant measure of entrepreneurial effectiveness, is a combination of the sales-profitability measure and an asset-utilization ratio. By calculating each component of the measure, it is possible to analyze more precisely the origins of the company's profitability: marketing or production. The two components of this calculation, sometimes called the DuPont formula because it was developed by the management of that company into an extensive analysis system, are:

$$\text{Return on Assets} = \frac{\text{Income}}{\text{Sales (or Revenue)}} \times \frac{\text{Sales}}{\text{Average Total Assets}}$$

$$= \frac{\text{Income}}{\text{Average Total Assets}}$$

When the component ratios are calculated for several years, it is easy to determine if profit margin (marketing) or asset turnover (operating efficiency) is having the greater impact on the return on the company's assets.

Although the ROA helps identify the relative contributions of the marketing and the production activities, it does not reflect the effects of financing on the stockholders' profitability. This is provided by the return on equity (ROE) ratio, which is the ROA times the leverage-on-equity ratio:

$$\text{Return on Equity} = \frac{\text{Income}}{\text{Assets}} \times \frac{\text{Assets}}{\text{Equity}}$$

> **KEY POINT:** In general terms, the sales-profitability ratio and its subcomponents are measures of marketing activity. The asset-utilization ratios measure operating management. The capital-leverage ratios are the finance department's responsibility. The return-on-equity ratio is a measure of the corporate effectiveness. The ROE, for a group of companies in diverse industries, should have much less variation than the individual components of the ratio because the equity investors ultimately price the return based on the risk. If returns are unusually high for the risk, more funds will flow to that sector of the economy, depressing the return (price competition). If returns are low, funds are withdrawn until the returns finally improve.

Other Ratios

Many ratios have been developed by trade associations, credit reporting agencies, security analysts, and other users of financial statements. Some ratios are peculiar to certain industries such as transportation, utilities, and insurance. Others are of a more general nature. If the analyst can find out which relationships are important to measure, a ratio can be developed to measure them.

INDUSTRY CHARACTERISTICS

The financial characteristics of an industry are closely related to that industry's production process, marketing activities, and financial practices and customs. The numbers already cited for The Distributing Company show the characteristics of a company in the wholesale business: large inventories but little long-term plant and equipment. The reverse would be true for an electric utility, which would be characterized by a very low asset-turnover ratio but a better profit margin. Many manufacturing companies would fall between the extremes of a utility and a merchandising firm.

For example, the major differences between retail food stores and a basic chemical manufacturing business are the following.

1. *Depreciation.* Manufacturing is more capital intensive, with owned fixed assets comprising a high proportion of total assets. Thus, there are more assets to be depreciated. In addition, many smaller retail stores lease their buildings for periods that do not require the leases to be capitalized. This leads to less depreciation and more rental payments. Long-term leases are often capitalized, however, so that the lease obligation will appear as long-term debt with a corresponding figure in the fixed-asset account. Retail chains with large stores generally sign long-term leases.

2. *Current Ratio.* Retailers usually do not carry accounts receivable because their customers pay cash or use credit cards, but accounts receivable is a significant item in the current assets of a manufacturing firm. Thus, retail stores may have lower current ratios than manufacturing firms. Because of the high proportion of inventory in a retailer's current assets, its acid test ratio also may be worse than a manufacturer's.

3. *Net Sales to Net Working Capital.* Net working capital in this context means current assets minus current liabilities. The retail food store turns its inventory (sales ÷ average inventory) much more rapidly than a manufacturing firm—and even than a furniture store. This, coupled with no receivables, leads to a much higher working-capital turn. If the manufacturing company had used LIFO for many years to calculate its inventory, however, the low valuation of the inventory might create an artificially high working-capital turnover. It would therefore not be a useful number to use in estimating increases in working capital that would be needed to support increases in sales.

4. *Net Profit Before Tax.* The manufacturing company turns its assets (sales ÷ assets) fewer times in a period than the retailing company

does. Therefore, to earn an adequate return on assets employed, the manufacturing company needs to earn more profit as a percentage of sales than the retailing company.

5. *Net Income to Net Worth.* Retail food stores, despite a much lower profit margin on sales, can have a higher return on net worth because they have a higher proportion of debt compared with equity and also a higher turnover of assets.

These industry comparisons illustrate the dangers of trying to apply universally accepted ratios. Each industry has its own characteristics that can affect ratios significantly. With practice in analyzing various industries, the analyst will become familiar with industry characteristics and interpret a company's financial ratios in the proper context. The Risk Management Association (www.rmahq.org) publishes the *Annual Statement Studies: Financial Ratio Benchmarks,* which provides ratio data by performance quartiles for a wide range of industries. Commercial banks use this information and may make the book available to customers. BB&T Bank, for example, offers small business owners a compact disk that contains performance data for similar businesses.

Other Analytical Techniques

Many other techniques can be used to evaluate a company's potential profitability and financial condition. Although a few are briefly described, see Chapter 4 for a more thorough discussion.

➤ *Cash Flow Statements.* Cash flow statements are more helpful than ratios in projecting a company's ability to repay debt, in projecting potential cash needs to support increased sales and capital expenditures, and in identifying patterns of corporate financial policy.

➤ *Projected Statements.* By projecting a company's financial statements under varying assumed conditions, you can learn the effects of the risks of the assumed conditions—economic slowdowns, strikes, heavy promotion efforts, or other variables that affect the company's operations. The results, however, are only as reliable as the underlying assumptions.

➤ *Break-even Analysis.* If a company's fixed and variable costs are known, it is possible to calculate the revenue volume needed to "break even." More important, given certain projected revenue volumes, it is possible to calculate the expected profit at these levels.

The break-even sales figure is the sales volume at which the contribution to fixed costs equals the fixed costs. Fixed costs are expenses that do not vary with sales. The company would have incurred these costs even if it did not open its doors. The contribution to fixed costs is the percentage of a sales dollar that is not used in out-of-pocket costs to produce the item and make the sale (these costs are commonly called the variable costs).

The break-even sales level is thus calculated by dividing the fixed costs by the contribution percentage:

$$\text{Break-Even Sales} = \frac{\text{Fixed Costs}}{(\text{Sales} - \text{Variable Costs}) \div \text{Sales}}$$

For instance, if variable costs are 40 percent of a dollar of sales and the company's fixed costs are $30,000, the company must sell $50,000 ($30,000 ÷ .6) to break even. At $50,000 sales, the variable costs are 40 percent, $20,000, leaving $30,000 to cover the fixed costs.

> **KEY POINT: Profit at any sales level can be calculated simply by multiplying the sales projection by the contribution margin and subtracting the fixed costs. This is a straight-line relationship, so it can be charted for convenient reference. It is important to reemphasize that profit is different from cash. As pointed out in the life-cycle discussion in Chapter 1, an enterprise in its growth stage can be profitable and still run a major cash deficit.**

Financial Analysis and Ratio Interrelationships

As indicated, the return-on-investment ratio can be derived as the product of the return-on-sales and the asset-efficiency ratios. This is one of many instances illustrating how ratios can be combined to produce important analytical insights. In recent years, the analysis has been extended to develop an approximate measure of the *sustainable growth rate.* The name of the DuPont company is associated with this type of analysis because that company's management pioneered in the development of these relationships and the interpretation of their meanings. Partly expanded sets of the DuPont ratios are presented in Exhibit 3-4.

The first set is the basic equation relating marketing efficiency, as the return-on-sales, to production efficiency, the sales-turnover ratio, to derive the return-on-assets measure. This ratio is a sign of the efficiency with which the company's funds are being put to work. We have already shown how each of these two component ratios can be broken down for further analysis into subcomponents, such as the gross margin and the days sales' outstanding.

The second and third equations introduce the effect of the company's capital structure into the analysis. The components of the profit-sales ratio are the responsibility of the marketing department, and the components of the sales-asset ratio are largely under the control of the production

EXHIBIT 3-4

"DuPont" Ratios Interrelationships

1. BASIC "DUPONT" RATIOS

Marketing Efficiency		*Production Efficiency*		*Funds Efficiency*
$\dfrac{\text{Profit}}{\text{Sales}}$	$\times$	$\dfrac{\text{Sales}}{\text{Assets}}$	$=$	$\dfrac{\text{Profit}}{\text{Assets}}$

2. CAPITAL LEVERAGE

Funds Efficiency		*Leverage on Capital*		*Return on Equity (Capital Efficiency)*
$\dfrac{\text{Profit}}{\text{Asset}}$	$\times$	$\dfrac{\text{Assets}}{\text{Capital (LTD + OE)}}$	$=$	$\dfrac{\text{Profit}}{\text{Captial (LTD + OE)}}$

3. LEVERAGE ON EQUITY

Return On Equity		*Retention Rate*		*Growth in Equity*
$\dfrac{\text{Profit}}{\text{Capital}}$	$\times$	$\dfrac{\text{Capital}}{\text{Equity}}$	$=$	$\dfrac{\text{Profit}}{\text{Equity}}$

4. GROWTH IN EQUITY ("SUSTAINABLE GROWTH RATE")

Return on Equity		*Retention Rate*		*Growth in Equity*
$\dfrac{\text{Profit}}{\text{Equity}}$	$\times$	$(1-\text{Dividend Rate})$	$=$	$\dfrac{\text{Increase in Retained Earnings}}{\text{Equity}}$

department, but a company's financial structure is the responsibility of the financial executives.

The second equation in Exhibit 3-4 illustrates how return-on-capital (long-term debt plus owner's equity) can be enhanced by use of current liabilities, such as trade accounts payable, commercial paper, and bank notes. A company that can get more assets for a dollar of capital (by implication, increasing the level of current liabilities) is using its capital more efficiently than a company that does not have this ability. More assets bring more sales and profits. Therefore, as shown in equation (2) of Exhibit 3-4, a higher return on capital will result. The use of such funds, of course, can create a higher level of financial risk (the analysis of this issue will be discussed in Chapter 8). In addition, the earnings on the business must be higher than the cost of the debt for a positive benefit to be obtained by using that form of financing.

Just as a company that can get additional current liabilities in proportion to its capital may, under favorable operating conditions, enhance its return on capital, a company that can get additional long-term debt (in one of its many forms) in proportion to its equity may enhance its return on equity. This relationship is shown in equation (3). Again, for the effect of the leverage to be favorable, the company must earn more than enough to pay the interest on the debt.

> **SMART FINANCIAL MANAGEMENT: The relationships spelled out in equations (2) and (3) can be compressed into one step by using the assets-equity ratio as the second component of equation (2). The product of the calculation is the return on equity (ROE), as in equation (3).**

The fourth relationship specified in Exhibit 3-4 is between the return on equity, a product of many complex interrelationships, and the growth in the equity account. The critical variable in this relationship is the proportion of the earnings retained in the business after dividends have been paid to the various classes of equity owners. For example, if a company earns 10 percent on its equity and pays no dividends, the earnings retained will increase the owners' equity by the full 10 percent. If the company pays out half its earnings in dividends, retaining only half, the increase will be half the return, or 5 percent. The rate of growth in the equity account, in general terms and ignoring the sale of additional equity, is thus the return-on-equity times the proportion-of-earnings-retained. Because the more common measurement of dividends is the proportion of profit paid out, or not retained, the retention rate is often written as (1 – payout rate).

> **KEY POINT: The rate of increase in the equity accounts is an especially important ratio because it is also the rate at which the company can comfortably increase its sales without having to alter its other financial policies.**

This rate has been called the *sustainable growth rate* (SGR). It is a useful measure because, first, it is easily derived. Second, it can quickly alert you to potential financial difficulty that should be investigated carefully. If the company's growth exceeds the sustainable rate, some aspect of its policies has to change. If it is growing at less than this rate, the company should be generating cash (or repaying debt). Investigation of the other ratios, over time, can be most helpful in figuring out the origin and extent of the problems, if any.

Although the demonstration that the growth in equity is the SGR is most commonly done in mathematical terms, a graphic illustration may be as efficient and more memorable. First, consider a very simple situation,

EXHIBIT 3-5

Chart Representing
DuPont Ratio Interrelationships

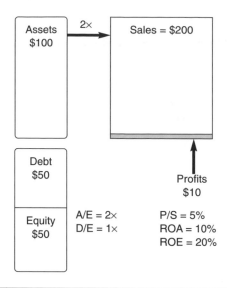

illustrated in Exhibit 3-5. The relevant summary ratios describing the company's operating and financial characteristics are as follows:

➤ Production efficiency: Sales ÷ Assets = 2 times
($1 of assets will generate $2 of sales; $0.50 of assets will generate $1 of sales).
➤ Marketing efficiency: Profit ÷ Sales = 5%
(An extra $1 of sales generates an extra $0.05 of profits).
➤ Equity efficiency: Assets ÷ Equity = 2 (in this instance)
(This is the product of the leverage on capital and the leverage on equity, simplifying the two components into one; note that the implied ratio of total debt to equity is 1:1).

As Exhibit 3-5 shows, these relationships produce a sales volume that is twice the total assets. The sliver of total sales remaining after all costs of operations and taxes is the profit. Assets are supported, as the graphic indicates, by sources of funds that are half debt and half equity.

The return on equity is the funds efficiency times the leverage on equity, an attractive 20 percent, derived as follows:

MARKETING EFFICIENCY		PRODUCTION EFFICIENCY		EQUITY EFFICIENCY		RETURN ON EQUITY
$\dfrac{\text{Profit}}{\text{Sales}}$	$\times$	$\dfrac{\text{Sales}}{\text{Assets}}$	$\times$	$\dfrac{\text{Assets}}{\text{Equity}}$	$=$	$\dfrac{\text{Profit}}{\text{Equity}}$
5%		2×		2×		20%

EXHIBIT 3-6

Illustration of Effect of Dividend Payout on Equity Growth

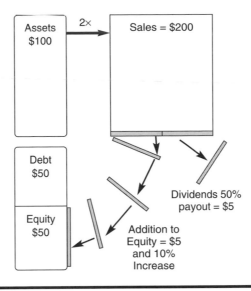

Exhibit 3-6 shows the effect of the dividend decision:

➤ Dividend payout ratio: 50%
(By subtraction, the retention rate is also 50%).

Funds (usually cash) amounting to half the profits are paid to the equity owners. The remaining half of net income is added to the equity account on the balance sheet. Consequently, the earnings retained create a 10 percent increase in the equity account. In terms of the formulas, this may be represented as:

RETURN ON EQUITY		RETENTION RATE		GROWTH IN EQUITY
				Increase in
$\dfrac{\text{Profit}}{\text{Equity}}$	$\times$	$(1 - \text{Dividend Rate})$	$=$	$\dfrac{\text{Retained Earnings}}{\text{Equity}}$
20%		50%		10%

The 10 percent increase in equity, given a debt-equity relationship of 1:1, will allow an additional 10 percent debt, as shown in Exhibit 3-7.

Because sources and uses must equal, the 10 percent increase in the liabilities-owner's equity (source of funds) side allows management to increase the firm's assets by 10 percent. Furthermore, for each $1 of new assets, the company can generate an additional $2 of sales. Because the sales are twice the assets, however, a $2 increase in sales is the same

EXHIBIT 3·7
Illustration of Effect of 10 Percent Growth

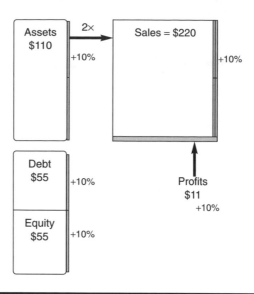

proportionate increase as a $1 increase in assets. Therefore, the 10 percent relationship carries all the way from the equity account to sales.

> **KEY POINT: The increase in the equity foundation of a soundly managed company allows a proportionate increase in debt, assets, and sales**

What happens if sales increase faster than the equity account can grow? This can occur if management is attempting to maintain the company's market share in a rapidly growing market or to enhance it in a more stable one. The demands of the market are large, and, rather than constrain the company's sales growth to a level proportionate with the equity account, sales are allowed to increase according to market demand.

Exhibit 3-8 illustrates this situation, using the interrelationships already established for the 10 percent growth example. Sales, the initiating variable in this illustration, have been allowed to grow by 40 percent, from $200 to $280. This requires a proportionate increase of 40 percent in assets. In absolute terms, the increase in the dollar amount of assets will be half the increase in the dollar amount of sales because of the sales-asset ratio of 2:1. Nevertheless, a 40 percent increase in assets (uses of funds) requires a 40 percent increase in sources, which must be equal dollar amounts.

Profits would be 5 percent of $280, $14 before dividends. After a 50 percent dividend payout, $7 would be added to equity, bringing the

EXHIBIT 3-8

Illustration of Sales Growth
Exceeding Equity Growth

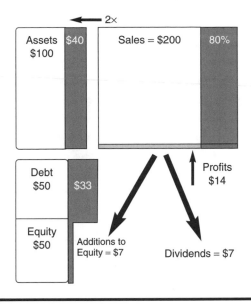

total to $57. Assets increased by $40, from $100 to $140. At a 1:1 debt-equity ratio, equity should be $70. It is $13 short, which must be made up by debt.

Debt thus increases from $50 to $83, creating a debt-equity ratio of 83:57, 1.4:1, as shown in Exhibit 3-8. On the margin, funds were raised at 33:7, nearly 5:1, which can quickly change the underlying total debt-equity relationship if new funds are repeatedly added in significant amounts at this proportion.

Even with the burst of new sales in the following years, it will take time to bring the debt-equity ratio back to 1:1. Suppose in the following year, sales were to grow by the traditional 10 percent, from $280 to $308. This sales level requires $154 in assets. It can generate profits of $15.4 and an addition of $7.7 to retained earnings after dividends. Equity will now be $64.7 ($57 + $7.7) versus a target of $77. The shortfall has been cut from $13 ($70 − $57) to $12.30 ($77 − $64.70). At this rate of closure ($12.30 ÷ $0.70), it will take more than 15 years for the debt-equity ratio to return to the target level.

By making the convenient assumption that the company's initial financial position was optimal and the profit after tax was 5 percent of sales, this discussion has avoided many complications of the real world. For example, if the company had initially been using less than optimal debt, it could have initially financed the high rate of growth by tempo-rarily using proportionately more debt than the ultimate target. Drawing more than proportionately on one source of funds, however, will quickly consume any spare funds that exist in that category. Even if no initial debt had existed in this example, the addition of debt at the incremental rate of 5:1 debt-equity will quickly bring the total debt up to the target of 1:1 with total equity.

> **SMART FINANCIAL MANAGEMENT: A temporary imbalance offers limited relief before the discipline of the sustainable rate of growth again must be recognized. For many rapidly growing companies, this discipline means a difficult choice. Management must choose to raise additional equity funds, to slow growth, or to risk potential serious financial difficulty and possible financial collapse if the creditors decline to provide further funds or demand repayment of funds already advanced.**

Analyzing Financial Statements

This chapter has introduced some widely used techniques and methods for analyzing financial statements. The techniques have been applied to statements prepared for public consumption. The basic techniques, however, also can be applied to internal management reports for any type of organization.

Ratios can be useful, especially for analysis of comparable periods (such as year-end to year-end) and when underlying operating results are stable from period to period. Ratios can be extremely misleading if some components are subject to major but routine fluctuations. If sales-to-date are used as the denominator of the calculation, the day's sales outstanding calculated for the accounts receivable of a department store as of January 31 will be quite different from the day's sales outstanding calculated as of September 30. This difference will largely be the result of the different sale levels in August-September and December-January, rather than a sign of any fundamental change in the store's operating characteristics. Chapter 4 discusses ways to analyze and appraise these differences in preparing a funds forecast and cash budget. Chapter 5 offers more detailed techniques for analyzing and forecasting accounts-receivable balances.

FORECASTING, BUDGETING, AND CASH MANAGEMENT

The most important rule for the financial management of smaller companies is not to run out of cash. Of course, this rule holds true for companies of all sizes. It is a more serious problem for the smaller enterprise because the smaller enterprise faces greater difficulties in raising cash. Small business owners must therefore watch the cash balance more carefully than the profit figure. It is lack of cash, not lack of profits, which forces firms into bankruptcy.

This chapter provides an overview of funds forecasting and budgeting to provide you with basic tools to plan your firm's cash management. Subsequent chapters provide more detailed tools for planning and managing your company's major assets.

A budget is how you *hope* the business will operate; a forecast is what you *think* will happen. Budgeting and forecasting mechanisms are the same, but the budgeting process comes first. Forecasts are made later, when the outlines of the future are better defined. At that point, a comparison between budget and forecast may suggest actions to be taken and adjustments to be made to bring them closer together.

A funds budget or forecast is constructed in the same way as a cash budget or forecast. The cash and funds budgets and forecasts have somewhat different objectives, however, as will be explained. Because the forecast—based on some indication of what is actually happening—is more important in cash and funds management than the budget, the emphasis in this chapter is on forecasting: what is likely to happen rather than what you hope will happen.

An introduction to forecasting tools requires detailed examples. Computer-based spreadsheets make the development of budgets and forecasts much easier today than for previous generations of managers. There are even software packages that provide forecasting tools, although these templates must often be modified to fit the needs of a particular business.

> **KEY POINT: Despite the availability of electronic assistance, the most critical element of cash and fund projections is the quality of the estimates made by knowledgeable managers in preparing them.**

Effective management of cash and credit relationships depends on good funds forecasting. Without funds forecasts, the treasurer will not know when to expect cash surpluses or deficiencies, the amount of the surplus or deficiency, nor the duration of the borrowing need or investment opportunity. Funds and cash forecasts may be made for short-range planning purposes on a daily, weekly, or monthly basis, or for long-range planning purposes, usually for one year or longer.

Two methods are used to forecast funds needs. If consistent assumptions are used, the two methods obviously provide the same estimates of fund requirements or surpluses. The criterion for choosing a method is which will give the information needed in the most efficient manner.

Basic Approaches to Cash and Funds Forecasting

The *Income-Statement/Balance-Sheet* (IS/BS) method provides the more comprehensive information about the disposition of *funds* in the business. This technique requires a forecast of the income statement and associated end-of-period balance sheet accounts in the detail appropriate for the analysis. The difference between the resulting forecast of assets (uses) and of liabilities and owners' equity (sources) is the estimate of spare funds available (if uses are less than sources) or of additional funds needed (if uses are greater than sources). The difference is often called the "plug figure."

> **SMART FINANCIAL MANAGEMENT: The IS/BS approach is particularly useful when a full picture of a company's financial position is needed. The complete financial statements allow you (and the banker) to see how asset and liability accounts change over the forecast (or budget) period. This information shows where the firm is allocating resources and how it expects to be funded.**

A lender for instance, may want to know whether the enterprise is gaining funds from other external sources and what external sources are getting net payments. A lender also may want to know whether funds are being generated from ongoing operations or by shrinking assets.

The *Cash-Receipts/Cash-Disbursements* (CR/CD) method is the more abbreviated technique. CR/CD focuses on the *cash* account, identifying all the deposits to and disbursements from it. It does not allow detailed insights to be obtained easily or clearly about where the rest of the funds are in the business. If cash at the end of the forecasting period is greater than the company's minimum operating cash balance, the excess is the amount of spare funds. If the forecast cash balance is smaller than the minimum operating balance, the shortfall is the amount of cash needed from an external source. This amount should be the same as the "plug figure" calculated by the IS/BS method. The CR/CD technique provides the same information for a company as your checkbook provides about your personal finances. The technique does not provide easy insight into asset, liability, or net worth positions.

> **KEY POINT: The CR/CD forecasting method is often easier to use because it involves fewer calculations: cash receipts and collections on accounts, payments to suppliers, payroll, taxes, and distributions to external sources of funds. It is the method often used by corporate treasurers to forecast a firm's short-term, day-to-day, or even month-to-month borrowing requirements. It will not easily show, however, what is happening to inventories or whether suppliers are being paid ahead of banks.**

FLOW OF FUNDS

Another technique is useful for analyzing the flow of funds over time. It is, however, cumbersome and difficult to use as a forecasting tool. A *Flow-of-Funds* (FOF) calculation is most appropriately applied to the analysis of historical financial statements or of projected financial statements already created by the IS/BS method.

> **KEY POINT: Because the application of the FOF technique to forecasts requires the existence of a complete IS/BS forecast, the FOF analysis adds no insights to the forecast of the plug figure already available. The FOF is useful, nevertheless, in helping analyze how a firm is receiving and using its funds.**

Defining "funds" is not easy. The funds available to a company is the sum of the credit it can obtain, the long-term debt it has available, the equity capital contributed by the owners, and the equity left in the business as retained earnings. The funds invested, in the largest sense, are the company's assets.

Funds *flow into and out of* a business as it *changes its scale of operations.* For example, a firm may increase its sales volume and thus its needs for assets (uses), credit, and equity (sources). A decrease in sales may decrease funds used. This effect often takes place because of a company's seasonal business pattern. As sales expand and contract, the funds used expand and contract.

Funds *flow within* a business during the production cycle, as it transforms its assets from cash to inventory to accounts receivable and back to cash again. There may be comparable changes during this cycle in the company's sources of funds from trade accounts payable to bank seasonal credit.

Preparing the Income-Statement/ Balance-Sheet Forecast

There are two basic approaches to preparing an IS/BS forecast. The more complex is the preparation of a *T-account* for each item, tracing sources and uses of funds to each account involved in a transaction. The second approach is easier. It uses the *historical ratios* between appropriate income and balance sheet accounts as the basis for the forecast. This method is useful if the relationships are stable and the level of detail needed is not great. Historical ratios, lacking more precise information, can provide a way of estimating at least the general size of a company's need for funds and the way the funds will be committed. The historical relationships must be adjusted, of course, for changes expected during the forecast period.[1] Because the ratios method is the easier technique to use, it will be illustrated first and then followed by a discussion of the T-account method.

USING RATIOS TO FORECAST FINANCIAL REQUIREMENTS

The use of ratios as tools for projecting financial statements will be illustrated by the Arc Company, a manufacturer of industrial products.[2] Exhibit 4-1 presents summary financial statements for Arc's last five years. Exhibit 4-2 provides a ratio analysis of accounts central to the forecast. In this example, an external analyst, the company's commercial banker, is preparing the analysis. Although the technique is the same, the forecast will not be as precise as if it were prepared internally. It is therefore possible to simplify the analysis by combining certain accounts and rounding to reasonable limits, which an internal analyst might not want to do. The internal analyst would use the same techniques but apply them to more detailed accounts. For instance, rather than using a ratio of costs to sales, the internal analyst might break out the labor and materials cost by product for the forecasted sales of each product.

In early 2004, Arc Company's management was slightly optimistic and told Arc's banker that a sales increase of 10 percent was expected for 2004. If the economy became stronger, sales might increase by as much as 15 percent. These two estimates are reflected in the "Low" and "High" columns of Exhibit 4-3, which contains the banker's forecast of Arc's funds needs.

Reviewing the company's historical income statements presented in Exhibit 4-1 and the percentage analysis shown in Exhibit 4-2, the banker

---

Financial Planning and Asset Management

1. Note, however, that relationships may be stable from comparable periods from year to year but may not be consistent from period to period within a year because of the pattern of seasonal activity.

2. Unlike a service business, a manufacturer will typically have significant balances in all major asset accounts. Even retailers, who tend to sell for cash (or credit card), will not have as well-distributed balances as a manufacturer. For illustrative purposes, therefore, a manufacturer makes a better example.

EXHIBIT 4-1

Arc Company, Inc. Financial Statements, Years Ended December 31, 1999–2003 (thousands of dollars)

INCOME STATEMENT	1999	2000	2001	2002	2003
Net sales	$211.2	$217.5	$203.4	$234.3	$256.2
Cost of sales*	135.0	145.2	135.3	145.8	162.3
Gross margin	$ 76.2	$72.3	$68.1	$88.5	$93.9
Total expenses	57.6	60.0	58.2	63.3	66.3
Net operating income	$ 18.6	$12.3	$9.9	$25.2	$27.6
Other expense net of other income	1.2	0.9	0.6	0.6	0.9
Income before tax	$ 17.4	$11.4	$9.3	$24.6	$26.7
Federal, state, and local income taxes	8.7	5.7	4.7	12.3	13.4
Net income	$ 8.7	$ 5.7	$ 4.6	$ 12.3	$ 13.3
Dividends–Preferred	$ 0.9	$ 0.9	$ 0.9	$ 0.6	$ 0.6
Dividends–Common	2.4	2.4	3.1	6.0	6.0
Additions to retained earnings	5.4	2.4	0.6	5.7	6.7
*Includes depreciation of	7.0	7.6	8.5	8.9	10.2

BALANCE SHEET

Assets

	1999	2000	2001	2002	2003
Current assets					
Cash	$ 9.6	$ 10.2	$ 8.7	$ 7.8	$ 9.3
Marketable securities	1.5	1.8	3.6	3.6	3.0
Receivables	18.6	19.5	20.1	25.2	24.6
Inventories	33.6	40.2	38.1	40.8	44.1
Total current assets	$ 63.3	$ 71.7	$ 70.5	$ 77.4	$ 81.0
Long-term investments	9.9	10.5	10.8	11.7	12.3
Property, plant, and equipment (net)	90.3	97.2	96.6	97.8	105.4
Other assets	3.3	2.7	2.4	2.1	2.7
Total assets	$166.8	$182.1	$180.3	$189.0	$201.4

Liabilities & Owners' Equity

	1999	2000	2001	2002	2003
Current liabilities					
Notes payable	$ 1.5	$ 3.9	$ 8.7	$ 2.1	$ 1.2
Accounts payable	18.0	27.6	27.0	28.2	29.7
Accrued liabilities	3.0	4.2	3.9	4.5	5.4
Federal income tax	—	—	—	6.3	7.5
Total current liabilities	$ 22.5	$ 35.7	$ 39.6	$ 41.1	$ 43.8
Long-term debt	30.6	30.3	24.0	22.5	25.5
Total liabilities	$ 53.1	$ 66.0	$ 63.6	$ 63.6	$ 69.3
Equity					
Preferred stock ($100 par value)	18.0	18.0	18.0	12.0	12.0
Common stock†	30.0	30.0	30.0	37.5	37.5
Paid-in-capital	3.0	3.0	3.0	4.5	4.5
Retained earnings	62.7	65.1	65.7	71.4	78.1
Total equity	$113.7	$116.1	$116.7	$125.4	$132.1
Total liabilities & owners' equity	$166.8	$182.1	$180.3	$189.0	$201.4

†1,000,000 shares 1999–2001; 1,250,000 shares 2002–03

Forecasting, Budgeting, and Cash Management

Arc Company, Inc.
Ratio Analysis of 1999-2003
Financial Statements

	1999	2000	2001	2002	2003
INCOME STATEMENT RELATIONSHIPS					
Net sales	100.00%	100.00%	100.00%	100.00%	100.00%
Cost of sales	63.92	66.76	66.52	62.23	63.35
Gross margin	36.08%	33.24%	33.48%	37.77%	36.65%
Total expenses	27.27	27.59	28.61	27.02	25.88
Net operating income	8.81%	5.65%	4.87%	10.76%	10.77%
Other expense net of other income	0.57	0.41	0.29	0.26	0.35
Income before tax	8.24%	5.24%	4.57%	10.50%	10.42%
Federal, state, and local income taxes	4.12	2.62	2.31	5.25	5.23
Net income	4.12%	2.62%	2.26%	5.25%	5.19%
ACTIVITY RELATIONSHIPS					
Cash ÷ Sales	4.5%	4.7%	4.3%	3.3%	3.6%
Days sales outstanding	32.1d	32.7d	36.1d	39.3d	35.0d
Days cost of sales in inventory	90.8d	101.1d	102.8d	102.1d	99.2d
Accounts payable ÷ Cost of sales	13.3%	19.0%	20.0%	19.3%	18.3%

developed a projected income statement for Arc. Cost of sales, for example, had risen from a low of 62.2 percent in 2002 to 63.3 percent in 2003. A continuation of this trend could bring the figure to 64 percent in 2004. If the higher sales figure appeared, the cost of sales percentages would probably be a little lower because of economies of scale. Cost of sales of 64 percent was used for the 10 percent increase in sales and 63.5 percent for the 15 percent increase.

The components of the other major item on the income statement, expenses, showed a variety of trends. Overall, expenses as a proportion of sales declined, with the recovery in sales following the 2001 recession. The banker was skeptical about whether this would continue: management might relax its control of expenses a little with a third year of improved results. Therefore, the banker split the difference between 2002 and 2003 to select an expense ratio of 26.5 percent for 2004. The other minor entries the banker estimated in total as about constant and used a figure of 50 percent for total income taxes.

To the banker's surprise, the net-income figure developed from this analysis for the 10 percent sales increase was $13,000, slightly lower than the $13,300 reported in 2003. Because management would not be pleased

EXHIBIT 4-3

Arc Company, Inc.
Projected Fininacial Statements for
the Year Ended December 31, 2004
(thousands of dollars)

ACTUAL 2003		PROJECTED 2004	
	ACCOUNT AND ASSUMPTIONS	**LOW**	**HIGH**
	INCOME STATEMENT		
$256.2	Net sales: increase 10% to 15%	$282.0	$295.0
162.3	Cost of sales: 64%, 63.5% of sales	180.0	187.0
$ 93.9	Gross margin	$102.0	$108.0
66.3	Total expenses: 26.5% of sales	75.0	78.0
$ 27.6	Net operating income	$ 27.0	$ 30.0
0.9	Other expenses net of other income	1.0	1.0
$ 26.7	Income before tax	$ 26.0	$ 29.0
13.4	Federal, state, & local inc. taxes: 50%	13.0	14.5
13.3	Net income	$ 13.0	$ 14.5
	BALANCE SHEET		
	Assets		
$ 9.3	Cash (minimum): 3.3% of sales	$ 9.3	$ 9.7
3.0	Marketable securities	—	—
24.6	Receivables: 35, 37 days sales	27.1	29.6
44.1	Inventories: 96, 94 days c.o.s.	47.4	48.2
12.3	Long-term investments: up $1	13.3	13.3
	Property, plant, and equipment (net): no net change at $282 sales;		
105.4	up $3 at $295 sales	105.4	108.4
2.7	Other assets: no change	2.7	2.7
$201.4	Total assets	$205.2	$211.9
	Liabilities and Equity		
$ 1.2	Notes payable: repay completely	$ —	$ —
29.7	Accounts payable: 18% cost of sales	32.4	33.7
5.4	Accrued liabilities: up $1	6.4	6.4
7.5	Federal income tax: 50% liability	6.5	7.2
25.5	Long-term debt: $3 annual retirement	22.5	22.5
$ 69.3	Total liabilities	$ 67.8	$ 69.8
12.0	Preferred stock: no change	12.0	12.0
42.0	Paid-in equity: no change	42.0	42.0
	Retained earnings: add net income and deduct dividends on preferred		
78.1	(.6) and common stock (6.0)	84.5	86.0
$132.1	Total equity	$138.5	$140.0
$201.4	Total liabilities and equity	$206.3	$209.8
	Plug figure (Liabilities and Equity less Assets)	1.1	(2.1)

to report these results, the banker guessed that Arc Company would try to control its expenses to be able to report at least $14,000 in profits. Unless the tax rate had been overestimated, Arc would have to cut $2,000 in expenses before taxes to achieve a $14,000 target. This effort would bring the expense-sales ratio down to 26 percent. This was not an unreasonable number, considering the 2003 results, but it would require a conscious effort on management's part.

The current-asset accounts were the first balance-sheet items the banker studied. Estimating (and budgeting) the minimum cash balance is a special challenge discussed later in the last section of this chapter. The lowest cash balance (excluding marketable securities, which presumably represented cash above the minimum needed for operations) as a percentage of sales had been 3.3 percent in 2002. The banker used this relationship.

Receivables and inventories had both been rising (to 2002) in proportion to the volume of business Arc Company was doing. The collection period was 35 days' sales on accounts receivable in 2003, down from the 2002 peak of 39.2 days but up from 32.1 days in 1999. Inventory numbers showed a similar pattern, with a 95.5 days' cost of sales in 2003. Because the company was planning for only a 10 percent increase in sales, the banker thought that any increase in sales above that level would likely reduce the inventory and thus cut the days' cost of sales held by the company. The banker therefore decided to use a 96-day figure for the lower sales estimate but to cut this to 94 days for the higher sales alternative.

The banker also thought that the extra sales, if they appeared, might be the result of Arc's taking on slower-paying customers. The banker decided that if the 35 days' collection period on receivables would hold at the lower sales volume, it would increase to 37 days with higher sales. The addition of $2,500 to the receivables balance on an extra sales volume of $13,000 did not seem unreasonable. It implied a 70-day collection period on these accounts ([$2,500 ÷ $13,000] x 365 days), compared with 35 days on the average account.

The other major asset account was property, plant, and equipment. Exhibit 4-1 shows that Arc had recently completed an expansion of its facilities, adding almost $8,000 to the net value of its plant. The previous expansion had been three years earlier, in 2000. The banker concluded, therefore, that it was unlikely that any major change would be required in 2004. The amount spent on capital equipment would be the same as the depreciation expense. To be on the safe side, however, the banker estimated a $3,000 extra facility investment if the higher sales number was realized.

No change was forecast in the other asset accounts, but it appeared that Arc Company had been adding nearly $1,000 a year to its long-term investments. Therefore, an allowance for a $1,000 long-term investment in 2004 was made.

Turning to the liabilities accounts, the banker calculated that the ratio of accounts payable to cost of sales had increased from 13.3 percent in 1999 to 18.3 percent in 2003, but this was a decline from a peak of 20 percent in 2001. Because 18 percent was still 66 days payable, the banker doubted that Arc's management would be allowed by its suppliers to stretch this ratio further. The banker therefore estimated accounts payable as 18 percent of cost of sales.

Estimates of the other liability accounts were based on past trends. Accruals were rising approximately $1,000 a year. The income-tax liability had been half of the taxes due as calculated on the income statement. Having not yet obtained a debt retirement schedule, the banker estimated that approximately 10 percent of the debt might be due, $3,000. Management could confirm this estimate.

Most of the equity accounts could be projected easily. No changes were anticipated in the preferred stock balance nor in the paid-in equity accounts. The only change would be to the retained earnings, which would increase by the net earnings of $13,000 or $14,500 and decrease by the preferred ($600) and common ($6,000) dividends Arc would probably pay.

Adding up the totals, the banker found that the sources were $1,100 larger than the projected uses at the $282,000 sales volume but were $2,100 smaller at the $295,000 sales volume. The banker thus saw little difficulty facing Arc Company if it made the lower sales volume. Notes could be repaid, and the firm would still have cash consistent with its prior balances. If the additional $1,000 in earnings appeared, Arc could reduce its payables even further.

The higher volume, however, presented several questions. Even with the extra $1,500 in retained earnings, the company would be $2,100 short of funds. This suggested that bank notes would have to be renewed and drawn. A vigorous effort to cut receivables back to 35 days would produce an extra $1,300 to add to cash. Curtailment of capital expenditures might also save funds. It was likely, however, that management would want to borrow on its credit line with the bank to provide at least part of the shortfall. Otherwise, all the actions mentioned would be required simultaneously to generate the $10,000 cash and marketable securities Arc had enjoyed in the past.

The banker therefore expected the company would at least want to roll over its existing bank line. A request for an increase to $3,000 might be received. The banker would discourage increasing the dividend on the common stock, although the company's financial position is strong.

KEY POINT: As this example has shown, useful financial estimates can be prepared even with very approximate information. In this illustration, the estimates will be materially improved once the banker knows the company's capital expenditure plans and the maturity schedule of the

long-term debt. Both figures are readily available to management and would certainly be available to the banker who asked for them.

Furthermore, once the income statement and balance sheet are estimated, a flow-of-funds analysis may be prepared if it would be useful. The techniques for developing FOF statements from the income statement and balance sheet will be discussed later.

SENSITIVITY ANALYSIS

Using ratios to prepare budgets and forecasts is helpful in developing "single-point" forecasts—forecasts based on a single estimate of the sales level. If you want to test the sensitivity of the forecast fund and cash needs to various levels of sales, as the banker did in the Arc Company analysis, specifying the relationships of the financial statements to the sales figure becomes more complex. For instance, to obtain more reliable forecasts of costs of sales and administrative costs, you must estimate the fixed costs— the costs that will not vary within the ranges of sales volumes that might occur. An estimate of the variable costs as a percentage of sales is also necessary. The total costs for each level of sales will thus be the fixed costs plus the variable costs associated with that sales level.

The income statement is more complex to estimate than the balance sheet, however. The current assets and liability accounts will typically be given ratios of their related income-statement accounts unless management makes the explicit decision to alter them, such as by extending more generous credit terms to customers. (A change in credit terms, of course, may be the reason for greater sales.) Most of the other balance-sheet accounts are more certain, such as payments on outstanding debt and depreciation.

DANGERS IN FORECASTING WITH RATIOS

The relative ease with which forecasts based on historical ratios can be prepared must not blind you to the dangers inherent in the method. In the first place, future relationships may not be the same as past relationships. Second, certain mechanical problems arise in using ratios when the underlying physical activities of the firm change from period to period because of seasonal, cyclical, or secular factors. For example, inventories for a retail store may be very high at the end of September as a percentage of the third quarter's sales because of stocking up for the Christmas season. Similarly, receivables at the end of December may be very high as a percentage of the year's sales, at least in comparison to the percentage outstanding at the end of September. Chapter 5 discusses how using averages will generate a very inaccurate projection if seasonal and cyclical effects on accounts receivable are not allowed for. Similar problems occur in making accurate forecasts of inventories and accounts payable.

T-Account Forecasting Techniques

In instances where relationships may not be the same with respect to the average or constant with respect to each other—as often happens over the course of a season or a business cycle—other budgeting and forecasting methods than annual ratios must be used. One approach is to prepare a more detailed set of ratios. For example, it might be that although the balance in outstanding accounts receivable varied wildly as a percentage of sales to date, it was always 100 percent of the most recent month's sales and 50 percent of the prior month's sales.

When precision is required, such as when preparing monthly IS/BS budgets or forecasts, estimates are necessary of how individual transactions will take place and of what financial accounts they will affect. For instance, it may be well established that certain large accounts will be paid on certain days or receivables collected in a similarly established pattern.

> **SMART FINANCIAL MANAGEMENT:** The T-account method—the best way to deal with this type of detailed budgeting and forecasting—starts with the opening balance in each account on the financial statements. The analyst then adds or subtracts amounts reflecting the real physical activities of the enterprise anticipated during the period under study. The sum of the beginning balance and the forecasted changes to an account equals that account's ending balance. (Of course, the additions to and subtractions from an account may simply be summed and the net figure used to adjust the balance.) The income statement, in effect, serves this purpose for the retained earnings account on the balance sheet.

The T-account budgeting and forecasting technique will be illustrated using the example of the Ledo Manufacturing Company, Inc. Exhibit 4-4 presents the actual balance sheets for the company for December 31, 2000 and 2001. In addition, it shows a projected balance sheet for December 31, 2002, which will be derived using the T-account forecasting procedures. Exhibit 4-5 presents Ledo's income statement for the year ending December 31, 2001. It also shows a projected income statement for the year that will end December 31, 2002.

The background information needed for the preparation of a T-account forecast comes from the company's operating budget (sometimes called the profit plan or the income-and-expense budget). The starting point for the operating budget and the funds forecast is the revenue or sales projection, which is reported for Ledo in Exhibit 4-5. Estimates must also be made of all other aspects of a firm's operations. Exhibit 4-6 thus provides a list of significant projected operating and financial activities for Ledo for the 2002 operating year. These are summary figures, which would be

EXHIBIT 4-4

Ledo Manufacturing Company, Inc.
Balance Sheets: Actual 12/31/00, 12/31/01 and Projected 12/31/02
(thousands of dollars)

	ACTUAL 12/31/00	ACTUAL 12/31/01	PROJECTED 12/31/02
ASSETS			
Cash in bank	$ 44.1	$ 53.4	$ 44.4
Trade receivables (net)	73.2	84.7	101.7
Raw materials	26.0	17.1	14.1
Work-in-process	56.0	32.3	43.3
Finished goods	130.8	86.0	110.0
Manufacturing supplies	12.5	9.5	11.5
Manufacturing plant, and equipment (net)	450.0	462.5	517.5
Total assets	$792.6	$745.5	$842.5
LIABILITIES AND OWNERS' EQUITY			
Notes payable	$ 73.0	$ 75.0	$150.0
Payables and accruals	62.6	38.6	45.6
Federal income tax liability	22.2	11.0	30.0
Long-term debt	210.0	180.0	150.0
Capital stock	300.0	300.0	300.0
Retained earnings	124.8	140.9	166.9
Total liabilities and owners' equity	$792.6	$745.5	$842.5
Memo:			
Net income		$ 31.1	$ 44.0
Dividends		15.0	18.0
Depreciation		34.1	45.0

extensively supported in detailed operating budgets and capital expenditure and financing plans. (These detailed reports have not been reproduced here but are prepared in the same manner as the data shown.)

Projecting the income statement and balance sheet may be accomplished in different ways. The less formal the requirements and the more skilled the analyst, the less formal the estimating process. The worksheet format for projecting 2002 statements, which is provided in Exhibit 4-7, will be used to illustrate a comprehensive method for the beginning analyst. As the analyst's experience and skills develop, the analyst can tailor the format to the needs and develop appropriate shortcuts. At this point, however, it is worthwhile to be thorough and complete.

The worksheet in Exhibit 4-7 begins with the December 31, 2001 balances transferred from the balance-sheet accounts. Note that these figures

EXHIBIT 4-5

Ledo Manufacturing Company, Inc.
Statement of Income and Retained Earnings:
Actual for the Year 2001;
Projected for the Year 2002
(thousands of dollars)

	ACTUAL 2001		PROJECTED 2002	
Net sales		$510.2		$570.0
Cost of goods sold		341.7		346.0
Gross profit		$168.5		$224.0
Selling, general & administrative expenses	$111.4		$130.0	
Interest expense	15.0	$126.4	20.0	$150.0
Profit before income tax		$ 42.1		$ 74.0
Federal income tax		11.0		30.0
Net profit for year		$ 31.1		$ 44.0
Add: Retained earnings at beginning year		124.8		140.9
Less: Dividends		15.0		18.0
Retained earnings at end of year		$140.9		$166.9

agree with the figures in Exhibit 4-4, the financial reports, except trade receivables. In Exhibit 4-4, trade receivables and estimated uncollectible accounts were combined to create the net receivables figure of $84,700: $90,000 trade receivables less $5,300 estimated uncollectible accounts. In Exhibit 4-7, both numbers are shown.

The next step is to enter into the proper columns the details of changes that will result from the projected 2002 operations of the company. The net result of the planned changes, added to or subtracted from the December 31, 2001 balances, will be the December 31, 2002 balances. A forecast of a full year will be used to illustrate the development of the projected balance sheet and income statement in Exhibits 4-4 and 4-5. The monthly detail given in Exhibit 4-6 is not required for this forecast. That detail will be used later in developing a monthly budget or forecast of cash receipts and disbursements. It could also be used to create monthly income statements and balance sheets.

As noted, a T-account forecast begins with an estimate of sales or revenues. Exhibit 4-6, Activity A, indicates that sales for the 2002 year are estimated to be $580,000. What balance sheet accounts will this affect? Trade receivables of $580,000 will be entered on the books because of sales on account. The second entry, needed to maintain the integrity of the "Assets = Liabilities + Owners' Equity" equation, is an increase in retained earnings

EXHIBIT 4-6

Ledo Manufacturing Company, Inc.
Projected Operating and Financial Activities
For the Year Ending December 31, 2002
(thousands of dollars)

ACTIVITY	DESCRIPTION OF ACTIVITIES
(A)	Sales to be made on account: $580.0. Monthly sales expected be: $46.0, 47.0, 47.0, 48.0, 48.0, 49.0, 50.0, 50.0, 50.0, 50.0, 48.0, 47.0.
(B)	Cash to be collected from customers: $550.0, representing payment on $560.0 gross receivables net of $3.0 cash discounts and $7.0 sales allowances. Monthly collection expected to be: $44.0, 44.0, 44.0, 45.0, 45.0, 46.0, 46.0, 46.0, 47.0, 48.0, 48.0, 47.0.
(C)	2002 provision for estimated uncollectability of customer accounts: $3.0.
(D)	Raw materials, $60.0, and manufacturing supplies, $25.0, to be purchased on account.
(E)	Raw materials, $63.0, and manufacturing supplies, $23.0, to be issued to the factory.

(F) Cost in the factory to be incurred on account:

➤ Direct Labor	$120.0
➤ Indirect Labor	50.0
➤ Maintenance, Utilities, etc.	86.0
	$256.0

(G) Property, plant, and equipment to be purchased for cash: $100.0. Payments made: $20.0 in April, $25.0 in June, and $55.0 in September.

(H) Annual depreciation on property, plant, and equipment charged to:

➤ Factory	$ 39.0
➤ Selling, general, and administrative	6.0
	$ 45.0

(I) Transfer of finished goods from factory to finished goods warehouse: $370.0.

(J) Cost of finished goods to be shipped from warehouse: $345.0.

(K) Selling, general, and administrative expenses to be incurred:

➤ For cash ($2.0 January–November; $3.0 in December)	$ 25.0
➤ On account	$ 96.0
	$121.0

(L) Cash to be paid on payables and accruals: $430.0. Monthly payments as follows: $32.0, 34.0, 40.0, 36.0, 36.0, 30.0, 48.0, 35.0, 35.0, 35.0, 34.0, 35.0.

ACTIVITY	DESCRIPTION OF ACTIVITIES	
(M)	Cash to be paid: $154.0 as follows:	
	➤ To meet notes payable due	$ 75.0 in March
	➤ To reduce long-term debt:	
	30.0, to be repaid	$ 15.0 in June
		$ 15.0 in December
	➤ For interest on debt,	
	$20.0, to be paid	$ 2.0 in March,
		$ 10.0 in June
		$ 8.0 in December
	➤ On Federal income tax liability	$ 11.0 in March.
	➤ For dividends to stockholders:	
	$18.0 to be paid	$ 4.0 in March
		$ 4.0 June
		$ 4.0 September
		$ 6.0 in December
(N)	Federal income tax accrual on 2002 income: $30.0	

of $580,000.[3] This pair of entries has been made on Exhibit 4-7. The reader is encouraged to review these items entry by entry and to verify that all entries to the retained earnings account in Exhibit 4-7 also appear on the projected income statement in Exhibit 4-5.

After the projected activities are posted in the change columns, the two sides of the column are "netted out" to calculate the net planned changes. For example, cash in bank is calculated as shown in Table 4-1.

The net result of these activities is a decrease of $159,000. This amount, deducted from the beginning cash balance of $53,400, gives an estimated negative closing balance of $105,600.

➤ **IMPORTANT: In the United States, banks are not allowed to establish overdraft facilities for their customers. A company requiring more cash than it believes will be available during an operating period must arrange in advance with a bank or other financial source to provide the necessary funds, reduce its planned commitment of funds to assets, or both.**

(text continues on page 90)

---

3. This is a convenient method of avoiding the use of an income statement. All charges that would normally be made through the income statement can be recorded as direct increases or decreases in the equity accounts. As a final step, the income statement can be made up from these entries. Normally, the income statement is used to record these changes. The net profit or loss figure is used to make only one entry to retained earnings.

EXHIBIT 4-7

Ledo Manufacturing Company, Inc.
T-Account Funds Forecasting Worksheet for 2002
(thousands of dollars)

NAME OF ACCOUNT	BALANCE 12/31/01 ASSETS	LIABS.	DETAIL OF PLANNED CHANGES IN FUNDS USES +A/-L	SOURCES +L/-A	NET CHANGES PLANNED IN FUNDS USES +A/-L	SOURCES +L/-A	PROJECTED BALANCE 12/31/02 ASSETS	LIABS.
ASSETS								
Cash in bank	$ 53.4	$ —	(B) $550	(G) $100	$ —	$159	$ (105.6)	$ —
				(K) 25				
				(L) 430				
				(M) 154				
Trade receivables	90.0	—	(A) 580	(B) 560	20	—	110.0	—
Est. uncollectability	—	5.3	—	(C) 3	—	3	—	8.3
Raw materials	17.1	—	(D) 60	(E) 63	—	3	14.1	—
Goods-in-process	32.3	—	—	—	11	—	43.3	—
Raw material used			(E) 63					
Mfg. supplies used			(E) 23					
Direct labor			(F) 120					
Indirect labor			(F) 50					
Maint., utilities, etc.			(F) 86					
Depreciation			(H) 39					
Transfer to fin. goods				(I) 370				

Finished goods	86.0	—	(I) 370	(J) 346	24	—	110.0	—
Manufactg. supplies	9.5	—	(D) 25	(E) 23	2	—	11.5	—
Prop., plant, and equipment—net	462.5	—	(G) 100	(H) 45	55	—	517.5	—
LIABILITIES & EQUITY								
Notes payable	—	75.0	(M) 75	—	75	—	—	0.0
Payables & accruals	—	38.6	—	(D) 85	—	7	—	45.6
Fed. inc. tax liability	—	11.0	(L) 430	(M) 11	—	19	—	30.0
Long-term debt	—	180.0	(M) 30	—	30	—	—	150.0
Capital stock	—	300.0	—	—	—	—	—	300.0
Retained earnings	—	140.9	—	—	—	26	—	166.9
Sales	—	—	—	(A) 580	—	—	—	—
Cash discounts	—	—	(B) 3	—	—	—	—	—
Sales allowances	—	—	(B) 7	—	—	—	—	—
S,G, & A uncoll. accts.	—	—	(C) 3	—	—	—	—	—
S,G, & A. deprec.	—	—	(H) 6	—	—	—	—	—
Cost of goods sold	—	—	(J) 346	(F) 256	—	—	—	—
S,G, & A	—	—	(K) 121	(K) 96	—	—	—	—
Interest	—	—	(M) 20	—	—	—	—	—
Dividends	—	—	(M) 18	—	—	—	—	—
Provision for 2002 taxes	—	—	(N) 30	—	—	—	—	—
Totals	$750.8	$750.8			$217	$217	$700.8	$700.8

TABLE 4-1

T-account Forecast of Ledo's Cash Account, 2002 (thousands of dollars)

CASH INCREASED BY		CASH DECREASED BY	
Activity B	$550	Activity G	$100
		Activity K	25
		Activity L	430
	____	Activity M	154
Total	$550		$709

In Ledo's case, the forecast shows that management will need to find $105,600 in funds *plus* whatever funds Ledo will require for its minimum operating balance in the cash account. With this information, the treasurer can decide how to obtain the necessary funds. A variety of ways are open to Ledo:

➤ Reducing planned asset levels such as a reduction in inventory
➤ Raising additional equity by a new stock issue or a reduction in the dividend
➤ Obtaining a short- or long-term loan
➤ Stretching out the company's accounts payable

This illustration assumes the treasurer decides to ask Ledo's bank for a loan of $150,000, which will give Ledo a projected year-end cash balance of $44,400, as shown in Exhibit 4-4.

The new totals in the accounts shown in Exhibit 4-7 (adjusted for the new debt) become the figures used in the projected balance sheet for December 31, 2002, as shown in Exhibit 4-4. The trade receivables and estimated uncollectible account figures are netted to show net receivables of $101,700.

Projecting a Flow-of-Funds Statement

A flow-of-funds (FOF) statement is a useful analytical tool, but a poor tool for projections. Over the last three decades, the accounting profession has been mandating increasingly elaborate FOF presentations for inclusion in a company's audited financial statements. The FOF statements are now very complex, but many situations can be usefully analyzed more simply.

❯ **KEY POINT: The purpose of the FOF statement, originally called "where-got, where-gone" by its developer, is to show the sources of a**

company's funds and where the funds were used. In a specific circumstance, the analyst may need to modify the standard accounting presentation to ensure that important funds-flow aspects are not lost in the details.

A simplified FOF statement for Ledo, prepared from the information contained in Exhibit 4-7 with a few adjustments to the Net Changes Planned in Funds columns, is shown in Exhibit 4-8. FOF statements also can be prepared from a pair of balance sheets and an income statement, which is how external analysts generally prepare them.

The "detail" and "net" change columns of the worksheet are subtitled "Uses +A/−L" and "Sources +L/− A." Because the asset side of a company's balance sheet represents the way it invests or uses funds and the liability

EXHIBIT 4-8

Ledo Manufacturing Company, Inc.
Flow of Funds Statements
Actual for the Year Ending 12/31/01;
Projected for the Year Ending 12/31/02
(thousands of dollars)

	ACTUAL 2001	PROJECTED 2002
FUNDS WERE PROVIDED BY:		
Income after tax but before depreciation	$ 65.2	$ 89.0
Decrease in cash	—	9.0
Decrease in raw materials	8.9	3.0
Decrease in work-in-process	23.7	—
Decrease in finished goods	44.8	—
Decrease in manufacturing supplies	3.0	—
Increase in notes payable	2.0	75.0
Increase in payables and accruals	—	7.0
Increase in federal income tax liability	—	19.0
Total	$147.6	$202.0
FUNDS WERE USED FOR:		
Increase in cash	$ 9.3	$ —
Increase in trade receivables (net)	11.5	17.0
Increase in work-in process	—	11.0
Increase in finished goods	—	24.0
Increase in manufacturing supplies	—	2.0
Acquisition of property, plant, and equipment	46.6	100.0
Decrease in payables and accruals	24.0	—
Decrease in federal income tax liability	11.2	—
Decrease in long-term debt	30.0	30.0
Payment of dividends	15.0	18.0
Total	$147.6	$202.0

side represents the sources of these funds, an increase in an asset is a use of funds and a decrease is a source. An increase in a liability or in the owners' equity account is a source of funds and a decrease is a use of funds. For example, if Ledo buys raw materials on account (Activity D), it increases assets (use of funds) and increases payables and accruals (source of funds). When Ledo transfers work-in-process inventory to finished goods (Activity I), one asset is decreased (source of funds) and another is increased (use of funds). This represents a change of funds from one use to another but no change in total funds used. When Ledo pays its creditors (Activity L), it decreases cash in bank (source of funds) and decreases payables and accruals (use of funds).

Most of the net changes from the Net Changes Planned in Funds columns in Exhibit 4-7 can be carried directly to the funds statement in Exhibit 4-8. In this instance, as usual, adjustments must be made to two accounts to develop a comprehensive picture of the flow of funds. The two accounts are retained earnings and property, plant, and equipment. Another adjustment is necessary to allow for the way the projected cash balance is made equal to the minimum operating balance.

RETAINED EARNINGS

Exhibit 4-7 shows a net change for the balance in retained earnings after allowing for payment of dividends. Because it is often useful to know the size of the dividend paid in relation to the net income generated, these two are usually shown separately in funds statements. To make the adjustment for Ledo, the $18,000 dividend payments are restored to the change in owners' equity account on the one hand (increasing that source) and then shown as a separate use on the funds statement. The effect of this alteration is usually to increase the change in owners' equity to the amount of income after tax, under which name it appears in many funds statements.

PROPERTY, PLANT, AND EQUIPMENT

Depreciation is the allocation to expenses of the cost of a lasting asset over the time it is expected to generate sales and earnings for the company. The funds usually used to acquire the asset were committed at the time of purchase. The depreciation charge in any accounting period, therefore, does not represent a cash expense. It is known as "noncash expense."

To develop an accurate picture of the movement of funds within the company, an adjustment must therefore be made to reflect the noncash nature of the depreciation charge to the income statement and against the property, plant, and equipment account. This adjustment will allow a more useful statement of the total amount (net) shown in Exhibit 4-4. Exhibit 4-7 shows an increase of only $55,000, whereas Activity G specifies that $100,000 is to be spent for capital expenditures during 2002. The difference is the charge of $45,000 for depreciation.

TABLE 4-2

Adjustments to Ledo's "Net Changes Planned in Funds Projection" Required in Preparation of a "Flow-of-Funds Statement" (thousands of dollars)

CHANGES IN SOURCES OF FUNDS			CHANGES IN USES OF FUNDS	
Increase in owners' equity		$26.0	Add payment of dividends	$18.0
Restoration of dividends	$18.0			
Restoration of depreciation	45.0		Increase by listing acquisition of property, plant, and equipment rather than the change in the net balance in the property, plant, and equipment account	
Total change		$63.0		
Adjusted increase in owners' equity (now more accurately called income after tax but before depreciation)		$89.0		45.0
			Total change	$63.0

These adjustments may be shown in several ways. The method used in Exhibit 4-8 is to list the gross additions to plant and equipment as a separate item under uses of funds. The amount of the depreciation charge in total, including the amounts allocated to cost of goods sold and to selling, general, and administrative expenses, is added back to the income-after-tax figure to produce a figure for earnings after tax but before depreciation.[4] In many statements, however, the depreciation figure and the income-after-tax figure are shown separately as provisions of funds. The changes outlined here are summarized in Table 4-2.

Adjustments for noncash charges other than depreciation, such as amortization of organization expense, patent costs, and "goodwill," may be made similarly to the depreciation change. The amortization amount is restored to the income figure and to any net change for the particular asset involved.

With these two major adjustments completed, the statement of projected financial changes is finished, as shown in Exhibit 4-8.

Projecting a Statement of Cash Receipts and Disbursements

The IS/BS projecting technique and the FOF statement are most useful for longer-term financial statements. For short-term projections, many

---

4. The previous section showed how to adjust the net changes in retained earnings to produce the income-after-tax amount.

EXHIBIT 4-9

Ledo Manufacturing Company, Inc.
Cash Receipts and Disbursements Forecast Monthly for the Year 2002
(thousands of dollars)

	JAN	FEB	MAR	APRIL	MAY	JUNE	JULY	AUG	SEPT	OCT	NOV	DEC	TOTAL
PROJECTED RECEIPTS													
Collection on account (B)	$44.0	$44.0	$44.0	$45.0	$45.0	$46.0	$46.0	$46.0	$47.0	$48.0	$48.0	$47.0	$550.0
PROJECTED DISBURSEMENTS													
Property, plant & equip. (G)	—	—	—	20.0	—	25.0	—	—	55.0	—	—	—	100.0
S,G & A expend. (K)	2.0	2.0	2.0	2.0	2.0	2.0	2.0	2.0	2.0	2.0	2.0	3.0	25.0
Payables and accruals (L)	32.0	34.0	40.0	36.0	36.0	30.0	48.0	35.0	35.0	35.0	34.0	35.0	430.0
Notes payable (M)	—	—	75.0	—	—	—	—	—	—	—	—	—	75.0
Long-term debt (M)	—	—	—	—	—	15.0	—	—	—	—	—	15.0	30.0
Interest (M)	—	—	2.0	—	—	10.0	—	—	—	—	—	8.0	20.0
Federal taxes (M)	—	—	11.0	—	—	—	—	—	—	—	—	—	11.0
Dividends (M)	—	—	4.0	—	—	4.0	—	—	4.0	—	—	6.0	18.0
Total disbursements	$34.0	$36.0	$134.0	$58.0	$38.0	$86.0	$50.0	$37.0	$96.0	$37.0	$36.0	$67.0	$709.0
Net inflow (outflow)	$10.0	$8.0	$(90.0)	$(13.0)	$7.0	$(40.0)	$(4.0)	$9.0	$(49.0)	$11.0	$12.0	$(20.0)	$(159.0)
CASH AND LOAN FORECAST													
Beginning cash balance	53.4	63.4	$71.4	$31.4	18.4	25.4	60.4	56.4	65.4	16.4	27.4	39.4	53.4
Change in bank loan	—	—	50.0	—	—	75.0	—	—	—	—	—	25.0	150.0
Ending cash balance	$63.4	$71.4	$31.4	$18.4	$25.4	$60.4	$65.4	$65.4	$16.4	$27.4	$39.4	$44.4	$44.4

companies use a daily, weekly, or monthly budget, or a projected statement of cash receipts and disbursements (CR/CD). Using the information from Exhibit 4-6, Projected Operating and Financial Activities, a projected monthly CR/CD statement can be prepared for Ledo for 2002. This statement is shown in Exhibit 4-9.

Projected receipts, in this example, consist of collections on accounts as described in Activity B, Exhibit 4-6. For some companies, cash receipts might also include proceeds from the sale of capital stock or long-term debt or the sale of used equipment or other assets. Normally, the largest recurring receipts would be cash sales and collections on account.

❯ SMART FINANCIAL MANAGEMENT: Collections on account can be projected by relating customers' typical paying practices to the dates shipments were made. This average expectation should be tempered with judgment of the paying habits of individual customers when the dollar value of the individual items sold is significant compared with the total.

Under projected disbursements, some items, such as property, plant, and equipment acquisitions, long-term debt payments, and dividends, are *scheduled disbursements.* Others, such as payables and accruals, depend on the level of operating activity, when goods are purchased, payment terms, and the level of financing.

The format of Exhibit 4-9 shows the difference in receipts and disbursements for each month. If, when this net balance is added to or deducted from the beginning cash balance, the result differs from the minimum cash balance, it is a sign that short-term loans can be repaid (balance larger than minimum) or need to be increased (balance smaller than minimum).

For example, in March, $90,000 more is forecast to be paid out than is collected. With a beginning cash balance of $71,400, Ledo would have a negative cash position of $18,600 without more short-term debt. In recognition of this cash requirement, the treasurer plans to borrow an additional $50,000 in March. In effect, the treasurer will only reduce Ledo's net outstanding debt by $25,000 ($75,000 repaid, $50,000 reborrowed).

Many companies set a minimum cash balance as one of their financial policies. If this is done, the minimum cash balance can be shown in the projected statement. Each month the exact amount of borrowing needed or the surplus cash available for investment or debt reduction can be calculated. The example in Table 4-3 restates Ledo's figures for January through June 2002 under the assumption that the treasurer always wishes to have at least $25,000 in cash on hand.

If there are wide fluctuations in a company's daily receipts and disbursements, a statement similar to Exhibit 4-9 should be prepared for a shorter period, such as a week or a day. The amount of cash involved and

TABLE 4-3

Surplus or Deficit Cash Position of Ledo Assuming a $25.0 Minimum Balance (thousands of dollars)

	JAN	FEB	MAR	APR	MAY	JUNE
Net inflow or (outflow)	$10.0	$ 8.0	$(90.0)	$(13.0)	$ 7.0	$(40.0)
Plus: Cash balance, beginning of month	53.4	63.4	71.4	(18.6)	(31.6)	(24.6)
Equals: Total cash available	$63.4	$71.4	$(18.6)	$(31.6)	$(24.6)	$(64.6)
Less: Minimum cash balance	25.0	25.0	25.0	25.0	25.0	25.0
Equals: Cumulative cash surplus (or deficit) after debt repayment but before new borrowing	$38.4	$46.4	$(43.6)	$(56.6)	$(49.6)	$(89.6)

the size of the fluctuations will determine the period and the detail needed for the projected cash receipts and disbursement statement.

To be useful, actual results should be compared to the projection regularly and revisions made whenever the actual results are significantly different from the projected figures.

Budgeting and Forecasting: Summary

Three cautionary observations are necessary in concluding this section:

1. *Reliance on historical relationships is extremely dangerous when the economy or a particular company is undergoing major change.* During inflationary periods, for example, producing and selling the same number of units requires more funds than before to support the necessary inventories and receivables balances. During deflationary episodes (which can be localized as in the rapid fall of personal-computer prices), even if margins can be held, absolute dollars of profit will decline. The key to adequate cash generation in this circumstance is the reduction of accounts receivable and inventories. Reduction of inventories is particularly important because the value real assets declines in a deflationary environment.

2. *The application of relationships to different periods in a company's production cycle than those from which the relationships were*

derived may not provide meaningful information about the firm's financial needs. When significant changes are inherent or occur in a company's operating pattern, it is essential to base forecasts on information from comparable times in the past. Financial forecasts must fully reflect the realities of the production and marketing process.

3. *In preparing a budget or forecast, it is important to use analytical time wisely.* That often means making rough estimates of immaterial accounts to have the time to concentrate on those items whose size or significance means they will have the greatest impact on future developments.

Analytic Considerations in Cash Management

ESTABLISHING A MINIMUM CASH BALANCE

If a company could sell all of its goods for cash and pay cash for all purchases on a daily basis, it could operate with a "zero" cash balance. This would be an ideal situation, because the lower the investment in cash (or any other asset), the higher the return on the entrepreneur's investment.

It is not easy to figure out the "minimum" cash needed at any one time because of a second, conflicting objective in managing cash. Besides the desire for profitability, there is need for liquidity. Liquidity, in the form of a large cash balance (or, less certainly, a line of credit), provides the firm with the ability to handle unfavorable variances from projections. The conflict between these two objectives is another instance of an "eat well, sleep well" decision: A small cash balance means higher income. A large cash balance means less risk of financial embarrassment.

Forecasting techniques aid in resolving the conflict by helping determine your company's cash needs or surpluses and the likely variation in these estimates. The less accurate these forecasts, the higher the level of financial flexibility needed for a given level of "sleep well."

One way of maintaining financial flexibility is to increase the cash balances above the minimum operating level shown by the forecasts. The forecasts cannot give an exact answer, however. The minimum-cash-balance decision is one that requires skilled managerial interpretation of the figures.

Another way of setting a minimum cash operating balance is to plan to maintain sufficient cash to cover disbursements during a period in which the company's receipts might be interrupted for some reason. A company located in a region where weather can block mail for several days, but which must pay local suppliers and employees despite the weather, might typically hold an additional week's cash disbursements in its balance as a buffer "cash inventory." If a company's business requires investments of large sums on short notice in raw materials, management might elect to maintain many times one week's typical disbursements in the checking account or as very short, riskless investments such as five-day Treasury bills. A company whose customers are unreliable in paying their bills will require more operating cash on the average than a company such as a retailer whose customers generally pay cash or use credit cards.

Another factor affecting the level of the cash balance is a company's banking relationships. The number of banks used and the types and quantity of bank services needed affect the size of the cash balances that must be carried with the banks. A company may keep more than one bank account for a variety of reasons:

➤ Widespread geographical plant locations
➤ Geographical location of customers
➤ Political and personal considerations
➤ Special accounts for payroll and other types of disbursements
➤ Control over funds
➤ Desire to have multiple suppliers of credit familiar with the company

Finally, your own risk preferences are important. Some business owners prefer to arrange a loan and then draw down the full amount even though no immediate need requires the funds. The rationale is that it is easier to borrow when it is not necessary than when it is. Other business owners elect to hold large cash balances even if the company has no debt because having cash makes fund management less stressful than not having cash. Conversely, some business owners, particularly if the company is growing rapidly and cash-hungry, try actively to manage cash to a minimum to reduce the funding needed to support the aggressive growth.

An analyst must take these dimensions into account when budgeting or forecasting the minimum-cash component. If the enterprise has shown a stable relationship between cash and sales or cash and cost of sales, it is an appropriate ratio to select for a minimum balance. For new enterprises, rapidly growing ones, or companies in distress, a review of the company's history may indicate the absolute minimum cash with which management has made do in the past. This amount can be used as the estimate for minimum future cash needs. A third approach is to set a minimum cash balance at one or two weeks' cash disbursements. Lacking disbursement figures, one or two weeks' cost of goods sold plus selling, general, and administrative expenses is a reasonable approximation of this estimate of minimum cash needed.

MANAGING THE CASH POSITION

Having multiple banks usually means a company will maintain a higher minimum level of cash than if it has only one bank. Bankers have nevertheless been remarkably creative in creating funds-transfer mechanisms that squeeze funds out of the banking system and make them available to their clients for investment. Ways have been found to speed up receipts processing and to control disbursements so they are made at the last possible minute. Often this has meant creating centralized cash-balance controls, techniques with which some banks have developed specialized capabilities. These features are particularly attractive to a company whose operations are spread over a wide geographic area. These methods may be too expensive to benefit smaller companies, but entrepreneurs should be alert to their potential use as the company grows.

Among the methods used to speed up collection are lock-box systems and the concentration of cash balances in a few banks. Lock-box systems reduce the elapsed time between the customer's mailing a check and the receiving company's obtaining collected funds in its bank. Managing accounts payable involves the timing of vendor payments and the taking of discounts. In short, payments are not made until the last moment it is still possible to take all discounts, which, if missed, would result in a higher effective interest rate than other available sources of funds. Managing accounts payable is a technique available to companies of all sizes.

Cash Management Summary

Cash is an investment with characteristics similar to the investment in inventory, receivables, and property. Effective management of cash position can increase your company's profitability. Ineffective cash management can be costly and even threaten the company with insolvency. The preparation of funds budgets and forecasts is essential to the efficient use of cash and arranging financing for the additional cash needs or for investing cash surpluses.

SMART FINANCIAL MANAGEMENT: Long-term cash and funds forecasts are important in highlighting major financing needs so the proper planning for the best financing alternatives can be done. Short-term forecasts are needed to manage the day-to-day cash position to make sure that cash is available for necessary disbursements and that the most appropriate investments are considered for excess cash.

CHAPTER 5

MANAGING ACCOUNTS RECEIVABLE

Effective management of accounts receivable includes not only evaluating and authorizing trade-credit extensions but also constantly supervising your credit customers' accounts. In routine cases, this means enforcing credit terms and ensuring that payment discounts are taken only if deserved and that payments are made promptly according to the terms granted.

> **WARNING: The volume of accounts receivable must be carefully managed. Otherwise, it can grow to such a point that your company will lose significant profits as customers use its funds free of charge. Even the best credit risks may take advantage of a supplier that is lax in collecting Its accounts.**

Potentially more damaging is that a customer with a significant outstanding balance may fail. In that event, you may collect nothing. Even if some portion of the account is eventually paid, eventually can be much too long for the smaller company to wait.

Credit management is a complex function that requires a thorough knowledge of the industry and a good deal of tact. Unfortunately, it is also usually conducted with a limited amount of information. In contrast to commercial bankers, who are constantly in touch with their clients, credit managers receive reports infrequently—and usually after a delay. The horse is out of the barn before the credit manager learns the door might be open.

The credit management function has two components. The first is how to decide whether to grant a credit request from a marginal customer. Requests from good customers or from clearly bad ones do not require much analysis. The second is a method for evaluating accounts-receivable management, using aggregate data that may be more easily available to an outsider. The credit manager may find these data helpful when reviewing a customer's credit worthiness. From the same data, a business owner can learn how the company's suppliers and bankers might be using and misusing information about the firm's receivables.

Basic Mechanics of Credit Management

TERMINOLOGY

Credit terminology can be extremely confusing, and terms differ from industry to industry. It is therefore difficult to define exactly how a set of credit terms should be interpreted. Even experienced individuals in one industry become confused when quoted terms in another. When in doubt, ask for clarification.

In the current practice of selling on "open account," as opposed to the practice years ago of taking a customer's note when a sale was made, the seller states when payment is due. The customer, by entering into the transaction, accepts these terms. Typical payment terms are 30, 60, and 90 days after the date of the invoice.

The seller also often offers its customers a discount for prompt payment. A common discount is 2 percent on bills paid within ten days of the invoice date, with payment due within 30 days in any event. These terms might read: "2/10, net 30." Another form provides for payment to be made within ten days after the end of the month in which the invoice is rendered. These terms might be stated: "10 days EOM" or "10EOM." If a discount is also offered, it could read "2/10EOM." "Proximo" is another term to designate the month following the invoice date—"10 prox." is the same as "10EOM."

For example, in some industries a wholesaler or distributor is billed at the price the wholesaler is expected to charge the retailer for the merchandise. The wholesaler is given a distribution discount as well as a prompt-payment incentive. For instance, suppose a manufacturer sells both to retailers and wholesalers. The retail terms are "2/10, net 30." The manufacturer bills the wholesalers at the same price charged the retailers, but wholesalers are also allowed 8 percent for their distribution services. This set of wholesale terms might read: "8/2/10, net 30." Whether the 8 percent is deducted before the 2 percent is taken is peculiar to each industry. In volume, of course, it makes a substantial difference if total discounts are 10 percent of the invoice or only 9.84 percent.

COST

The cost of granting discounts for prompt payment can be considerable, and the cost of failing to take those terms can be equally expensive.

If a company forgoes a 2 percent discount, delaying payment from the 10th to the 30th day, it has lost 2.04 percent of the net cost to gain 20 days extra credit. There are approximately 18 20-day periods in a year. At slightly more than 2 percent for each period, the annual rate is about 37 percent.

Stated another way, if the firm borrowed from its bank at a 10 percent annual rate, the cost per day would be 10 percent ÷360, or .028 percent a day. For 20 days, this would amount to 0.56 percent. By failing to make prompt payment, the firm is giving up 2.04 percent for a net cost of 1.48 percent (2.04 − 0.56) for 20 days or over 25 percent a year.

Granting credit discounts is equally costly to the supplier that can afford to borrow at low rates to support its accounts receivable but whose customers take their discounts. The customer makes 25 percent a year by paying promptly. The supplier loses a comparable amount by granting the discount terms rather than simply collecting on the 30th day.

The supplier is often motivated in extending credit by considerations other than interest rates. Credit terms are often used as aggressive competitive tools, providing better customers with disguised discounts in much less obvious form than direct price cutting. The better-financed customers have a clear advantage on this score because of their ability to take discounts. Similarly, better-financed suppliers can offer more generous terms that less well-financed competition may not meet.

ACCOUNTING FOR BAD DEBTS

At this point, a brief comment on the niceties of bad-debt accounting is appropriate. Many smaller companies may charge the estimated amount of the uncollectible account against income simultaneously with writing down the accounts-receivable balance. Then, when the proceeds, if any, are eventually received, income would be increased along with the cash balance.

> **SMART FINANCIAL MANAGEMENT: If actual write-offs can be of radically differing sizes and if ultimate collections are lumpy in occurrence, even a smaller company may wish to avoid distortions in its reporting by using a "reserve method" for bad-debt accounting. This technique, used for financial rather than tax reporting, assumes that a certain proportion of sales typically cannot be collected. Although the proportion may vary from period to period, over time it will be stable. Thus, each year a charge is made against sales of that proportion, say 1 percent.**

The reduction in income must be balanced with a second entry to maintain the integrity of the double-entry accounting system. This is accomplished by establishing a "reserve for bad debts" or uncollectible accounts as a liability account on the balance sheet. This is an accounting reserve, an allocation of what would otherwise be an increase in the retained earnings account, and does not directly involve the cash account. For reporting purposes, the reserve is normally subtracted from the accounts-receivable balance, which explains what is meant by a statement that reads: "Accounts and notes receivable, net."

Under this system, when a bad debt is discovered it is not deducted directly from the income statement. Rather, it is charged against the accounting reserve. Accounts receivable are decreased. The reserve for bad debts is also decreased, leaving the accounts-receivable (net) balance unchanged.

Similarly, if cash is eventually collected on a previously written-off account, these receipts are not recognized as income under the reserve system. The reserve is merely increased to reflect the amount of cash taken in to the cash balance, thus providing belated recognition that the amount originally written off was excessive.

Evaluating Credit Risks

The decision to grant credit to a doubtful account requires an assessment of whether the account is one of a group for which, as a group, profits after bad-debt losses will allow for at least a minimally acceptable return on investment. This decision is difficult. It depends, first, on the evaluation of the credit risk—on an assessment of the likelihood of getting repaid or of losing the goods shipped on credit. This is not the entire process, a fact that may escape the unsophisticated manager.

The second step is to figure out what the profitability of the account will be if it proves successful. The more profitable the account is likely to be, the greater the credit risk that can be taken. The same customer might be refused credit to purchase low-margin commodity items but have little trouble getting credit on high-margin proprietary products. Similarly, a high-risk customer may not get credit from banks, which traditionally operate on a very low margin, but can get ample lines from finance companies, which price their money much higher.

Certain types of credit risks have been found amenable to formula or "factor" evaluations once the relevant credit characteristics have been identified. The smaller the typical account and the larger the number of accounts, the easier it is to develop and apply formulas with some certainty that the law of averages is in the creditor's favor. Thus, most formula credit extension is used in the consumer-credit area. Most business credit is still granted only after an individual evaluation of a credit request, although major banks have begun to use a factor approach in analyzing and granting small-business loans of up to $250,000. Credit-card companies have also adopted the technique to enter the small-business loan market.

This approach cannot be applied directly to customers whose business is so significant to the enterprise that it does not represent a group. Playing the odds does not work well on only one bet. Credit should thus be granted more conservatively to these major customers relative to their financial quality—but, the larger customers *should* be more financially sound.

BUSINESS CREDIT EVALUATION

Evaluating business credit applications is easy when an applicant displays outstandingly strong characteristics:

- ➤ Profits represent a high percentage of sales and capital.
- ➤ Moderate growth.
- ➤ Excellent balance-sheet ratios (both working capital and capital structure).
- ➤ A large cash balance.
- ➤ Low payables.
- ➤ A record of prompt payment and taking discounts.

The difficulty of making these assessments accurately was graphically and expensively illustrated by the Enron situation. The company tumbled into financial difficulty while carrying prime credit ratings from leading credit-evaluating firms. Similarly, it does not take much skill to decide that a firm is a poor credit risk, especially if it is not paying its bills to other suppliers.

KEY POINT: The major challenge is correctly assessing the degree of risk in a marginal firm, considering the type of business the customer is likely to do with the creditor. It is in this evaluation process that good credit decisions make a major contribution to company profits. Correct decisions mean the development of profitable business that a less accurate credit assessment would decline and rejection only of those accounts that would turn into unprofitable problem customers.

The skills required to make these decisions are difficult to acquire and describe. They are developed by mastering the subject in textbooks, by developing an understanding of the characteristics of the industry in which the firm is doing business, and by a knowledge of the trends of the industry and the types of companies in it. Except for the first factor, the others are best acquired by experience under the direction of a capable manager. It would be presumptuous to try to give rules of thumb that would apply always to all industries.

A major problem is finding current information about a customer. A potential customer may be asked for recent financial statements and references. Once the relationship is established, however, the information is often updated only after long intervals. Public companies release information quarterly, two months after the quarter's end. Private companies may not release it at all.

Your company may subscribe to a credit-reporting service, such as Dun & Bradstreet, to obtain information about customers' credit standings. These reports may provide financial information, often minimal about private companies, and report how a sample of suppliers is being paid. A lengthening of payment times or an increase in the number of suppliers reporting slow payment is generally a sign that the account needs to be watched carefully.

If sufficient income and balance-sheet information is available, the customer's ratios can be compared to the ratios typical for the customer's industry. Some ratio information is available in the *Annual Statement Studies* published by the Risk Management Association. These data are calculated from information provided by banks about companies in a variety of businesses. Ranges of data are also provided, showing the ratios for the upper and lower quartile performers as well as for the average. Although these data are admittedly not perfect, they are among the best available. (The book is available in business-oriented libraries or, possibly, from your bank contact. Banks often use the book in loan assessments and will be happy to help you build a strong receivables portfolio.)

CONSUMER OR RETAIL CREDIT

In contrast with large retail stores, smaller retailers seldom grant credit. Formerly, they accepted only cash; now, they may accept credit cards. Even large retail operations, which made the extension of credit a selling tool and a profit center, have been forced by customer demand to accept general-purpose credit cards. The retailer pays for this service, presumably passing the costs on to the consumer as higher prices.

Retailers have learned, however, that accepting a credit-card transaction approved by the card issuer does not eliminate all credit risk. The card issuer only accepts credit risk if the card is presented in person to the seller by the authorized card signatory. The issuer does not accept credit risk for mail, telephone, or electronic orders if the purchaser is not physically present for the transaction.

> **WATCH THIS: If your firm ships in response to a telephone or mail order and the customer defaults on the credit-card charge, the card issuer will charge that loss back to you even if the card issuer had authorized the transaction. You then have to pursue the defaulting customer, which is often an impossible task for the smaller enterprise.**

Swindlers have been quick to exploit this opportunity. They have become skillful in establishing a relationship by putting in small orders and paying the credit-card bills promptly. They then place a large order, often asserting an urgent need for immediate shipment of the merchandise. The supplier fills the order with few questions because of the favorable experience with that customer. The swindler then disappears, having provided false identification information.

This fraud is similar to a technique used by established businesses that, perhaps because of financial difficulty, fall into the hands of "street-corner lenders." The business will place large orders with its suppliers, which are filled because of the long, favorable relationship with the customer. The business then files for bankruptcy, the merchandise allegedly having been sold at discount prices to generate cash to support the firm while it was failing.

Companies with weak financial positions must also be wary of unscrupulous customers who learn of their problems. Knowing the weak position of the supplier, the customer will place a large order at an attractive price. After the order is received, the customer will demand a significant price reduction. Because the supplier needs the funds immediately to pay production costs, it may be forced to agree to the extortion. If financial institutions become aware of a firm using this practice, they may alert their borrowers to the dangers of doing business with potentially problematic customers.

Evaluating Profitability

Evaluating profitability is also an assessment requiring considerable managerial experience, insight, and judgment. It is, perhaps, easier in this area to lay out a few rules than in the area of risk assessment.

The easiest approach is to look at the ratio of profits to sales for the products the customer wants. The higher the profit on sales, the more likely you will want to grant credit to a customer of a given risk profile. Other things being equal, this is true; but other things are seldom equal. Customer A, whose credit is not as good as Customer B's, may buy more than Customer B. Customer A may pay twice as fast as Customer B despite having some poorer ratios.

▶ KEY POINT: In short, the extension of credit, the commitment of funds to accounts-receivable balances, is an investment decision. It is thus appropriate to apply the same measure of attractiveness used in evaluating other asset decisions: return on investment.

The use of a return-on-investment measure requires that you develop information about both the return and the investment. Often, and accounts-receivable analysis is no exception, it is unclear which figures you should use. How to measure the return shall be discussed first, followed by consideration of the problem of measuring the investment.

ESTIMATING RETURN

Estimating Contribution

The most obvious return from an extra sale is the profit recorded on that sale.

> **KEY POINT: A sensible credit system will help you or the credit man-
> ager estimate the *contribution to fixed costs* and profits a sale will
> make rather than merely the standard profit allowed.**

This approach is particularly important if the standard costs incorpo-rate a variety of fixed costs and overhead. For a manufacturing company, the standard gross profit, less selling and delivery variable costs, is the least amount of contribution a marginal sale might make. Actual contri-bution is probably more because of fixed costs built into the standard costs. A retail or wholesale firm can derive a contribution estimate by deducting variable selling expenses from the gross margin.

In concept, the contribution is the sales figure less actual out-of-pocket cost associated with producing what is sold. Assuming the product would not be made if it could not be sold, materials and much of the direct labor costs will be true out-of-pocket costs for most credit decisions. A certain proportion of overhead will also be variable, but clearly such items as depreciation and most salaries and other overhead expenses do not vary with a specific credit sale. If your sales representatives are on commis-sion, part of the selling costs will be variable, although frequently most of these costs are fixed. Finally, it makes no sense to charge an average bad-debt allowance to a given credit decision.

For instance, a product whose standard costs total 90 percent of the selling price, as shown in Exhibit 5-1, might have a variable production cost of 45 percent, miscellaneous variable overhead of 15 percent, and variable selling expenses of 10 percent. The remaining 20 percent is contribution to fixed overhead, research, advertising, depreciation, and similar items that are fixed in the situation under consideration. This 20 percent should be added to the 10 percent profit when the credit ques-tion is considered.

At the extreme, if a marginal credit risk requests credit to buy scrap of a type that cannot otherwise be sold, the contribution is almost 100 per-cent of the sales price. Ample credit, if required to move the goods, would be justified in that instance.

> **SMART FINANCIAL MANAGEMENT: Estimating the return figure also
> requires an allowance for time and volume. Many new customers, if
> arrangements prove satisfactory to both parties, will become repeat
> buyers. It is therefore necessary to look at the total volume of business
> and at the total contribution the customer will make over time. Even with
> marginal customers, who may fail within a certain period, it is sometimes
> possible to do enough business and collect enough contribution to cover
> both the entire possible loss and earn a handsome profit as well.**

EXHIBIT 5-1

Contribution Calculation from Standard Cost Data

STANDARD COST AND PROFIT PER UNIT

Sales price	$10.00	100%
Standard costs of production		
Variable production costs	4.50	
Variable production overhead	1.00	
Fixed production costs	1.00	
Total	$ 6.50	65%
Gross margin	$ 3.50	35%
Standard selling and admin. costs		
Variable selling costs	1.00	
Variable S&A overhead	0.50	
Fixed S&A overhead	1.00	
Total	$ 2.50	25%
Standard profit	1.00	10%

CONTRIBUTION CALCULATIONS

Alternative 1			Alternative 2		
Sales price	$10.00	100%	Standard profit	$1.00	10%
Less: Variable costs			Plus: Fixed costs		
Production	4.50	45	Production	1.00	10
Production overhead	1.00	10	S&A overhead	1.00	10
Selling	1.00	10			
S&A overhead	0.50	5			
Total	$7.00	70%	Total	$2.00	20%
Contribution	$3.00	30%	Contribution	$3.00	30%

Exhibit 5-2 shows an example of an account that buys $1,000 an order of merchandise with a total contribution of 30 percent. Even if the customer fails after five purchases, the first four transactions will pay for the loss on the fifth extension and generate $500 extra contribution. The ideal decision would be to refuse the fifth shipment and suffer no loss. If no shipments had been made, however, the selling company would have lost income. With each credit extension, therefore, some estimate must be made of likely repeat business.

One problem, faced particularly by companies with divisional structures, is the difference between the total contribution the company will earn from a sale and the profits that will be recognized by the last profit center, the one making the credit decision. For instance, a company may have a "captive" wholesale subsidiary. Its responsibility is to undertake

Managing Accounts Receivable

109

EXHIBIT 5-2

Contribution from Credit Extension

ASSUMPTIONS:
Customer buys $1,000 an order
Customer buys 5 times a year
Contribution to seller is 30%

FIRST YEAR	CREDIT REFUSED	CUSTOMER SURVIVES	CREDIT GRANTED CUSTOMER FAILS, YEAR END 5TH ORDER SHIPPED	5TH ORDER REFUSED
Revenues	none	$5,000	$4,000	$4,000
Costs	none	3,500	3,500	2,800
Contribution	none	1,500	500	1,200

aggressive missionary selling of a type the company's independent wholesalers cannot afford. If the company transfers goods to its own wholesaler at the same price it sells to its outside wholesalers, then it should evaluate the operation of its missionary wholesale department differently from its cautious independents. Considering the narrow margin usually allowed for wholesale distribution, a captive missionary wholesaler could run at a loss but generate adequate returns to the company as a whole from the contributions the production departments enjoy.

Estimating the Investment

Although it is tempting to evaluate the investment in accounts receivable at book value, the billed price to the customer, this approach usually overstates the company's actual incremental investment in trade credit. Its effect is to limit the company's profitable credit extensions.

Referring to the example in Exhibit 5-2, of the $1,000 credit sale of goods with a 30 percent contribution, the book balance in accounts receivable would be the full $1,000. In actuality, $300 of this figure is the margin over out-of-pocket costs paid out, a margin for standard allocations of overhead, other nonvariable expenses, and profit. The overhead costs will be spent and eventually be charged against income regardless of whether this particular $1,000 sale is made. Therefore, the true investment is only the $700, the amount the company will be out-of-pocket if the sale is made as opposed to if it is not made. Contribution per transaction will be $300, and the maximum exposure is $700.

If the customer pays on extended terms, reducing the balance periodically until its next order, the average balance will be even lower.

Return on Investment

Thus, the correct measure of profitability is usually the contribution on the out-of-pocket investment. In the example above, if five transactions occurred a year, with each bill paid only as a new order is placed, the supplier's investment would be $700 and its return $300 × 5, or $1,500. Return on investment is 214 percent.

Why are no interest or bad debt costs assessed against the return? Interest costs were excluded because comparing the return from a credit investment to the company's total capital cost is more appropriate than comparing it merely to its interest cost. It is tempting to relate credit extensions as fund uses directly to bank lines as sources of funds. Such a comparison, however, commits the fallacy of ascribing specific fund sources to specific uses, of identifying a given dollar brought into the business with a given dollar of assets. Instead, it is the total source structure that supports the total use of funds. Individual association of assets and liabilities often cannot be logically supported.

For example, banks probably would not be willing to extend credit to the marginal credit risks a company will consider. One reason these marginal risks have to rely on supplier credit is they are unable to get bank financing. The bank's incentive to lend, with its effective net spreads of perhaps 3 to 5 percent on marginal accounts, is clearly less than a supplier's incentive with a return of more than 200 percent. Consequently, banks prefer to lend to suppliers than to the suppliers' doubtful customers. The bank knows the supplier is committing part of its resources to supporting the bank line and thus the extension of credit to its customers. A mix of capital is clearly involved in the transaction, and the bank interest rate is too low a cutoff return.

> **KEY POINT: The credit manager must evaluate whether the return in a given case is adequate compensation for the specific credit extension— not whether it is merely enough to recover an allocated bad-debt charge based on an average credit experience. This is best done by omitting interest and bad-debt allocations and looking at the returns and the risks on the specific account under consideration.**

Payback Assessment

For especially risky accounts, the credit manager can translate the return into a payback estimate. By this method, the manager can calculate the number of transactions that must be made and repaid before the company has recovered its investment. This is the break-even series of transactions. Using the example above, if the company extends credit of $700 and nets $300 from each transaction, then fewer than three transactions must be completed before the investment has been recovered. If it is likely this marginal customer will last longer than three turns, the supplier may wish to take the risk of a credit extension.

Playing the Odds

On an aggregate basis, if the company has enough similar accounts, the credit manager can calculate the minimum chance that an account must survive a year, on average, to keep a loss from being incurred. Without becoming diverted by the arithmetic, we shall call (p) the probability that an account will survive the year and $(1-p)$ the probability that it will fail immediately after the first shipment. The sum of (p) and $(1-p)$ is, by definition, one. Therefore, the expected gross profit (to use the term loosely) is the dollar profit times the probability it will be realized. The expected loss is the probability of the loss times the amount lost. The equations then appear as:

$$\text{Gross expected profit} \ = \ (p) \times (\text{dollar profit})$$

$$\text{Gross expected loss} \ = \ (1-p) \times (\text{dollar loss})$$

$$\text{Net expected profit} \ = \ [(p) \times (\text{dollar profit})] - [(1-p) \times (\text{dollar loss})].$$

By setting the net expected profit at zero and filling in the appropriate dollar figures, it is possible to calculate the probability that an account, on the average, must last for one year for the supplier to break even.

To elaborate further with the example, the account is expected to turn over five times a year, generating a profit of $1,500. If it fails immediately, the supplier will lose variable costs of $700. Thus, we solve for (p) when:

$$(p) \times (\text{dollar profit}) \ = \ (1-p) \times (\text{dollar loss})$$

$$(p) \times (\$1,500) \ = \ (1-p) \times (\$700).$$

In this example, (p) equals 0.318. If the account stands approximately a one-in-three chance of surviving *and* turns five times a year, it is worth extending the credit.

These probabilities might be altered modestly by a refinement that would add a capital charge to the potential loss figure to recover not only the minimum amount of out-of-pocket cost but also an opportunity cost for the capital involved. If the company required a 20 percent return before taxes, the loss figure would be increased to 120 percent of $700, or $840. This would alter the required odds to about 0.36.

Evaluating Receivables Management

Entrepreneurs, by definition, have a strong marketing orientation. You probably seldom find a customer you don't like. The tendency to make every sale, however, can bring considerable distress if the proceeds are not collected promptly. Fraud, already discussed, can be one source of problems. Granting unprofitable credit can be another. Failing to discipline collection of receivables is a third. A source of difficulty often overlooked by the business owner is simply the financial requirement to support the receivables, however sound, of a growing business. Business owners have grown into bankruptcy because they took in more orders than the firm's finances could support. You must therefore understand not only the sales process but also how to monitor the collection process.

REVIEW OF THE CREDIT DECISIONS

Earlier we suggested that the best test of credit policy and accounts receivable management was if credit was being extended to the point that the return on investment from the most marginal accounts was just sufficient to cover the capital costs involved. It is difficult to judge when and if this point has been reached. Therefore, it is extremely hard to figure out whether the credit department is performing effectively.

> **IMPORTANT: One of the least effective ways to attempt this evaluation is to look at the total level of bad debts. This measurement technique by itself would simply signal the credit department to avoid all bad debts. The best way to avoid bad debts is not to grant credit to marginal accounts. Thus, profits on the marginal accounts that would have survived are lost to the competition.**

Some credit managers have tried to identify the "calculated risk" accounts, the accounts that promised to be difficult to control but also offered compensating profit potential. Analysts can identify difficult accounts as they are evaluated for credit. They also can be flagged if their characteristics fit a preestablished set of criteria, such as low current ratio, high debt, and poor profits compared with industry standards. The profits on sales to this group of accounts can then be estimated and compared to the investment required. Based on this return on investment, you can judge whether the gains compensate for the risks. The opportunity for managerial game playing is present, but careful managers will be interested in studying their own performances. At least for that purpose, the credit manager will want to develop the most effective system available.

APPRAISING COLLECTION PRACTICES

The external analyst, who does not usually have as much information available as does corporate management, often evaluates the credit extension activity by comparing the volume of receivables outstanding to the sales level.

If your business has significant seasonal or cyclical features, you must recognize their effects on the business and be ready to explain them to financial sources. Many standard measures of receivables management are poor measures when seasonal or cyclical factors are present. You should not be surprised if an external analyst comes to an incorrect conclusion about your company's receivables management because the analyst is using an inappropriate measure. You need to educate the analyst and perhaps even the company accountant.

The internal manager is also concerned with whether the receivables are being collected as rapidly as possible. You may know that the accounts are not in danger of default, but a slow account ties up the supplier's funds for a longer time and reduces the profits that can be made on those funds. If your company suffers from a funds shortage, its sales volume is apt to be reduced when your customers begin to pay more slowly. As receivables increase, inventories will be cut to provide the necessary funds. Lower inventories, in turn, mean stockouts and sales lost because of an inability to deliver within competitive times.

For example, if sales increase from $1 million to $2 million and the accounts receivable balance remains at 10 percent of sales, the balance should double from $100,000 to $200,000. If a reduction in collection speed occurs, the balance might rise to $300,000, or 15 percent of sales. The first $100,000 increase is to be expected, although entrepreneurs sometimes forget to allow for it in their enthusiasm for growth. The second $100,000 increase is a cause for worry, but it is also often the result of a growth effort that grants more lenient terms. This change reflects the typical entrepreneur's sales orientation.

By measuring these factors in terms of collection time, a graphical illustration of the impact of volume and collection changes can be developed, as illustrated by Exhibit 5-3. Sales of $1 million a year and $2 million a year represent sales per day of $2,740 and $5,480 respectively, shown on the horizontal axis as points D and F. The collection period, in terms of sales per day, is calculated by dividing sales per day into the balance of outstanding receivables:

$100,000 ÷ 2,740 = 36.5 days

$200,000 ÷ 5,480 = 36.5 days

$300,000 ÷ 5,480 = 54.7 days

EXHIBIT 5-3
Managing Accounts Receivable

**IMPACT ON BALANCE IN ACCOUNTS RECEIVABLE
OF CHANGES IN VOLUME AND COLLECTION EXPERIENCE**

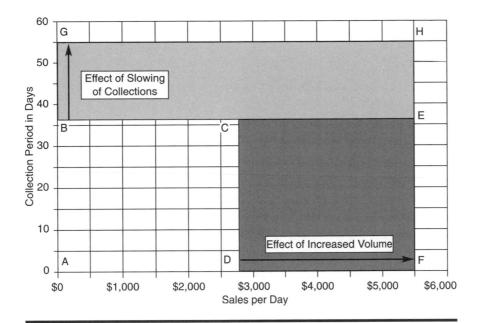

The first two collection periods are indicated by point B, the third by point G.

Because the total volume of receivables is the sales per day times the collection period, the area of the rectangles shown in Exhibit 5-3 is a graphic representation of this balance and its components. If the collection period does not change, the increase in the balance will be proportional to the increase in sales. In this example, a doubling of sales (and thus sales per day) produces an area ABEF, which is twice the size of the original area ABCD.

A lengthening of the collection period, which would be represented by an increase of $200,000 on an increase of sales of only $1 million, would have the effect of increasing the balance more than proportionally. A simultaneous change of this sort creates a major increase in receivables, adding the area BGHE to the DCEF created by volume increase alone.

> **IMPORTANT: If the extra sales have been stimulated in part by a more generous credit policy, which often must also be extended to existing customers, you must be careful to anticipate the extra funds that will be required. You also must evaluate carefully whether the extra investment in receivables is justified by the extra profit earned.**

SEASONAL COMPLICATIONS FOR THE ANALYSIS OF RECEIVABLES MANAGEMENT

It is particularly difficult to compare the results of different months for companies that experience pronounced seasonal sales patterns. A similar problem is present in the evaluation of companies that operate in longer cyclical patterns. The end of one year may be near the peak of a sales cycle and the end of the next year part way down a trough. Total sales in both cases may be the same, but the working-capital positions may be strikingly different. This discussion is devoted to receivables measurement in a seasonal setting. The reader is left to extend the case to the cyclical situation.

An Example of Constant Collection Experience

Exhibits 5-4 and Exhibit 5-5 will be used to illustrate the common methods of evaluating receivables management and the problems associated with them. These exhibits show the collection experience of the Chamberlain Company, a manufacturer of lawn and casual furniture. Exhibit 5-4 lists the monthly sales, which are at a low and level rate of $50,000 a month from September through January. Sales then begin to rise, slowly at first and then steeply to a peak month of $300,000 in June. Sales decline more rapidly after June than they rose, reaching the $50,000 off-season level again in September.

Chamberlain's collection experience, however, is very stable. As shown in Exhibit 5-4, no sales are collected during the first 30 days, during the month in which a sale is made. Fifty percent of the sales are collected between 30 and 60 days after sale. During the 60- to 90-day period, an additional 40 percent are collected. The final 10 percent is paid during the 90- to 120-day period, the third month after sale. The weighted average of day's sales outstanding in the accounts receivable balance is shown in Table 5-1.

Alternatively stated, during any given month, collections consist of 50 percent of the prior month's sales, 40 percent of the second prior, and 10 percent of the third prior month's sales.

Exhibit 5-5 develops the balance of accounts receivable given the information on sales and collections provided in Exhibit 5-4. The balance is calculated in two ways. Part A shows a balance calculated by applying constant percentages to the appropriate months, as shown in Table 5-2.

❯ KEY POINT: A calculation displaying this information and relating the outstanding balances to the sales of those periods in which the balances were created is known as an *aging of receivables*. In the Chamberlain Company's case, the aging would show a constant pattern of 100 percent, 50 percent, and 10 percent relating balances to the periods in which the sales had been made.

(text continues on page 119)

EXHIBIT 5-4

Chamberlain Company
Collection Experiences with Collection Period Constant but Fluctuating Sales
Collection Schedule: 0% current month, 50% prior month, 40% next prior, 10% third period.

	PY*	JAN	FEB	MAR	APR	MAY	JUNE	JULY	AUG	SEPT	OCT	NOV	DEC	TOTAL
Sales made in:	50	50	80	100	150	250	300	100	70	50	50	50	50	1300
Will be collected in:														
January	50	—	—	—	—	—	—	—	—	—	—	—	—	50
February	25	25	—	—	—	—	—	—	—	—	—	—	—	50
March	5	20	40	—	—	—	—	—	—	—	—	—	—	65
April	—	5	32	50	—	—	—	—	—	—	—	—	—	87
May	—	—	8	40	75	—	—	—	—	—	—	—	—	123
June	—	—	—	10	60	125	—	—	—	—	—	—	—	195
July	—	—	—	—	15	100	150	—	—	—	—	—	—	265
August	—	—	—	—	—	25	120	50	—	—	—	—	—	195
September	—	—	—	—	—	—	30	40	35	—	—	—	—	105
October	—	—	—	—	—	—	—	10	28	25	—	—	—	63
November	—	—	—	—	—	—	—	—	7	20	25	—	—	52
December	—	—	—	—	—	—	—	—	—	5	20	25	—	50
														1300

* Column includes collections this year on sales made in prior year.

EXHIBIT 5-5

Chamberlain Company
Accounts Receivable Balance

	JAN	FEB	MAR	APR	MAY	JUNE	JULY	AUG	SEPT	OCT	NOV	DEC
A. Accounts outstanding from:												
2nd prior month (10%)	5	5	5	8	10	15	25	30	10	7	5	5
1st prior month (50%)	25	25	40	50	75	125	150	50	35	25	25	25
Current month (100%)	50	80	100	150	250	300	100	70	50	50	50	50
Total	80	110	145	208	335	440	275	150	95	82	80	80
B. Balance, beginning												
of month:	80	80	110	145	208	335	440	275	150	95	82	80
Less: Collections	50	50	65	87	123	195	265	195	105	63	52	25
Plus: Sales	50	80	100	150	250	300	100	70	50	50	50	50
Balance, end of month	80	110	145	208	335	440	275	150	95	82	80	80

TABLE 5-1

Calculation of Weighted Average Day's Sales Outstanding

50% take 30 days to collect	=	15 day's sales
40% take 60 days to collect	=	24
10% take 90 days to collect	=	9
Average outstanding	=	48 days' sales

TABLE 5-2

Illustration of Proportion-of-Sales-Outstanding Calculation

PROPORTION OUTSTANDING	AS OF MAY	AS OF SEPTEMBER
100% of the month just ended	$250 (May)	$50 (Sept.)
50% of the prior month	75 (Apr.)	35 (Aug.)
10% of second prior month	10 (Mar.)	10 (July)
Total	$335	$95

Exhibit 5-5, Part B, proves these characteristics by showing they are consistent with the usual method of calculating the balance in accounts receivable: beginning balance less collections plus sales, all as shown in Exhibit 5-4.

Exhibit 5-6 shows the types of errors and distortions that result when an attempt is made to use various common measures of receivables management in a situation characterized by fluctuating sales levels. It is important to reemphasize that these distortions are caused *solely* by the fluctuations in sales and not by changes in the collection pattern, which is constant as described above.

Day's Sales Methods

A common way of measuring a company's collection experience is to calculate the number of days' sales represented by the receivables balance. As indicated earlier, this figure is computed in two steps as follows:

1. Sales per Day = (Total Sales) ÷ (Number of Days in the Period) (when using one year's sales, divide by 365; for one month's, divide by 30)
2. Day's Receivables = (Balance in Accounts Receivable) ÷ (Sales per Day)

EXHIBIT 5-6

Chamberlain Company
Alternative Measures of Accounts Receivable Management

	JAN	FEB	MAR	APR	MAY	JUNE	JULY	AUG	SEPT	OCT	NOV	DEC
Sales	50	80	100	150	250	300	100	70	50	50	50	50
Accounts receivable balance	80	110	145	208	335	440	275	150	95	82	80	80
1. Average day's sales (1,300,000 ÷ 365 = 3,560 sales per day)	22d	31d	41d	58d	94d	124d	77d	42d	27d	23d	22d	22d
2. Most recent month's day's sales	48d	41d	44d	42d	40d	44d	82d	64d	57d	49d	48d	48d
3. Most recent 3 month's day's sales	48d	55d	57d	57d	60d	56d	38d	29d	39d	43d	48d	48d
4. Percentage of assets (assuming assets constant at 2,000)	4%	6%	7%	10%	17%	22%	14%	8%	5%	4%	4%	4%
5. Percentage of receivables more than 30 days old	38%	27%	31%	28%	25%	32%	63%	53%	47%	39%	38%	38%

Alternatively, a simpler computation is:

$$\text{Day's Receivables} = \frac{\text{Accounts Receivable Balance}}{\text{Sales}} \times \text{Days in Period}$$

▶ **IMPORTANT: Remember that the number of days used must be consistent with the period for which the sales figure is derived. For a full year's sales, 365 or 360 is the proper number of days. For six months sales, a figure of 180 days is required.**

Rows 1, 2, and 3 of Exhibit 5-6 show three alternative ways of computing the number of days in the accounts-receivable balance. Row 1 uses a figure for sales per day based on the average for the entire year: $1,300,000 ÷ 365 = $3,560. The number of days' sales in receivables varies wildly with this measure because the average daily sales based on the entire year's sales volume is very different from the daily sales experienced in any one month.

In Row 2, the receivables balance is compared to the most recent 30 days' sales. This method shows variations because the balance in the accounts receivable includes not only sales of the most recent month (of which 100 percent are still outstanding) but also a significant proportion of the prior month's sales (40 percent). Row 3 shows the results of using a three-month average sales per day figure. This calculation is high when the current month's sales figure is low and is low when the current monthly figure is high.

Percentage Approaches

Two other methods are often used to evaluate receivables management, but they are subject to the same distortions described for the day's-receivables methods. These techniques are based on percentage calculations.

Exhibit 5-6 shows the percentage of the Chamberlain's assets invested in receivables as the year progresses, assuming that total assets are constant at $2 million. The percentage of receivables to total assets is only 4 percent at the low point, rising to 22 percent at the peak. This result is entirely due to the calculation method and not to any change in collection experience.

A second common percentage method relates receivables outstanding for more than a specified time (30, 60, or 90 days) to the total receivables' balance. A shift in this percentage is supposed to signify a deterioration of collection and perhaps of credit standards. As shown in Row 5, the percentage of receivables over 30 days varies drastically compared to the total balance in the account. The reason, again, is the fluctuation in sales. When current sales are high compared with prior sales, the percentage due from over 30 days is low. When current sales are low compared to prior sales, the percentage due from over 30 days is high.

If comparisons are made between comparable periods, say June of one year to June of the next, if the company's sales levels are proportionate in corresponding periods, and if its collection experience holds constant, then the results of any of these five calculations we have described should be comparable. These are several "ifs," but for many companies they are sufficiently true for the analyst to compare one year-end statement with another without distortion. If Chamberlain ended its fiscal year in July, for example, an outside analyst using average sales for the year would calculate that 77 days' sales were outstanding. Provided approximately 77 days were outstanding the year before, the analyst would conclude that the company was not losing control of its credit.

For companies that suffer serious cyclical patterns of more than one year in duration, even such year-end comparisons are difficult. Suppose Chamberlain ended one year's operation in a cyclical position typical of the July figures, with 124 days (average annual) sales outstanding. If it had happened to end the previous year with a cycle in a December stage, showing only 22 days' sales, the analyst could become needlessly concerned about the credit position.

A True Aging Method

The discussion so far has concentrated on common, but flawed, methods for assessing the collection experience. Is there a correct way? The answer is, "Yes"—but the outside analyst often cannot apply it because the necessary information is available only to insiders.

> **KEY POINT: Internal management has no excuse for not establishing its information system so that the proper information for evaluating the collection process is available. You are well advised to use this internal information to explain your company's collection history to financial sources.**

The most accurate method is that shown in Exhibit 5-4 and in Part A of Exhibit 5-5, where a true aging of accounts is displayed. With this information, the analyst could calculate either the collection pattern (when sales made in a given month are collected) or relate the outstanding balances at the end of each month to the sales of the month in which they were made. If the analyst calculated collections, as in Exhibit 5-4, the analyst would find the 50 percent, 40 percent, 10 percent pattern is consistent. In a situation where collection experience is good, some minor variation would naturally be expected—but no slipping over time. If the typical 50 percent of sales collected in the second month dropped to 45 percent and finally to only 30 percent, however, this would be a sign of credit deterioration. Confirmation would be a corresponding increase in collections after 60 days. A positive sign would be an increase in the proportion of sales collected in the first 30 days.

Smart Financial Management

The general rule, which applies to most current asset and current liability accounts, is that particular care is required in interpreting the sales volume and account balance relationships to ensure that they are analyzed in the light of most current business conditions. Comparisons of unlike periods for highly seasonal companies are especially fraught with danger. Misinterpretation of accounts receivable figures by an external analyst can undermine a financing relationship. If you do not understand receivables evaluation, your company can get into deep financial trouble.

CHAPTER 6

MANAGING INVENTORIES

Inventories are the most difficult of a company's physical assets to manage. If mismanaged, they are the quickest way for a company to get into trouble. They are hard to measure and value, their value may change very quickly, and they are subject to fraud. At least one turnaround authority has said that he has never seen a troubled company that did not have an inventory problem. Frequently, inventory was where the trouble started. Marketing executives, and particularly dynamic entrepreneurs, never want to miss a sale and thus can never have enough inventory. Of course, production executives also like to have inventory to reduce the likelihood of having production interrupted because materials are missing. Frequently, it is only the treasurer, worried about the hidden costs of carrying inventory and return on investment, who finds inventory a cause for concern.

> **KEY POINT: The rules for recording inventory on your firm's books are simple in concept and enormously complex in application. The concept is that inventories should be valued at the lower of cost or market, with a market valuation being low enough to allow for the proper gross margin at the time the inventory is sold.**

This rule may not be too difficult to apply in a wholesale or retail business, although complexities can quickly multiply when items have been purchased at different prices at different times. However, it is far more difficult to apply in a manufacturing setting, where judgments must be made about what overhead and fixed costs should or should not be included in the product cost at various stages of the production process. Furthermore, if market value is to be assessed, how is that to be determined for a specialized and partly completed product?

A physical count is also very difficult to perform because it is not easy to stop the sales or production process while the count is going on. The inventory may be scattered among many physical locations. At best, the valuation of the inventory is thus an educated guess.

There is also more potential for fraud in inventory management than in most other assets. Fraudulent sales require the creation of fictitious customers and a variety of other complexities, but fraudulent inventory management can be done in a variety of ways. One is to fiddle the inventory records so that more cost remains in inventory than should be there, thus lowering current period costs and enhancing profits. Damaged goods can be kept as work in process. Obsolete inventory can be kept at its full cost. Inventory can be moved from one location to another so it is counted twice. Labels on boxes can misrepresent the contents. The auditor's efforts to apply random tests can be subverted.

Still, most inventory problems do not arise because of fraud. They arise because management buys or produces too much of the wrong merchandise at the wrong price. This can be the result of overoptimistic management: you expect sales the next period to rise dramatically and build inventory accordingly. Then, sales grow more slowly than anticipated or even decline if the economy softens or as consumer tastes change. Style changes can be sudden: a women's-wear style termed the "wet look" evaporated before the merchandise reached the retail shelves. "Firm" orders are suddenly canceled. Merchandise is returned because of real or alleged quality issues. As an executive of a retail chain noted, "When sales fall off, we don't even bother claiming quality problems. We just pack the stuff up and send it back and don't pay. We can argue about the settlement later."

Our description of inventory management starts with consideration of a manufacturing operations–management perspective. (This discussion will not deal directly with retail inventories because they are similar to the finished goods inventory of a manufacturer and are subject to the same analytical approach.) First, you need to consider the financial aspects of inventory management and its risks. The financial characteristics of inventory should then be related to the nature of the business and its economic function. Then, review managerial decisions that involve inventory and the types of problems those decisions can create. The better informed you are about the risks and rewards, the more likely you will make the correct decision on inventory management.

The Operations Perspective

The main responsibility of an operations manager is to provide the quantity required of the quality required when it is required at the lowest cost. How this is accomplished depends largely on the nature of the production process.

THE EFFECT OF THE PRODUCTION PROCESS ON INVENTORIES

At one extreme are industries with *continuous production*. Paper mills are designed to operate at a certain speed 24 hours a day, 7 days a week. They are down a week or two for annual maintenance, but otherwise they produce continuously. Chemical plants and petroleum refineries operate in the same manner.

Continuous-production operations have several advantages. First, the raw material inputs are easy to plan. The same amount may be required day after day. Thus, the main managerial question is how much raw-materials inventory must to be on hand to buffer delays in receiving the daily delivery from suppliers. Second, there is very little work-in-process. Wood or oil is dropped in one end. Paper, chemicals, or gasoline comes out the other a couple of days later.

> **KEY POINT: The major inventory problem that continuous-production operations have is what to do with the finished goods if demand falls. Finished goods can build up quickly. Storage space is often expensive and limited, even if the product does not spoil physically or economically. The result is price cuts that encourage consumers to substitute the product for other products whose production can be more easily curtailed. A drop in oil prices may encourage more use of oil and less of electricity.**

There is no problem if demand rises because continuous-production industries generally require large plant and equipment and have low sales-to-asset ratios. This characteristic means that new capacity takes time to come on stream. If demand rises but capacity is fixed, prices and profits rise.

At the other extreme of the production spectrum is the company that produces a large and unique product, such as aircraft carriers, top-end residences, and even works of art. This type of product, sometimes classified as a *project,* has a different inventory situation than the continuous-production product. Because the project is unique and often requires a long production period, most of the project's inventory is a work-in-process. To support production, producers require progress payments at various stages as the work is completed. There is virtually no finished-goods inventory because the final product is turned over to the customer when it passes whatever tests have been mandated. The raw-material inventory also can be closely controlled because of the certainty about what is in the production process.

Job-shop products have a faster production cycle than aircraft carriers but are similar in that they are produced to order. Many textiles fall into this category, as does upholstered furniture. Paper-bag makers, for example, usually produce only to order because of the need to print the outside of the bag to the customer's specification. The bag production process is short. Raw material may not be as easy to plan because the customer may not provide advanced warning of its requirements. There will be little finished-goods inventory, however, unless the bag company offers storage as a service to its customers. This inventory is not the result of the production characteristics but of a marketing decision.

Some manufacturing processes are strictly *assembly* in nature. Raw materials, purchased from other manufacturers, are the bits and pieces that must be snapped into place. Assembly is accomplished with little plant and equipment. It can be as simple as a long table with employees pushing boxes of the product to the next person once the assembly operation for a station is completed. It can be as complex as several technicians building a large electronic unit at one station over several months. The common characteristics are that most parts are purchased and only assembly is performed. An assembly operation's inventory depends more on the nature of its product (such as special order, seasonal demand, and unique components) than on the nature of the production process itself.

❯ **KEY POINT: Most manufacturing facilities contain characteristics of several of these categories. They can alter their production somewhat in response to changes in demand. Nevertheless, they may have to start production before orders have been received because low-cost production demands longer runs and fewer setups. In addition, having the capacity to produce to demand may mean having a much larger plant than is needed on average. This capital equipment is expensive. Thus, the inclination is to produce more efficiently even if it means taking the risk of carrying some intermediate or finished goods.**

THE TRADEOFFS

The preceding discussion hinted at the nature of the tradeoffs from the operations perspective. The operations manager wants to keep the production cost as low as possible, which means few setups or changes, long production runs, and a stable workforce. This combination can create finished goods ahead of firm orders along with generous work-in-process inventories.

❯ **IMPORTANT: The accumulation of inventory in any form means funds are tied up that otherwise could be invested in marketable securities, used to repay debt, or even returned to the shareholder. It also means capital must be invested in facilities to store the goods. There are costs of handling the items in inventory: putting them in to storage when a manufacturing stage is complete and taking them out for the next stage or when they are shipped. It even may be necessary to move finished goods around while they are in storage to make room for or to get at other items. The more times the finished product is handled, the greater the chance for accidental damage. The more finished goods in stock, the more**

vulnerable the inventory is to theft because the finished goods are usually the most valuable of the inventory components.

Another risk presented by finished-goods inventory is that of obsolescence, either physical or economic. *Physical obsolescence,* or spoilage, is characteristic of items with a short shelf life. Fresh fruits and vegetables are perhaps the most dramatic examples (when they are ripe, they must either be sold rapidly or trashed). Other natural products, such as nuts, grains, and soybeans, may keep longer under proper conditions. Nevertheless, farmers who store even this produce for too long will find it has degenerated. Pharmaceuticals and chemicals are often products that deteriorate with time, occasionally becoming dangerous if not just ineffective.

Economic obsolescence occurs when demand for the product dries up even though the product is physically as good as when it was produced. Clothing has traditionally been one of the products most susceptible to economic obsolescence. Jackets bearing the name of a professional sports team may be in such demand one year that they sell out instantly but hardly sell at all the next. Women's-wear fashions can change dramatically. On one memorable occasion, the department stores were heavily advertising a peasant-with-veil look one week and a tailored look the next. Even standard items, such as men's slacks, are vulnerable to style changes—color, pleats, and fabric.

The increased speed of technical development contributes more to hard-good obsolescence than before. The silver-based photographic process had hardly changed for more than one hundred years although there were continual improvements in its performance. Cameras had new features, but their basic function was to record the effect of light on film in an irreversible process. Video cameras were the first to challenge the traditional photographic industry, recording the image on tape that could be erased and reused. Digital cameras do not even use tape but can record the image on disks or strips or in a computer memory. Similar, but faster, changes have occurred in all aspects of the computer industry and in many communications industries. Finished goods that had value one day could have no value the next, as was the case when the Federal Communications Commission authorized additional channels for citizen-band radios. The inventories of CB radios with the smaller number of channels instantly became virtually worthless.

> **KEY POINT: You therefore have the challenge of balancing the savings from longer (and perhaps speculative) production runs against the costs of carrying the inventory—including handling, financing, and obsolescence.**

ECONOMIC ORDER QUANTITY

Fortunately, the optimal economic order quantity (EOQ) can be computed mathematically. Unfortunately, the results are only as good as the estimates on which the calculations are based. These estimates are often difficult to make accurately.

The formula will not be derived here, but the derivation can be found in the comprehensive financial-management texts. The *sales* component is self–explanatory; it is the annual dollar sales volume. The *cost per setup* should include whatever costs are involved in beginning a production run. The *direct costs* required to set the machines for the run may be obvious, but a variety of *variable overhead costs* in engineering and production planning should be included. In addition, *training costs* and the *cost of scrap* may be generated during the startup process.

The *carrying cost* for a unit of inventory is even more complex because it incorporates all the miscellaneous costs, such as financing, damage, theft, and obsolescence. These are calculated as percentages of a unit's cost (for example, interest at x percent and damage at y percent). The percentages are added and then applied to half of a unit's out-of-pocket cost. The result is a dollar figure that can be used in the final calculation.

The carrying costs can be significant. One major accounting firm's studies show the carrying cost for consumer goods is in the range of 20 to 30 percent a year. It is much higher for goods with high economic obsolescence.

▶ **SMART MOVE: Based on this information, the firm encourages its clients to liquidate inventory at the end of a season rather than hold it over for the next year.**

The EOQ formula itself is:

$$\text{EOQ} = \sqrt{\frac{2 \times \text{Sales} \times \text{Cost per Setup}}{\text{Carrying Cost}}}$$

Although the previous discussion has been couched in manufacturing terms, retailers may also use the EOQ formula to determine how much to order at a time. Because their setup costs will be lower, the retailer's reorder quantity will generally be a much lower percentage of sales volume than the manufacturer's. Consequently, the retailer's ordering frequency will be higher. If the retailer can return unsold merchandise, however, its EOQ will be larger and its orders less frequent.

ADDITIONAL CONSIDERATIONS

If everything worked perfectly, the average inventory would be half of the EOQ. New inventory would arrive just as the last unit of the previous order was being sold. Unfortunately, even with just-in-time supply practices, reality is seldom this perfect. Buffer stocks are thus necessary at many stages in the production and retail process to guard against interruptions in supply. Even in the information era, bad weather, disasters, strikes, and other unexpected variables can delay delivery.

With more efficient communication and low-cost computing power, it is possible to get accurate data in time to take corrective action if delays crop up or if sales deplete an inventory more rapidly than expected. Similarly, inexpensive and fast air transportation has made it possible to source supplies from much farther afield with little loss in delivery time. Long supply chains, however, are more vulnerable to interruption. This development ironically requires larger-than-expected buffer stocks to prevent loss of production or sales.

Setting buffer stocks is even more an art than estimating the variables necessary to calculate the EOQ. It is an "insurance" decision—balancing the cost of having the extra inventory against the cost of stocking out. If the stockout cost is low, there is no need to carry much inventory in the buffer. Furthermore, the amount of inventory in the buffer, given a stockout cost, will vary according to the length of the potential delay. The longer the probable delay, the greater amount of inventory needed in the buffer.

> **SMART FINANCIAL MANAGEMENT: One approach to setting a buffer stock at a given point in the production and sales process is to develop a simple Monte Carlo simulation, a feature available on some spreadsheet programs. By specifying the relevant costs of having inventory and of stocking out, together with the chance of delay, a probable cost can be calculated for various levels of buffer stock. The inventory level with the lowest cost would be the most efficient level, but it would not guarantee that no stockouts would occur. The same data also will permit calculation of the additional costs of holding a higher buffer stock to reduce or virtually eliminate the chance of stocking out.**

An additional factor needs to be considered about the effect of loading up a job-shop or assembly production process. The normal assumption is that this type of production facility will gain efficiency as it nears capacity. Costs will be lower because there are no delays at any of the work stations. Delivery also will be more certain.

Case in Point: A study of a major job-shop facility in the aerospace industry confirmed this was true over a wide range of capacity utilization. At higher rates, however, the effects of greater efficiency were offset by a sudden increase in the ratio of work-in-process to production. The study found the relationship was constant for capacity utilization ranging from 50 percent up to the upper 80s: if production rose by x percent, work-in-process rose by the same percentage. Once capacity use had reached the upper 80 percents, however, the work-in-process rose dramatically more than production utilization.

Investigation showed this unexpected result stemmed from the need to have larger than proportional work-in-process inventories to avoid the marginal delays at the high operating rates. In addition, the plant became so cluttered that necessary inventory was located under other inventory or could not be found. Thus, further buffer stock was needed.

> **KEY POINT: The moral of this finding for financial management is that pushing for greater operating efficiency by greater capacity use may require more funds for work-in-process than anticipated if calculations were based on production utilization lower than 85 percent. At some point, a tradeoff will arise between the working-capital requirements and additions to plant and equipment when it will become more efficient to use funds for plant expansion rather than working capital. It also may be easier to finance the physical assets on a longer-term basis.**

The Financial Perspective

The relationship between capacity use and funds allocation leads to the subject of financial perspective on inventory management. Central to this issue is the characteristic of the business—the volatility of demand, the seasonal nature of demand, and whether the business can build to order or must build inventory on speculation. These critical dimensions determine the carrying cost of inventory, which includes not only the cost of financing the inventory but also such other costs as obsolescence.

VOLATILE DEMAND

As a rule, the higher the volatility of demand and the accompanying uncertainty of demand, the greater the potential loss to a business from its inventory.

Businesses, such as women's wear clothing or any product with high-fashion content that is characterized by volatile and uncertain demand, must find ways to avoid building inventory, or they will not survive. The ideal is to build only to order, but this technique is not without other problems.

A second way of dealing with uncertainty is for an industry to divide into unintegrated, flexible components whose total capacity is likely to match the total volume of the goods or services required.

Case in Point: The textile industry is one example. It is virtually unintegrated. The retailers and designers do not integrate back into production. If a designer's products are in high demand, the designer and the designer's emulators simply contract with more mills to weave the fabric and with more cutters and sewers to produce the finished product. Individual cutters and sewers, in turn, may lease more loft space and sewing equipment as required. This additional capacity may not even be necessary because the products of another designer, perhaps last season's hot designs, will have fallen out of favor. Resources devoted to the previous year's hot lines are free to shift to this year's hot lines.

Integration is usually a disaster for companies in this type of industry. In good years, they cannot meet production requirements. In poor years, they cannot cover overhead. An entrepreneur in this type of business should be very cautious about the temptation to integrate. It would be better to set up a separate business to service different stages in the production process and run them independently.

A third approach is to have the capacity needed at the time it is needed. This is an expensive alternative because it means the resources are unlikely to be used at optimal capacity at times but may be stretched at others. *Examples:* Processing produce and other seasonal foods, such as fish, falls into this category. When the fruit is ripe, it has to be processed quickly. The cannery may work at full capacity during this period. What cannot be processed spoils and is discarded. The rest of the year, the cannery may shut down.

> **KEY POINT: The financial problems of inventory management created by volatility thus depend on how funds can be used most efficiently. The least efficient is building capacity to produce on demand at the last minute. A better approach is for an industry to be structured so adequate resources are available and can be brought to produce whatever products are in demand. This structure may require sacrifice of some efficiency for an increased chance of survival. Entrepreneurs like yourself, being optimists, must be wary of indulging in capacity that can more efficiently be obtained from others.**

SEASONAL DEMAND

A second characteristic central to the financial management of inventory is seasonal demand. This problem is similar to the those of volatile demand because of the tradeoff between capacity and finished-goods inventory. Where there is little uncertainty but a strong seasonal component, such as in the Christmas-tree lights and desk-calendar industries, then sensible financial management comes down on the side of efficient production and investment in finished-goods inventory.

Unfortunately, most seasonal products do not enjoy a stable demand. The market may not be quite as volatile as an industry that has multiple seasons each year (clothing), but there may still be considerable uncertainty about the level of demand (lawn furniture) and the product (toys). A variety of financial strategies are used to reduce this type of risk.

Smart Move #1

One strategy is to provide incentives for customers to order and accept delivery early. In effect, convert finished goods to accounts receivable. This practice has several advantages:

> ➤ It makes the customer's commitment more certain. The customer must do more than order. It must provide storage and take care of the product while it is in the customer's inventory.
> ➤ Filling the customer's warehouse or store with products makes it more difficult for the competition to place its product.
> ➤ The manufacturer's need for finished-goods inventory space is reduced.
> ➤ There may be fewer times the inventory must be handled, thereby reducing the chances for damage.
> ➤ Financial institutions are more willing to lend against accounts receivable at a lower interest rate and a higher draw rate than they are against inventory. It may even be possible to borrow the entire cash production cost if a receivable is pledged. A loan secured by inventories is usually half the total production cost. A loan secured by a high-quality receivable may be as much as 85 percent of the amount due.

The incentives themselves can be expensive, as explained in Chapter 5. An easy incentive to administer is the offer of additional trade discounts for firm advance orders. The earlier the order is placed, the greater the discount. In addition, manufacturers may also offer deferred payment terms. A toy manufacturer, for instance, may allow its customers to pay by December 15 for any merchandise they take possession of by September 15 (this practice is sometimes called *dating*). Payment is due on more conventional terms for shipments after September 15.

At an extreme, suppliers whose production level is difficult to vary (such as chemicals) may offer customers in seasonal businesses dating terms that require payment only once a year. The payment date may be set to fall at the end of the customer's selling season, when collections from accounts receivable have begun to roll in. These delayed-payment terms may require a compensating accommodation by the customer, such as accepting regular shipments each month.

Smart Move #2

It can be more efficient for you to use your financial resources to provide these incentives than to use the same funds to build finished-goods inventory. Although nominal return on investment may be lower, the risk-adjusted return may be higher.

Furthermore, a firm with sound finances may use its financial resources to compete effectively against competitors whose lack of funds forces them to compete on price. The customer may value the credit and having the inventory on hand much more than a price cut. A small retailer, for example, may have limited access to debt and a much higher funds cost than a large, well-financed supplier. In many parts of the world, small firms are financed by suppliers' permitting lengthy trade terms.

Smart Move #3

Another approach for efficiently using capacity is to arrange for production first of products with the least uncertain demand.

This reduces the risk of finished goods becoming obsolete and allows capacity to be available to produce the most volatile or new products closer to receipt of firm orders. This arrangement does cut the risk, but it does not have as many advantages as persuading customers to take early delivery. It requires a stronger financial base because funding is needed for finished-goods inventory rather than receivables and because the chance of loss from obsolescence is greater.

STABLE DEMAND

Where demand is very stable, even if it is seasonal, it is possible to reap the benefits of integration and stable, long-run level-production practices. The structure in these industries substitutes finished-goods inventory for plant and equipment. Level production also cuts labor costs because the retraining and layoff costs associated with changes in production rates are avoided. Finally, a stable production process can allow the manufacturer to negotiate better prices from its suppliers, particularly if its suppliers are continuous-process firms. They put a premium on having customers willing to take delivery on a uniform, level schedule.

Products qualifying for level production, such as garden hoses, fencing, or Christmas-tree lights, do not degenerate physically or economically. If they do not sell one year (as happened to Christmas-tree lights during the oil crisis of the early 1970s, which struck in the fall), they can be stored for the next at little cost. The reorder rate on desk calendars, for instance, is approximately 95 percent. The setup time for a given calendar model is extensive, but, given the stable demand, the entire annual production of that model can be completed in one run. The calendar company can use its financial resources to support the finished-goods inventory (and accounts receivable if its customers are willing to take advanced shipment) rather than plant and equipment.

▶ **KEY POINT: The production level must be set at the close of a season to produce inventory during the low period for sale during the peak. This requires you to estimate, perhaps six to nine months in advance, what the peak seasonal sales will be.**

Regrettably, insight into the true nature of the peak season may not be clear until after the season has begun. It is at this point that the seasonal buildup in finished-goods inventory is already at its highest level. Thus, by the time it is clear that sales will be softer than expected, perhaps because a cyclical downturn has developed, the finished-good inventory has already been built. (The reverse problem, higher than expected demand, is less serious. Price can be raised. Production can be put on overtime. Even subcontracting can be used.)

INVENTORY REDUCTION

There are only two legitimate ways to reduce inventory levels. The first is to sell the merchandise (or give it to charity to receive a tax deduction of the normal selling price, earnings permitting).

> **KEY POINT: Selling inventory at a discount is wise if the merchandise is subject to obsolescence of any type.**

Selling merchandise at a discount, however, can damage existing distribution relationships. If the sales cannot be made outside normal channels and without damage to them, it may be wisest to use the second way to reduce inventories.

You also must be sure the sale of the inventory will bring in as much as the lender has allowed the company to borrow against it. If the company has borrowed 50 percent against the inventory but can only realize 40 percent in a distressed sale, inventory reduction will create a cash drain. If sale of the inventory would actually reduce funds and increase external financing needs, the second way out is also indicated.

The second way is to cut production below the expected level of demand for the next season. The size of the cut depends on the reduction required in the finished-goods inventory. The size of the cut will also depend on the speed with which adjustments in the production process can be made.

> **KEY POINT: Cutting production may take longer than a fire sale to reduce inventories and free up funds, but it is less likely to damage a brand image and the distribution channels.**

Cutting production does have disadvantages, however. First, changes in production levels are expensive. Skilled employees may not return when the firm wants to ramp production back up. Second, the firm's capital will be tied up longer. If the company uses a seasonal bank loan to finance the working-capital cycle, the inventory buildup may prevent the company's paying down the loan completely at the end of the season.

This failure may alarm the bank, which could be experiencing loan-quality problems itself because of the same poor economic environment.

Smart Move

It is therefore wise to begin frank discussions with the relationship manager at the bank as soon as the problem is identified. These discussions should include review of the production revisions and forecasts of when the loan will return to a fully seasonal basis.

BUILDING TO ORDER OR FOR SPECULATION

It is the lucky company, such as one that builds ships, that can build only to order. By definition, a company that *builds to order* has firm orders in hand when production is started. The finished goods are typically shipped and invoiced when they are completed. A company that builds to order thus will have little finished-goods inventory. Its inventory will be primarily work-in-process. It can minimize its raw-material inventory because the certainty of the production process makes just-in-time delivery of raw materials and components possible.

> **IMPORTANT: Lenders distrust work-in-process as collateral. Its value is hard to assess and usually plummets if problems arise. For large projects, the customer may have to help finance the production by providing progress payments as the manufacturer attains prespecified targets.**

A company with sufficient financial resources may compete by offering its best customers a build-and-hold program. The manufacturer thus provides part of the finished-goods inventory function for its customer. This function may be more valuable to the customer than a lower price, a competitive method that ill-financed companies have no choice but to use.

Powerful retailers are now demanding that suppliers take over management and financing for the finished goods on the retailers' shelves. Computer scanning permits such accurate and fast bookkeeping that the supplier only gets paid when merchandise actually goes by the cash register. These practices blur the distinction between building to order and building for speculation. Although production may build to the retailer's order, the retailer may not take responsibility for paying the bill if the merchandise does not sell. The transaction is less than a sale and more of a provision of inventory on consignment.

Financial institutions prefer to lend against accounts receivable, provided the receivable is due from a customer whose credit is good. Indeed, a major problem the produce-to-order firm has is whether the orders can be canceled and, if so, with what compensation. A second major problem is the conditions under which the merchandise can be returned. Is the order really a sale? Or, is it more accurately considered a consignment?

The answer to these questions may depend in part on the relative bargaining position of the supplier and the customer.

If the supplier is weak, one of many supplying that merchandise, and with a narrow relationship to its customer, firm orders can be much less firm than they appear. A customer placing an order with a marginal supplier in a time of shortage expects to pay a premium. The customer might even be willing to accept product that does not quite meet typical standards. Should market conditions weaken, however, the customer will return merchandise to this supplier, alleging any number of real or imagined problems as an excuse not to pay for it.

A final concern for the produce-to-order firm is the quality of the receivable. This concern is shared by all companies that offer credit terms, so it is not unique. The first problem is assessing the ability of the customer to pay. The produce-to-order firm, however, has to make this assessment much earlier in the production process than the firm that can evaluate the credit as the product is shipped. It is another reason the customer may be asked for a deposit, periodic progress payments, or even a letter of credit.

Building for speculation, production in anticipation of orders, is common particularly in businesses with strong seasonal demand. It is also common where the product is in constant demand and the turnover is very fast. Grocery stores, for example, may order several times a week, but the producer of soft drinks knows the orders will be coming. Building finished-goods inventory ahead of orders, as discussed above, can be critical in keeping production costs low and competitive.

The resulting inventory profile is typically different from the profile of a company that produces to order. The finished-goods inventory is a much more significant asset for the firm producing inventory on speculation.

The level of finished goods may vary, of course, depending on the season. If the season is particularly pronounced, finished goods immediately before the season may be almost equal to the company's total cost of sales. This is likely to be the case for companies producing seasonal foods or goods such as Christmas fruit cakes or Fourth-of-July fireworks. In other food processing industries, such as fruit canning, the finished-goods build up occurs because the raw material is only available for a brief time but sales are made over an extended period.

> **KEY POINT: Although the company that must produce before orders are received is riskier than one that produces against firm orders, there are some compensating advantages. The main one is that lenders prefer to lend against the security of finished goods than work-in-process. It may be easier for a company with a short work-in-process cycle, producing ahead of orders, to gain external financing than for a firm that produces to order but has only in-process inventory.**

Managerial Decisions and Their Dangers

Throughout the preceding discussion, suggestions have been made about how inventory can be a competitive tool. This is an important managerial decision. Price cutting is a very blunt instrument, available to all but used often by companies in distress. It is an obvious technique, with little protection against retaliation.

SMART MOVE

If your company has funds, it is often effective to use them to compete in a subtle way that your customers may find more useful than price cuts.

One technique is to offer build-and-hold accommodations for good customers. This integrates the manufacturer's inventory with the customer's, which can be to the advantage of both.

Another technique, already mentioned, is providing incentives to customers to order early and accept early delivery by giving special payment terms. As discussed, this technique helps get customer commitment in uncertain markets and helps the supplier maintain a more level and lower-cost production schedule.

A second managerial decision is how far to produce in advance of expected orders—the speculative-inventory decision. At one extreme, absolutely level production will keep production costs low at the expense of potentially high costs for inventory loss. At the other extreme, production can be done at the last minute but at a high cost.

> **KEY POINT:** Where along the spectrum your firm should operate is your choice. Your decision must allow for the nature of the production process, the product, and the customers. The nature of the risks associated with the production decision, however, is different and must be considered. You should be cautious about indulging your natural entrepreneurial enthusiasms to build inventory.

A third management decision is whether to make shipments on pseudoconsignment. The shipments may technically be counted as sales, but, if return conditions are sufficiently generous, the transactions are more nearly consignments.

> **WATCH THIS:** Although shipping on pseudoconsignments can be a useful strategy for entering a new and untested market, it also can be dangerous precisely because the market is new and untested. It should be undertaken very cautiously and watched closely. It is particularly danger-

ous if accompanied with generous trade terms that give the customer little incentive to market the product aggressively, let alone to report to the supplier the actual sales to the ultimate consumer.

A final managerial decision that can bring grief, often unintended and unexpected, is the treatment of pipeline inventory. When a new product is introduced, a portion of initial sales usually will go to filling the inventories at the various levels of distribution. During this period, sales to the ultimate consumer may be hard to detect.

> **WATCH THIS: Unfortunately, customer purchases will determine production schedules once the pipeline inventories are at the desired levels. Thus, initial high demand may fall when shipments are made primarily to fill the consumer's ongoing demand.**

A similar problem can arise when a firm decides to introduce new channels of distribution for an existing product or line. Again, many initial shipments may merely be for pipeline inventory. The volume of actual retail sales may be much less than initial orders to the manufacturer.

Less sophisticated entrepreneurs may fail to appreciate these situations. Elated by the initial sales volume, they will set production levels to maintain that level of shipments. When demand falls to a sustainable level, finished goods build up rapidly.

> **WATCH THIS: A different type of problem is the failure to understand the asset turnover of your business. As orders arrive, you are tempted to buy raw material and boost the production volume. Unfortunately, if collections on accounts receivable are not fast enough to generate cash to pay the suppliers and the employees, your firm will run out of cash. It will grow to death.**

Compounding these decisions can lead to very serious problems. Adopting a high rate of level production, encouraging the distribution system to order early by giving attractive terms, providing incentives to sales representatives to put inventory into the distribution system, and giving the distributors and retailers little reason to manage their inventories and payables can over several years create an enormous problem of finished goods inventory at the factory and in the field. Instances have occurred where as much as three-year's inventory was in the distribution systems before the problem was discovered. Reducing this inventory without serious cash loss is a major managerial challenge.

Smart Inventory Management

Although the change to the service economy has reduced the importance of inventory management to the economy as a whole, inventory is a critical asset for those who have it. Inventory is one of the most difficult assets to manage because of the problems of controlling and valuing it. The natural tendency of a sales-oriented entrepreneur is to increase the level of inventory to avoid stockouts. On the other hand, return on investment can be increased by reducing funds tied up in inventories. Better data systems make inventory management easier, and more flexible production systems reduce the need to take chances with inventories.

Nevertheless, as a foundation for planning the proper financing, you must assess carefully the nature of inventory that your company requires. This chapter has reviewed the approaches to setting economic production quantities and inventory levels. These calculations must be related to the managerial decisions that underlie the business strategy and the resulting production and marketing dimensions. These must be related to the structure of the industry, the nature of the production processes that are economically sensible, and the ways that inventories are positioned in the distribution channels.

Important dimensions include the volatility and predictability of demand, the obsolescence characteristics of the product, whether the product is produced to order or on speculation, and what marketing decisions are made to help reduce the production costs. Because of the slippery nature of inventory management, ill-considered decisions can quickly produce inventory problems of dangerous dimensions. Thus, although the trend is away from manufacturing and toward service industries, companies that do have inventories will seldom find that ignoring them is bliss.

CHAPTER 7

CAPITAL BUDGETING AND CORPORATE VALUATION

Capital Budgeting

When your company invests in a new asset, the asset usually appears on the balance sheet rather than being immediately charged against income as an expense. The asset is then charged against income through depreciation expense over its estimated useful life. This expense is supposed to match the timing of the income generated by the asset. Because there are often differences between depreciation for tax and accounting purposes, it may be necessary to create a liability account for deferred taxes if the tax depreciation is greater than the financial-accounting depreciation.

Although the income statement provides some indication of the profitability of the business, it provides little indication of the true return on invested capital or whether a particular capital investment is worthwhile. A project may provide a positive return but the return may be too small to justify the investment. The return on capital invested must be measured on a cash-flow basis and take time into account. That is the purpose of capital investment analysis, also called capital budgeting.

> **KEY POINT: Capital budgeting involves the analysis of project proposals and the ranking and selection of those projects suitable for investment. It is an integral part of a company's strategic-planning process. Capital budgeting is a process of analyzing expected cash flows and expected risks in a disciplined, quantitative way against a backdrop of overall corporate strategy.**

For a company of any size, an overriding concern of management is to increase the owners' value. To do so requires investing in projects that return more than the cost of capital. That idea is the foundation for performance metrics such as *economic value added*, which was discussed in Chapter 1.

Capital budgeting deals with the asset side of the balance sheet. It is concerned with what investments should be made, not how the projects

Capital
Budgeting
and
Corporate
Valuation

143

are financed. Inevitably, those two decisions overlap in the minds of a company's CFO and treasurer. A simple comparison of the next project to the next financing can be misleading, however, particularly if that financing includes debt with tax-deductible interest payments. You and the CFO should take a broad look at all of the company's investment opportunities and all of its capital sources, including both debt and equity, when making capital-investment decisions.

In theory, the company should increase your (and any other owners') worth by investing in all projects earning more than the firm's cost of capital, adjusted for project risk. In reality, however, you will usually limit the number of projects you are willing to oversee at a given time because your company will be stretched thin with too many projects. As the owner of a privately held company, you may be reluctant to seek outside financing for additional projects if such financing would dilute your ownership or control.

> **SMART FINANCIAL MANAGEMENT: Capital budgeting involves quali-
> tative as well as quantitative analysis. You must consider how well
> each project fits into the company's business strategy, how much man-
> agement time it will absorb, whether forecasted returns justify assuming
> identified risks, and how that project might affect other projects under
> consideration.**

Capital budgeting requires assumptions about the future. To decide how a proposed project compares with other investment opportunities and to identify risks and pitfalls, you should ask for the insights of thoughtful individuals from different departments and different professional experience. In addition to sharing their views on whether a project should be a strategic priority, these individuals may review items in the project proposal, such as raw material costs, labor costs, the market for the product to be produced, when the product will become obsolete, price points, competition, and terminal value of the capital assets.

From a quantitative perspective, the key concepts are:

➤ The time value of money
➤ Discounted cash flow analysis
➤ Four methods for evaluating projects:
   o Net present value
   o Internal rate of return
   o Payback
   o Profitability index

TIME VALUE OF MONEY

The time value of money is based on a simple truism: a dollar received today is worth more than a dollar received a year from now because today's dollar can be invested and will be worth more a year later. A dollar deposited in a 5-percent savings account will have a *future value* of $1.05 a year from now and $1.1025 two years from now. Conversely, the *present value* of $1.05 a year from now or $1.1025 two years from now is $1.00. In this case, 5 percent is variously called the *reinvestment rate,* the *opportunity cost of funds,* or the *hurdle rate.* A dollar is worth 5 percent a year to an investor who can either invest at that rate or retire existing capital costing that rate. As will be discussed later, the hurdle rate a company uses for capital budgeting is approximately equal to its cost of capital.

> **IMPORTANT: A commonly used hurdle rate is 12 percent. This rate may be too low for smaller enterprises. It is certainly too low for startups, whose debt and equity are very expensive. It would be a rate appropriate for safe investments.**

Table 7-1 shows how present values and future values are related and calculated. On the first line, $1.00 is invested at Year 0, the beginning of Year 1, and reinvested each year at 12 percent. It compounds to $1.76 at the end of Year 5. On the second line, $1.00 is divided by the future value of $1.00 to calculate a *present-value factor.* The present value (today's value) of $1.00 received at the end of Year 5, using a 12 percent discount rate, is the $1.00 times the present-value factor for the end of Year 5, or $0.57. In a capital budgeting analysis, as illustrated below, the present-value factor for each year is multiplied by a project's net cash flows for that year.

TABLE 7-1
**Present and Future Value Calculation
at 12 Percent**

YEAR	0	1	2	3	4	5
Future value	$1.00	$1.12	$1.254	$1.405	$1.574	$1.762
Present value = 1 ÷ Future value	1.00	0.893	0.797	0.712	0.635	0.567

Discounted Cash Flow Analysis

Discounted cash flow analysis is the quantitative base used for capital budgeting. It is a method for identifying all of the cash outflows and inflows relevant to a project and adjusting them for both risk and the time value of money. *Cash outflows* include all of the cash necessary to fund the project, such as the cost of the property, plant, and equipment; legal fees; working capital needs; and taxes before the assets are put into use.

Capital
Budgeting
and
Corporate
Valuation

145

Cash inflows include net income from the project; tax benefits from depreciation of project assets; tax benefits from amortization of project assets such as patents; and the *terminal* or *residual value,* the estimate of the project's value at the end of the analysis period.

NET PRESENT VALUE

A project's *net present value* (NPV) is the sum of the present values of all its projected cash outflows and inflows, including all investments made and returns realized. A positive NPV suggests a financially attractive proposal.

To illustrate the technique, consider a manufacturing company with a 12-percent hurdle rate having an opportunity to invest $100,000. The machine being purchased is projected to produce estimated savings of $30,000 per year over the next four years. Management's "base case" estimates the machine's terminal value will be $20,000, its worth at the end of the five-year period. The $100,000 investment is shown as a negative number in the Exhibit 7-1 analysis because it is a cash outflow. The cash inflows and the residual value are positive figures. In Exhibit 7-1, first, the present values are calculated for each year's flows. These annual figures are then added to determine the NPV of $2,469.

EXHIBIT 7-1

Net Present Value Calculation for Cost-Saving Machinery Project at a 12 Percent Discount Rate

YEAR	0	1	2	3	4	5
Present-value factor @ 12%	1.0000	0.8929	0.7972	0.7118	0.6355	0.5674
BASE CASE						
Cash flows	($100,000)	$30,000	$30,000	$30,000	$30,000	$20,000
Present value	($100,000)	$26,786	$23,916	$21,353	$19,066	$11,349
Net present value $2,469						
SENSITIVITY ANALYSIS: LESS FAVORABLE ASSUMPTIONS						
Cash flows	($100,000)	$25,000	$25,000	$25,000	$25,000	$10,000
Present value	($100,000)	$22,321	$19,930	$17,795	$15,888	$ 5,674
Net present value ($18,392)						

The NPV of $2,469 for the base case is an estimate of how much the project will add to the net worth of the business in today's dollars. (The actual increase over time would be the sum of the undiscounted flows, but there would be no year-to-year correlation with the annual figures shown in Exhibit 7-1.) Because the NPV is positive, the project clears the 12-percent hurdle rate.

SENSITIVITY ANALYSIS

The base case, of course, is only a forecast. Actual results likely will be different. One way of testing the effects of alternate results is to vary assumptions within the likely ranges. For example, in a more difficult economic environment, the annual savings for Years 1 through 4 might be only $25,000 and the residual value only $10,000. Under these assumptions, the NPV at a 12 percent discount rate is a decidedly negative $18,392, as also shown in Exhibit 7-1.

> **SMART FINANCIAL MANAGEMENT: Having prepared two calculations of this type (or as many as necessary to provide a clear representation), you must then think about the probability of each alternative outcome. If you think the base case is highly likely, you may want to go on with the project. On the other hand, if you assign a 50 percent probability to each of the two alternatives, the resulting probability-adjusted NPV is negative, as shown below in Table 7-2. You should not go ahead unless there are compelling nonfinancial reasons for the investment. It is not unusual for a corporation to calculate half a dozen alternative situations In this way, assigning them probability factors that add up to 1.**

These NPV calculations are important but not the only part of the decision process. Equally important is your consideration of the relative probability of each alternative and all the strategic and other nonfinancial reasons for considering the investment.

TABLE 7-2

Adjusting Alternate Outcomes for Their Probability

NET PRESENT VALUE	PROBABILITY FACTOR	PROBABILITY-ADJUSTED NPV
$ 2,469	.50	$1,234.50
(18,392)	.50	(9,196.00)
		($7,961.50)

Capital
Budgeting
and
Corporate
Valuation

147

Comparing Different Investment Opportunities

NPV is a particularly useful calculation for comparing investment opportunities that have different schedules of investments (cash outflows) and returns (cash inflows). This type of analysis is useful in ranking investment opportunities.

> **KEY POINT: Of course, ranking capital investments is never done on purely quantitative grounds; there are always strategic, marketing, competitive, risk, legal, regulatory, human resources, environmental, and other qualitative factors to consider for each proposed investment.**

Exhibit 7-2 compares three different investment opportunities. The first alternative is the base-case cost-saving machinery project from Exhibit 7-1. Exhibit 7-2 includes an analysis of two other projects—an efficiency-improvement project and a plant-expansion project. The efficiency-improvement project is a two-stage investment, $50,000 now, in Year 0, and another $50,000 at the end of Year 1. The NPV of $274 just clears the 12-percent hurdle rate.

The plant-expansion project requires cash outflows of $150,000 in Years 0 and 1 and $50,000 in Year 2. The increased cash flow estimated to result from this project begins with $100,000 in Year 2, followed by $120,000, $140,000, and $170,000 in the three succeeding years. In Year 2, therefore, there is both a cash outflow of $50,000 and an estimated cash inflow of $100,000. In a spreadsheet format, it is convenient first to list estimated cash flows individually. Then, net out multiple cash flows in a single year when necessary. Finally, multiply the net cash flow for each year by the present-value factor. The plant-expansion project appears very attractive, with a positive NPV of $26,780. It may be significantly more risky than the other two projects, however, which must be considered in selecting the final portfolio of investments.

INTERNAL RATE OF RETURN

A calculation related to NPV is the *internal rate of return* (IRR). This is the reinvestment or hurdle rate at which the NPV is zero. You can calculate IRR on an iterative, trial-and-error basis, by testing the effect of different discount rates until the one is found that results in a zero NPV. One way to reduce the calculations needed is to compute the NPV at two rates, chart the results on a graph, and extend the line connecting the two points until it crosses the zero point on the vertical axis. Most spreadsheet programs, however, have functions that will calculate the NPV of a series of numbers and also calculate the IRR. (Internal rates of return for the effi-

EXHIBIT 7-2

Analysis of Alternative Investment Opportunities Discounted at a 12 Percent Rate

YEAR	0	1	2	3	4	5
Present-value factor @ 12%	1.0000	0.8929	0.7972	0.7118	0.6355	0.5674

COST-SAVING MACHINERY PROJECT

Cash flows	($100,000)	$30,000	$30,000	$30,000	$30,000	$20,000
Present value	($100,000)	$26,786	$23,916	$21,353	$19,066	$11,349
Net present value	$2,469					

EFFICIENCY-IMPROVEMENT PROJECT

Cash flows	($50,000)	($50,000)	$35,000	$35,000	$35,000	$35,000
Present value	($50,000)	($44,643)	$27,902	$24,912	$22,243	$19,860
Net present value	$274					

PLANT-EXPANSION PROJECT

Cash flows	($150,000)	($150,000)	($50,000)	—	—	—
Cash flows	—	—	100,000	$120,000	$140,000	$170,000
Net cash flows	($150,000)	($150,000)	$50,000	$120,000	$140,000	$170,000
Present value	($150,000)	($133,929)	$39,860	$85,414	$88,973	$96,463
Net present value	$26,780					

ciency and the expansion project are shown in Exhibit 7-3.) Several pocket calculators, such as the Hewlett-Packard HP-12C, also have programs that will calculate these measures.

> **KEY POINT: One important distinction between NPV and IRR is the different implicit reinvestment-rate assumption each has for the reinvestment rate applied to the cash flow generated each year by the project. The NPV calculation assumes that a dollar can be reinvested at the hurdle rate, the rate used for discounting the cash flows. The IRR, on the other hand, assumes that a dollar can be reinvested at the IRR. For a project**

Capital
Budgeting
and
Corporate
Valuation

EXHIBIT 7-3

Trial-and-Error Calculation of Internal Rate of Return

YEAR	0	1	2	3	4	5
EFFICIENCY-IMPROVEMENT PROJECT						
Cash flows	($50,000)	($50,000)	$35,000	$35,000	$35,000	$35,000
Present-value factor @ 12%	1.000	0.8929	0.7972	0.7118	0.6355	0.5674
Present value	($50,000)	($44,643)	$27,902	$24,912	$22,243	$19,860
Net present value $274						
Present value factor @ 13%	1.000	0.8850	0.7831	0.6931	0.6133	0.5428
Present value	($50,000)	($44,248)	$27,410	$24,257	$21,466	$18,997
Net present value ($2,118)						

Estimated by interpolation: 12.1% = (1% × 274/[274 + 2,118]) + 12%

YEAR	0	1	2	3	4	5
PLANT-EXPANSION PROJECT						
Cash flows	($150,000)	($150,000)	($50,000)	–	–	–
Cash flows	–	–	100,000	$120,000	140,000	$170,000
Net cash flows	($150,000)	($150,000)	$50,000	$120,000	140,000	$170,000
Present-value factor @ 15%	1.000	0.8696	0.7561	0.6575	0.5718	0.4972
Present value	($150,000)	($130,435)	$37,807	$78,902	$80,045	$84,520
Net present value $840						
Present-value factor @ 16%	1.000	0.8621	0.7432	0.6407	0.5523	0.4761
Present value	($150,000)	($129,310)	$37,158	$76,879	$77,321	$80,939
Net present value ($7,013)						

Estimated by interpolation: 15.1%

with an IRR significantly above the company's normal hurdle rate, that assumption might not be realistic.

PAYBACK

A simple capital budgeting measure, sometimes used alone but often used with NPV or IRR, is the *payback*. This measure is simply the number of years required for the project's cash inflows to repay the capital investment. If two projects have about equal NPVs and IRRs, the one with the shorter payback probably has lower risk.

To illustrate how payback is calculated, a project with an initial cash outlay of $300,000 and a positive cash inflow of $100,000 per year for five years will have a payback of three years. A similar project with a three-year life also has a three-year payback although it is clearly an unattractive investment.

> **SMART FINANCIAL MANAGEMENT: Payback is thus a useful comparison measure for longer-lived projects and for projects with lives of similar lives.**

PROFITABILITY INDEX

The *profitability index* is another measure used to compare projects. This measure is a ratio of the present value of cash inflows divided by the present value of cash outflows. A profitability index greater than 1.0 indicates the project's IRR is greater than the discount rate and it has a positive NPV. The profitability indexes for the cost-saving machinery project, the efficiency improvement project, and the plant-expansion project are illustrated in Exhibit 7-4. This analysis suggests that a present-value dollar invested in the expansion project is the most productive. For every present-value dollar invested, the project returns $1.08 present-value dollars.

Calculating a Hurdle Rate

The hurdle rate a company uses in its capital budgeting analysis is usually close to its *weighted average cost of capital* (WACC). Although there are other considerations, theoretically you should be receptive to projects that return more than the WACC and turn down those that return less.

A company's WACC is the weighted average of its long-term debt and its equity costs. An example of how a company's WACC is calculated is shown in Table 7-3.

The equity component is the most complicated part of this calculation. The cost of equity is often calculated using the *Capital Asset Pricing Model* (CAPM).

Capital
Budgeting
and
Corporate
Valuation

151

EXHIBIT 7-4

Profitability Index Calculation at a 12 Percent Discount Rate

YEAR	0	1	2	3	4	5
Present-value factor @ 12%	1.0000	0.8929	0.7972	0.7118	0.6355	0.5674

COST-SAVING MACHINERY PROJECT

	0	1	2	3	4	5
Cash outflows	($100,000)	—	—	—	—	—
Present value, cash outflows	($100,000)	—	—	—	—	—
Cash inflows	—	$30,000	$30,000	$30,000	$30,000	$20,000
Present value cash inflows	—	$26,786	$23,916	$21,353	$19,066	$11,349

Cash inflows $102,469

Cash outflows $100,000

Profitability index   1.02

EFFICIENCY-IMPROVEMENT PROJECT

	0	1	2	3	4	5
Cash outflows	($50,000)	($50,000)	—	—	—	—
Present value, cash outflows	($50,000)	($44,643)	—	—	—	—

Total present value, cash outflows   ($94,643)

	0	1	2	3	4	5
Cash inflows	—	—	$35,000	$35,000	$35,000	$35,000
Present value, cash inflows	—	—	$27,902	$24,912	$22,243	$19,860

Total present value, cash inflows $94,917

Cash inflows $94,917

Cash outflows $94,643

Profitability index   1.0029

YEAR	0	1	2	3	4	5
PLANT-EXPANSION PROJECT						
Cash outflows	($150,000)	($150,000)	($50,000)	—	—	—
Present value, cash outflows	($150,000)	($133,929)	($39,860)	—	—	—
Total present value, cash outflows	($323,788)					
Cash inflows	—	—	$100,000	$120,000	$140,000	$170,000
Present value, cash inflows	—	—	$79,719	$85,414	$88,973	$96,463
Total present value, cash inflows	$350,568					
Cash inflows	$350,568					
Cash outflows	$323,788					
Profitability Index	1.08					

TABLE 7-3

Weighted Average Cost of Capital (WACC) Calculation

COMPONENT	MARKET VALUE	WEIGHT	PRE-TAX COST	AFTER-TAX COST	WEIGHTED COST
Debt	$3,000,000	37.5%	8%	5.6%	2.10%
Equity	5,000,000	62.5	15	15.0	9.38
Total	$8,000,000				11.48%

CAPITAL ASSET PRICING MODEL

The Capital Asset Pricing Model is a technique for calculating the cost of equity capital. The formula is:

Cost of equity = Current risk-free rate + (*beta* × market risk premium for common stocks)

The risk-free rate, as its name implies, is the return available from an investment that carries no risk. In practice, U.S. Treasury bill rates often are

Capital
Budgeting
and
Corporate
Valuation

153

used as a proxy for the risk-free rate. Some companies, however, consider a longer-term Treasury bond rate to be a more appropriate risk-free rate to use in developing the cost of equity.

Beta is a measure of the risk of a particular stock compared to the entire stock market. It is the covariance of the stock with the market. It is derived by running a regression analysis between the returns on a specific stock and those of a broad index of stocks such as the S&P 500. A stock with a beta of more than one has greater volatility than the underlying market, and vice versa. The CAPM states the expected risk premium for a given stock is proportional to its beta. Although CAPM is widely used, the accuracy of betas for particular company stocks has been questioned in recent years.

> **WATCH THIS: A more difficult problem for you and other owners of private companies is that a beta for such companies cannot be calculated. There is no way to compare the performance of your company's value to the stock market as a whole. One approach to estimating a beta in this situation is simply to make a managerial judgment about how well the company's performance tracks the overall market. Another way to estimate a beta is to look for the betas of comparable companies that are traded. Calculations of betas are available from several sources, such as *Value Line.***

The *market-risk premium* is the incremental rate of return required by investors to hold a well-diversified portfolio of stocks rather than risk-free securities. The historical difference between the stock-market return and the risk-free rate, used in the formula above, is available in the frequently used yearbook, *Stocks, Bonds, Bills and Inflation,* published by Ibbotson Associates of Chicago. According to the 2002 Yearbook, the compound annual return for United States Treasury Bills between the end of 1925 and the end of 1998 was 3.8 percent. Over the same period, the compound annual return for large company stocks was 10.2 percent and for small company stocks 12.1 percent. Therefore, the market risk premium for large company stocks was 6.4 percent (10.2 minus 3.8 percent) and for small companies 8.3 percent (12.1 minus 3.8 percent).

The CAPM cost-of-equity calculation for a small company with a *beta* of 1.2 is calculated as: $3.8\% + (1.2 \times 8.3\%) = 13.96\%$.

ADJUSTMENT FOR HIGHER RISK OR UNCERTAINTY

For projects with higher than normal business risk, some adjustment to the hurdle rate is advisable. Some companies raise the discount rate by one or two percentage points for riskier projects. Others apply a probability adjustment, cutting projected future cash inflows by 5 or 10 percent. Based on a 1996 survey,[1] practice is evenly divided.

Corporate Valuation

Corporate valuation is central to all corporate financial activities. Management's most important objective is to create value for the owners by increasing the value of the firm. Nearly all business decisions are made with this duty in mind.

There is no single, correct method to value a company. Various parties, such as potential or actual investors, potential acquirers of controlling interests, CFOs and other managers, lenders, and vendors, use different methods depending on their reasons for valuing the company. Most will use several methods to validate assumptions and judgments. Some techniques base valuation on past performance, others on expected performance. Value may be based on assets, profits, or expected cash flow.

There are at least five commonly used methods to value a company:

1. Book value
2. Market value
3. Liquidation value
4. Replacement value
5. Discounted cash flow

BOOK VALUE

Book value is simply the value of total equity on the balance sheet, total assets minus total liabilities. Equity is created and increased by the sale of stock, and it is increased or decreased by additions or subtractions to retained earnings. Book value is backward looking. It is based on a company's historical performance, governed by the conventions of double-entry bookkeeping and generally accepted accounting principles (GAAP). Therefore, it does not reflect the changing worth of balance-sheet assets and liabilities or the company's future earnings potential as a going concern.

Book value is most used in regulated industries. For example, a bank's required ratio of capital to total assets is based on book value. The rates a public utility is permitted to charge are based on the book value of its assets and an allowable rate of return. Book value has greater importance for financial institutions than many other industries because of the predominance of financial assets on the balance sheet. The presumption is that financial assets are more likely worth their book value than machinery and intangibles.

> **SMART FINANCIAL MANAGEMENT: Book value is used also, however, for bank-loan covenants such as debt-equity ratios because lenders**

1. Henry A. Davis, *Cash Flow and Performance Measurement: Managing for Value* (Morristown, NJ: Financial Executives Research Foundation, 1996).

are concerned about worst-case problems requiring liquidation. Basing a loan on a percentage of book value typically results in a lower figure than the same percentage of current market value.

MARKET VALUE

Market value is the price of a company's stock multiplied by the number of outstanding shares. The market values of different companies may be compared with two ratios: market to book value and price-earnings ratio.

Market to book value is often used to compare the values of banks and other financial institutions. The stock of a bank with flat earnings growth and a high percentage of nonperforming loans might sell for only two-thirds of book value. The stock of a bank with good earnings growth, a high-quality loan portfolio, and significant non-credit service income might sell for two or even three times book value.

The *price-earnings ratio* (P-E ratio) is the ratio of a company's total value to its annual net income. This is often calculated as the ratio of its stock price to annual earnings per share. P-E ratios are easy to understand, easy to calculate, and widely used. Even for experienced securities analysts, they can be a convenient shorthand for more complicated valuation methods. A P-E ratio, however, is based on just one period's earnings, either recent past or forecasted.

❯ WATCH THIS: The use of an average or representative industry's P-E ratio to value a particular company, say at 15 times earnings, is judgmental at best. Despite these limitations, industry P-E ratios are often used in valuing private companies in the absence of a comparable transaction. Business brokers will usually know the P-E ratios at which local transactions are taking place.

LIQUIDATION VALUE

Liquidation value is the expected net proceeds, after all expenses and taxes, of selling the company's assets in an orderly liquidation. The more rapidly the liquidation must be accomplished, the smaller the proceeds are likely to be.

❯ KEY POINT: Liquidation value is often the absolute minimum value for a business. It is relevant for poorly performing companies; for lenders who are concerned with the liquidity of inventory, receivables, and other assets pledged to them as collateral; and for creditors when bankruptcy becomes a possibility.

REPLACEMENT VALUE

Replacement value is the amount a potential purchaser would have to pay to duplicate the company's assets at current market prices. As with liquidation value, replacement value is based strictly on a company's assets and does not consider its earnings or its potential as an operating business. In some circumstances, this value will set a maximum on a company's worth. A prospective buyer will start a new business if the price of an existing one is much more than its replacement value.

DISCOUNTED CASH FLOW

> **SMART FINANCIAL MANAGEMENT: A discounted cash flow (DCF) valuation is based on a company's forecasted future free cash flow discounted at a realistic reinvestment rate, such as its WACC. It is the most rigorous and conceptually sound method to value a company.**

DCF valuation is not as widely understood as are P-E ratios, however. It requires many assumptions and judgments about a company's future performance, assumptions whose validity may be difficult to assess with agreement by all parties.

The methodology for a DCF valuation of a company is similar to the present-value methodology described above for capital projects but is applied to the whole company rather than to an individual project. As with capital investment projects, a corporate valuation often recognizes the inherent difficulty in forecasting. It therefore considers several different alternative situations based on more and less favorable assumptions. Those alternatives can be probability weighted to create a risk-adjusted value.

The following basic financial relationships are central to applying the DCF methodology to valuing a company:

- ➤ Corporate value = market value of debt plus market value of shareholders' equity.
- ➤ Corporate value = net present value of future free cash flow.
- ➤ Shareholders' equity = corporate value minus market value of debt.
- ➤ Shareholders' equity = present value of future free cash flow minus market value of debt.

Free Cash Flow

Free cash flow represents all cash left from operating income after taxes and reinvestments necessary to continue growing the business—capital expenditures and additions to working capital—but before the payment of interest and dividends.

Capital
Budgeting
and
Corporate
Valuation

157

Free cash flow   =   Net income

+ depreciation and other non-cash deductions

+ after-tax interest

− increase in working capital

− capital expenditures

Alternatively:

Free cash flow   =   Earnings before interest and taxes (EBIT)

− taxes (on EBIT)

+ depreciation and other noncash deductions

− increase in working capital

− capital expenditures

Example of Discounted Cash Flow Valuation

The DCF method of valuation is best explained through an example. The most recent annual income statement of the Stalwart Manufacturing Company is shown in Exhibit 7-5. The company has long-term debt of $2 million, and its WACC is 12 percent. For the purpose of preparing a discounted cash flow valuation, Stalwart's CFO makes the following forecast:

> ➤ Sales will increase by 15 percent per year.
> ➤ The gross profit margin will remain at 40 percent.
> ➤ SG&A will increase at 12 percent per year.
> ➤ Depreciation will increase at 10 percent per year.
> ➤ Interest expense will increase at 15 percent per year.
> ➤ Taxes will remain at 30 percent.
> ➤ Incremental working capital will be 10 percent of incremental sales.
> ➤ Capital expenditures will be 12 percent of incremental sales.

Cash flow projections incorporating the CFO's forecast are shown in Exhibit 7-6. What happens after the end of the five-year forecast period? Rather than extending the cash flow forecast beyond the number of years for which reasonable forecasts may be made, most analysts use either a *perpetuity* or a *growing perpetuity* to reflect the *residual value,* the value of cash flows beyond the forecast period. An alternative is to estimate what the company might be sold for at the end of the period using a P-E ratio.

PERPETUITY METHOD The perpetuity method is based on the assumption that, after some point, the business no longer will generate investment opportunities that return more than its cost of capital. Therefore, it no longer will produce real growth in value. Further investment still will create income, but the present value of that income will be equal to the pres-

EXHIBIT 7-5

Income Statement,
Stalwart Manufacturing Company
(thousands of dollars)

YEAR	0	1	2	3	4	5
Net sales	$10,000	$11,500	$13,225	$15,209	$17,490	$20,114
Cost of goods sold	6,000	6,900	7,935	9,125	10,494	12,069
Gross profit	$ 4,000	$ 4,600	$ 5,290	$ 6,084	$ 6,996	$ 8,045
Selling, general, & Admin. exp.	2,000	2,240	2,509	2,810	3,147	3,525
Depreciation	500	550	605	666	732	805
Operating profit	$ 1,500	$ 1,810	$ 2,176	$ 2,608	$ 3,117	$ 3,715
Interest	200	230	264	304	350	402
Pre-tax income	$ 1,300	$ 1,580	$ 1,912	$ 2,304	$ 2,767	$ 3,313
Income taxes (30%)	390	474	574	691	830	994
Net income	$ 910	$ 1,106	$ 1,338	$ 1,613	$ 1,937	$ 2,319

ent value of the investment. Because further investment is unwarranted, all the cash flow generated can be capitalized at the appropriate discount rate. For example, an investor who requires a rate of return of 10 percent should be willing to pay $1,000 for an annuity of $100 per year. The present value of the residual can be calculated with the following formula:

$$\text{Present value of residual} = \frac{\text{Yearly free cash flow}}{\text{Discount rate}} \times \text{Present-value factor}$$

GROWING PERPETUITY METHOD The growing perpetuity is another frequently used method for calculating residual value. It assumes that free cash flow will grow at a given rate in perpetuity. The present value of the residual can be calculated with the following formula:

Present value of residual =

$$\frac{\text{Final year's free cash flow} \times (1 + \text{growth rate})}{\text{Discount rate} - \text{growth rate}} \times \text{Present-value factor}$$

Capital
Budgeting
and
Corporate
Valuation

159

EXHIBIT 7-6

Free Cash Flow, Stalwart Manufacturing Company (thousands of dollars)

YEAR	1	2	3	4	5
Sales	$11,500	$13,225	$15,209	$17,490	$20,114
Operating profit	1,810	2,176	2,608	3,117	3,715
Less:					
Taxes	543	653	782	935	1,115
Working capital increases	150	173	198	228	262
Capital expenditures	180	207	238	274	315
Plus:					
Depreciation	550	605	666	732	805
Free cash flow	$ 1,487	$ 1,749	$ 2,055	$ 2,412	$ 2,829

EXHIBIT 7-7

Discounted Cash Flow Valuation of Stalwart Manufacturing Company (thousands of dollars)

YEAR	1	2	3	4	5
Free cash flow	$1,487	$1,749	$2,055	$2,412	$2,829
Present-value factor @ 12%	0.893	0.797	0.712	0.636	0.567
Present value of free cash flow	$1,328	$1,394	$1,463	$1,533	$1,605
Total discounted five-year cash flow	$7,322				

Growing perpetuity, end of fifth year: ($2,829 × 1.04) ÷ (12% − 4%) = $36,776
Discounted to year zero: $36,776 × 0.567 = $20,868

Summary
Five-year discounted cash flow	$ 7,322
Plus Growing perpetuity	20,868
Equals Enterprise value	$28,190
Less Outstanding long-term debt	2,000
Equals Shareholder's equity	$26,190

This formula will not work if the growth rate is greater than the discount rate used to value the cash flows.

Exhibit 7-7 illustrates the calculation of discounted free cash flow from Stalwart's five-year forecast. It uses a growing-perpetuity analysis, assuming a 4 percent growth rate. The illustration also shows how the shareholders' equity is calculated by subtracting existing debt from corporate value.

Numerical Analysis

Capital investments are seldom wisely made solely because of the numerical analysis. You must consider how the capital investment fits with the corporate strategy, the company's financial planning, the risks associated with the investment, and your own (and the other owners') wishes and objectives.

> **SMART FINANCIAL MANAGEMENT: Careful numerical analysis, however, can help prevent unwise investment whose superficial appeal can result in excessive enthusiasm. It also can help you put the opportunities in perspective so you can rank them effectively when available funds are insufficient to finance them all. The same techniques are useful when you must value an entire business either to buy or to sell it.**

Finally, intangible assets and intellectual property create significant value for many companies. Although the cash expenditures to develop these assets are written off as current-period expenses rather than capitalized, the same analytic procedures apply to the analysis of these investments that apply to traditional investments in plant and equipment.

Capital
Budgeting
and
Corporate
Valuation

161

CHAPTER 8

BASIC CAPITAL-STRUCTURE DECISIONS

The capital-structure decision for the smaller company is both less complex and more critical than for the large corporation. It is simpler because there are fewer alternatives for nonequity financing. It is more critical because if there are financial-structure problems, the smaller company has much less room to maneuver. Its lenders, having little at stake, are less inclined to spend time working out the problem. Although the analytic approach to capital-structure decisions does not depend on the company's size, the relative weight placed on the decision's components may vary.

Before detailing how the capital-structure decision can be analyzed, it is useful to outline briefly the way that decision relates to the three other major decisions of corporate finance: the investment-in-assets, the dividend-payout, and the new-equity decisions. The basic financial and accounting identities will illustrate interrelationships.

The Relationship Among Assets, Capital Structure, and Dividends

A net increase in working capital and long-term assets (use of funds) can come from only two sources: an increase in long-term debt or an increase in equity (or a combination of the two). The increase in equity can be the result of an increase in preferred stock (not usually an alternative available to a smaller company except to high-growth ventures) or an increase in the common shareholders' equity (or both). Common equity, ignoring preferred stock as a specialized financial instrument, can come only from two sources: retained earnings or the issue of new common stock (or both). Retained earnings are the result of profits earned on the assets after distributions to the government for income taxes, to senior-security holders for interest and preferred dividends, and to the common stockholders as dividends. These relationships are diagramed in Exhibit 8-1.

The capital structure establishes the cost of capital, which should determine the investments that can profitably be made. On the other hand, there is evidence that the nature of the investments determines the

EXHIBIT 8-1
Basic Capital Structure Decisions

INTERRELATIONSHIP OF CAPITAL STRUCTURE DECISIONS

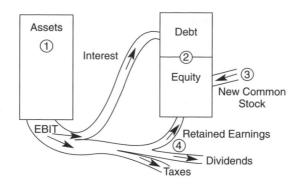

efficient capital structure. Given this circularity, the decision maker could start with either decision and work interactively with both to create the maximum value.

> **SMART FINANCIAL MANAGEMENT: Generally, and particularly with the smaller company, you make the asset decisions first. The opportunity to invest often creates the need for capital. In addition, investment decisions are typically easier to make, given a rough estimate of the entrepreneur's capital costs. Unlike the managers of a large corporation, you can directly assess the return you demand for an investment. You can balance the return against the risks you identify as associated with the project.**

Once the asset decisions are made, *Decision 1* on the diagram in Exhibit 8-1, the operating earnings are determined. The capital structure question, *Decision 2,* is how to divide the operating flows, the earnings before interest and taxes (EBIT), between senior and junior sources of capital and the government. How much the government takes in income taxes depends on the proportion of the stream paid out in a form that is deductible from the EBIT before the tax calculation is made.

Decision 3 is the decision about whether to issue new equity. As discussed later in this chapter, for privately held companies, the answer to this question is typically "No." That is the answer for many public companies as well unless the investments are extraordinarily profitable or the company is in deepest distress.

With three out of four decisions already made, *Decision 4,* the dividend-payout percentage, is set by default. For that reason, the dividend policy is often considered a residual decision. It distributes to the shareholders what is left after the other decisions have been made.

> **IMPORTANT: If the dividend decision is not the default decision, then another decision must be left as the residual. For example, if the asset decision and the capital-structure decisions are considered inviolable, then any equity shortfall must be made up by issuing new equity rather than by cutting the dividends.**

This action will dilute the ownership of the existing shareholders and dampen their per-share growth in value. If you believe the asset decision is essential but are unwilling to raise new equity to replace the dividends that exceed the maximum residual flows, debt must be raised to provide the missing capital. This action will increase the debt-equity ratio, a change not sustainable in the long run. Finally, if you believe that the debt-equity proportions should be maintained and no new equity raised, then the asset-investment program must be curtailed. This action creates the risk that the company will lose market position because it is underinvesting.

Example: Consider a company that requires $100,000 net additions to its assets. The firm's debt-to-capital policy is 40 percent, and debt is now at that proportion of the capital structure. The company can therefore raise only $40,000 from additional debt to finance the $100,000 addition to assets. The other $60,000 must come from equity.

If the firm's profits after taxes are $120,000, it can pay only $60,000 in dividends, a payout ratio of 50 percent. If management wishes (or has had the policy) to payout 60 percent of profits, the company will be $12,000 short of the equity it needs to fund the increase in assets. If this cannot be raised from new equity, a change must be made in either the asset-investment or the capital-structure policies.

Some companies have the luxury of slack financial resources: spare cash or debt capacity. This resource is only available once, however, and regenerating the spare resources takes a long time once it is used. Unwise expansions can prove major disasters when entrepreneurs extend their businesses into new locations not easy to control or get over their heads in new businesses they do not understand.

Therefore, you need to understand the considerations useful in setting up a proper capital structure. Part of the analysis will be static, assuming the asset side of the balance sheet is fixed and illustrating how to analyze the effects of different capital structures. Part of the analysis will be dynamic, showing how financing asset growth results in changes in future years as the effect of the investments appears in the income statement.

> **SMART FINANCIAL MANAGEMENT: The purpose of dividing a company's earnings flows to support various categories of securities, basically**

debt and equity, is to increase the total value of the company compared to the company's value in a plain, unadorned, total-equity version.

The chief financial officer's task thus contains a marketing component. The CFO is responsible for creating as much present value as possible by packaging and selling the company's prospective earnings in the most appropriate and valuable manner.

A Point of View

Where different consumers are concerned, different interests are involved. Where these interests are contrary to one another, as they often are when a limited resource is being parceled out, it is important to set up a point of view for the analyst. For whose interest is the CFO responsible? In this book, decisions are generally analyzed from the existing equity owner's position.[1] This perspective seldom presents a problem for the smaller company. Even if the managers are not the owners, the managers and the owners should be in close enough touch that the manager is working toward the owners' goals. If this is not so, then the responsibility for the problem has to be assigned to owners, who are not exercising proper oversight.

Finally, management should be concerned with *existing* shareholders. It is to those who already hold the stock that the manager owes first allegiance. The professional manager is naturally concerned to create a financial deal that will be fair to any new common stockholders, for the manager has to live with them, too. But, when a choice must be made, the manager should act for the existing shareholders. The prospective shareholders decide, given appropriate disclosure of financial information, whether they are willing to take a proposition. The existing shareholders have no such option; management must act for them.

The "FRICTO" Framework

The packaging devices management uses to increase its company's value involve changing the prospective gains and risks associated with financing alternatives. Funds are then raised in the proportions that promise the biggest total value.

---

1. There are pressures from other stakeholders, such as suppliers, customers, employees, and management that must also be balanced. This analysis assumes that these requirements have been satisfied to at least a minimal degree by the cost of sales, the general costs, and appropriate management of current assets and liabilities. Although the law traditionally made the directors responsible only to the *stockholders,* some states have altered their statutes to make the directors responsible for the health of the *company.* The implication is that an action that is for the good of the company is required even if it is harmful to the stockholders.

At one extreme, the common shareholder has the least security, the least protection from unfavorable events, but the most to gain if all goes well. Whatever is left after prior commitments are satisfied is available for the common shareholder. As the total earnings and value expand, the common shareholders get the entire increase once all other claims have been met.

> **KEY POINT: The least risky capital structure is one with all equity. The disadvantage of this choice is you and the other owners earn a lower return on your investment. You earn only the increase on your own funds rather than enjoying the extra earnings from the investments financed with fixed-rate debt. (Although the interest rate on most debt floats with changes in market rates, the rate is fixed in the sense that it does not change depending on the prosperity of the business itself.)**

The debt holder is at the other extreme, although debt comes in many flavors of seniority. The lender's contract with the company contains a variety of protective devices that restrict the ability of the borrower to commit its resources contrary to the lender's interest. The lender can go after the payments due, seizing (after the appropriate legal skirmishes) the company's property if necessary to get repaid.

In exchange for this protection and security, the lender must normally give up the chance to share in the company's earnings over a certain specified amount: the interest payment and repayment of debt. No matter how big the company "pie" gets, the size of the lender's piece is fixed in absolute terms, but it is well protected because the lender gets the first slice. The increase (and decrease) in the size of the pie goes to the account of less well-protected security owners, who must wait for their share until the senior securities have been served. A capital structure containing debt is thus more risky for the equity holder, but the benefits do not need to be as widely shared as if more equity had been sold.

The analysis of the position of the various parties is thus yet another variation on the risk-versus-return question. As a Rothschild is alleged to have asked when he was approached for investment advice, "Young man, do you want to eat well or sleep well?" The more senior a security, the more it is a sleep-well investment. The more junior the security, the more it appeals to an eat-well investor.

As outlined in Chapter 1, the factors that must be considered in appraising the risk and the return involved in the capital-structure decision can be grouped into six headings: five major ones and a sixth, all-inclusive category, which allows for the special aspects of situations. The factors, whose initials produce the FRICTO acronym, are **F**lexibility, **R**isk, **I**ncome, **C**ontrol, **T**iming, and **O**ther. The listing is strictly mnemonic, not in order of importance.

AN ILLUSTRATION: LITTLE GEM COMPANY

As an example for discussing the analytical tools in specific terms, consider the entrepreneur who is offered the opportunity to buy the Little Gem Company. Little Gem assembles and installs car-washing equipment, repairs the equipment, and supplies nonperishable items to the vending machines at the car washes. The business has annual sales of $2 million, generating an EBIT of $120,000. The owner will sell the business for $600,000 cash and will pay off all interest-bearing debt. Little Gem will thus be left with a small amount of accounts payable that provides permanent working capital if the volume of business does not decline.

The entrepreneur believes the existing owner, who wants to retire, has not been very aggressive in marketing the company's products and services. There is potential for increasing sales and earnings without additional investment, but there is also potential for the EBIT to decline. If the weather is either too dry or too wet, the demand for car-washing services declines. With less use, the equipment does not need repair as frequently. With less demand, new car-washing stations are not opened.

The entrepreneur must decide how best to raise the $600,000 to make the investment. At one extreme, the entrepreneur could provide the entire $600,000 from existing resources. By checking with local banks, the entrepreneur learned that some of the purchase price can be borrowed. The banks were willing to loan between $100,000 and $200,000 at 6 percent interest. This rate would float to the bank's funding index after three years. Repayment of the loan would not have to begin until three years had passed. The entrepreneur would have to provide a personal guarantee and a security interest in all assets of the company.

INCOME

This following analysis is couched in terms relevant to a privately held company and is, therefore, less complex than it would be for a company with public equity. The presentation thus emphasizes the effects of financing on the return on equity (ROE) rather than on earnings per share.

Exhibit 8-2 illustrates the effect of the different amounts of debt on the owner's ROE. Exhibit 8-3 is a chart of the relationship. With 100 percent

EXHIBIT 8-2
Little Gem Company Effect of Leverage on Return on Equity

Interest	6%
Tax rate	40%
Base Capital	$600,000

EBIT	$ 0	$36,000	$60,000	$120,000	$180,000	$240,000
LTD/Capital 0%						
Long-term debt $ 0						
Equity $600,000						
Interest	$ 0	$ 0	$ 0	$ 0	$ 0	$ 0
Taxes	0	14,400	24,000	48,000	72,000	96,000
Profit after tax	0	21,600	36,000	72,000	108,000	144,000
Return on equity	0.0%	3.6%	6.0%	12.0%	18.0%	24.0%
LTD/Capital 16.67%						
Long-term debt $100,000						
Equity $500,000						
Interest	$ 6,000	$ 6,000	$ 6,000	$ 6,000	$ 6,000	$ 6,000
Taxes	(2,400)	12,000	21,600	45,600	69,600	93,600
Profit after tax	(3,600)	18,000	32,400	68,400	104,400	140,400
Return on equity	−0.7%	3.6%	6.5%	13.7%	20.9%	28.1%
LTD/Capital 33.33%						
Long-term debt $200,000						
Equity $400,000						
Interest	$12,000	12,000	12,000	12,000	12,000	12,000
Taxes	(4,800)	9,600	19,200	43,200	67,200	91,200
Profit after tax	(7,200)	14,400	28,800	64,800	100,800	136,800
Return on equity	−1.8%	3.6%	7.2%	16.2%	25.2%	34.2%

EXHIBIT 8-3

Little Gem Company Effect of Leverage on Return on Equity

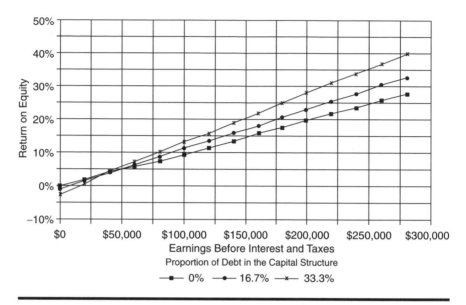

equity financing, the ROE at the current $120,000 EBIT level is 12 percent. If the business flourishes without requiring additional assets and investment, the ROE rises. At an EBIT of $180,000, the ROE is 18 percent. If the business encounters problems, however, and EBIT falls by one-half to $60,000, the ROE drops to 6 percent. The change in the ROE reflects perfectly the proportionate change in EBIT.

If the entrepreneur elected more aggressive financing, borrowing a third of the needed capital, net profits drop because of the greater interest charges. If the EBIT is $120,000, the ROE will be 16.2 percent. The decrease in the equity the entrepreneur must provide more than offsets the additional interest. If the business thrives with EBIT rising to $180,000, the ROE goes to 25.2 percent, 7 percentage points higher than with all-equity financing.

If EBIT drops, however, the ROE drops much faster under the debt-financed purchase than with the all-equity proposition. With an EBIT of only $60,000, the ROE drops to 7 percent. To break even, EBIT must be at least the cost of interest, $6,000, with the debt financing. With the equity financing, Little Gem would still be showing a profit, but a small one, at an EBIT of $6,000.

The relationship between EBIT and ROE is linear, as shown in Exhibit 8-3. A given change in EBIT produces a constant change in ROE. This can be easily seen in the all-equity case. An increase of $20,000 Little Gem's EBIT at any EBIT level creates an increase of 2 percent (*not* 2 percentage points) in ROE. The calculation is based on the income statement. ROE equals:

$$\frac{(EBIT - (\text{interest rate} \times \text{debt})) \times (1 - \text{tax rate})}{\text{Equity}}$$

In the all-equity case, the debt in the numerator would be zero and the equity in the denominator would be equal to the enterprise's capital. For a *given* financing alternative, the only change is in the EBIT. Thus, ($20,000 \times [1 - .4] \times $600,000) = 2$ percent.

The same formula is used to calculate the linear relationships for the other two alternatives as well. For example, if Little Gem is financed with 16.7 percent debt in its capital structure, the ROE will change 2.4 percent for each $20,000 change in EBIT. At a 33 percent debt structure, the change is 3 percent for each $20,000 EBIT change.

What is an advantage when EBIT rises is a disadvantage when it falls. ROE declines much more quickly when a capital structure is levered with debt. If EBIT falls low enough, the ROE is better with the all-equity financing. The cross-over EBIT is the point at which the before-tax return on capital (EBIT/(debt + equity) equals the interest rate on the debt. Above that point, the borrowed funds are earning more than their cost. The difference in earnings enhances the ROE. Below that EBIT, earnings on the equity base are helping pay interest on the borrowed funds: the ROE is being eroded to pay the interest. The crossover between the ROEs of the three alternatives for Little Gem occurs at an EBIT of $36,000 ($36,000 ÷ $600,000 = 6 percent).

> **IMPORTANT: A chart such as Exhibit 8-3, by itself, is not a magic device that tells the entrepreneur what capital decision to make. It does help the analysis by showing relative rates of change, positions, and points of relative attractiveness.**

This analytical approach is also valid once the entrepreneur has purchased the business and is considering an investment to expand it. The entrepreneur can invest enough additional equity to pay for the entire cost of the investment. Or, the entrepreneur can finance some or all of the investment with borrowed funds. The use of borrowed funds will have the effect of increasing the ROE if all goes well.

> **SMART FINANCIAL MANAGEMENT: To maintain the beneficial effects of leverage on the ROE, the debt proportion must be maintained.**

If funds are used to reduce the debt level over time, the ROE will gradually drop back to what it would have been if equity had been used in the first place—in effect, dropping from a higher line in Exhibit 8-3 to a lower one. Because remortgaging can be expensive, for example, the debt level is often adjusted when new assets are acquired. If the proportion of equity has built up, the new asset can often be financed with a higher percentage of debt (perhaps even purchased entirely with debt) than the company's average. This action will raise the company's leverage toward or even past the target level.

Because of this financing practice, many companies show a saw-tooth pattern in their capital structure. Debt is taken on temporarily in a proportion above the level the entrepreneur considers acceptable. It is then gradually reduced, often falling below the target capital structure before an opportunity occurs to releverage.

> **KEY POINT: Given this pattern, the initial boost in the ROE provided by a high proportion of debt financing will gradually decline as the capital structure reverts to the target levels. The entrepreneur should thus always ask whether the higher leverage will produce enough gain in the short run to justify the risks associated with it. If it does not, then a less aggressive financing mix will produce almost the same results in the end with less risk in the interim.**

Hidden Cost

Using only interest costs as a guide to the cost of financing ignores costs you may experience that do not appear on the company's income statement. These costs, sometimes called *hidden costs* or *joint costs,* are those adverse changes of value in the entrepreneur's assets that are the result of the financing decision. Hidden costs are therefore important to consider but difficult to identify.

The most obvious hidden costs are created by personal guarantees the owners must often provide when a closely held company takes on debt. These guarantees reduce the value of the entrepreneur's other assets because of the potential claim on them held by the lender to the company. This reduction in asset value is a hidden cost of the borrowing.

Another hidden cost can be in a reduction of the multiple at which the company's equity is valued. Even though the ROE is higher with greater leverage, a prospective purchaser may not have as much appetite for debt as the seller had when building the company. The purchaser may want an even higher ROE for taking on the risk of the debt. The purchaser can get that requirement only by lowering the price offered for the company.

Excess debt is also a potential problem for an entrepreneur who wants to take the company public. Prospective investors, who have no ability to reduce the level of debt to their liking, will reduce the multiple they will pay for the company's earnings. Other investors do not invest in companies that plan to use the funds to retire excessive debt.

The existence of hidden costs complicates the interpretation of the information in Exhibit 8-3. It is possible, for example, that hidden costs will reduce the implicit ROE of a high-debt alternative to a lower rate than with a lower- or no-debt alternative. Unfortunately, this assessment requires the entrepreneur's judgment of the hidden costs. That assessment does explain, however, why many entrepreneurs will not provide personal guarantees and accept lower debt proportions and consequently lower ROEs. The entrepreneur has implicitly assessed the hidden costs and concluded they are greater than the benefits of the debt.

An additional way to think about potential hidden costs is to consider how capital structure decisions affect risk and flexibility considerations.

RISK

Risk problems, defined somewhat arbitrarily, are caused by those potentially adverse irregularly recurring events whose impact can be evaluated with a degree of accuracy. The entrepreneur may not know when the next risk event will occur, but the entrepreneur has had experience in dealing with them. It knows what actions are likely to combat them, knows some danger signals, and can often reduce the impact of risk events. To use an organic analogy, risky events are like colds rather than serious lung problems. In the aerospace jargon, these would be "known unknowns." Risk events are usually dealt with by transforming assets into cash and using the cash to service senior financial obligations.

The most common type of risk situation is a business cycle, both on the down and on the upswing. These cyclical expansions and contractions first create strains as a company strives to meet demands of customers who, in good times, want delivery yesterday. Then strain is created as demand dries up. The company must scramble to trim back its operations, husband its resources, and prepare for the increase in demand that usually follows.

> **KEY POINT: You have no control over when a change in the cycle will occur. Management usually has an accumulation of information and experience dealing with the situation. You can therefore estimate the impact that development will have on earnings and cash.**

For instance, Exhibit 8-4 shows the sales, earnings before interest and taxes, and cash changes for The Minimax Company, a supplier of test equipment to the telecommunications business, over the period 1993 to 2003. Methods by which these data can be analyzed are illustrated in the following paragraphs. Similar information can be developed to aid in

EXHIBIT 8-4
The Minimax Company
Data for Cash-Flow Risk Appraisal
(thousands of dollars)

YEAR	SALES	EBIT	CHANGE IN CASH*
1993	$16,100	$1,000	$ –0–
1994	18,800	1,400	(100)
1995	22,900	1,800	(200)
1996	27,800	2,430	(1,000)
1997	28,400	2,800	(200)
1998	31,500	2,950	(100)
1999	34,300	4,350	(600)
2000	31,700	2,225	(1,000)
2001	20,500	875	2,000
2002	28,200	2,620	(700)
2003	30,000	3,000	(800)

* Less increases in short-term debt and plus decreases in short-term debt

analyzing other types of risky circumstances such as strikes, bad weather, and poor model years.

Earnings Coverage and Cash Generation

Lenders often look to earnings-coverage ratios to measure a firm's ability to meet its commitments to pay interest and repay principal. These measures are constructed in a variety of ways, some discussed in Chapter 3, to relate fixed senior debt to the earnings generated. But, *cash* is required to pay back debt. The funds generated by earnings are not useful for debt service until they have been converted into cash.

> **SMART FINANCIAL MANAGEMENT: The question, therefore, is not only how much a company can earn, but how much of those earnings will end up in the cash account after the other balance sheet changes take place. These cash uses must be studied in the risk situations the company is likely to encounter. This analysis will determine how well the firm can meet its obligations and what financial leverage it can afford.**

Earnings and the cash balance do not always move in the same direction, let alone by the same magnitude. In 1996, for instance, Minimax's earnings increased significantly, but the cash balance dropped drastically. The same pattern occurred in 2002, but the reverse took place in 2001.

Although information is not available to identify the precise causes for Minimax's results (large capital expenditures? changes in credit terms? changes in inventory?), this inverse relationship is not uncommon. As the business cycle enters a period of strength, the requirements for funds in the receivables and inventory accounts frequently increase faster than the volume of funds generated by accounts payable and earnings. New plants also must be constructed.

When the business cycle turns down, on the other hand, capital expenditures are curtailed. They may be less than current depreciation charges, which results in an absolute decline in plant and equipment. Sales fall or level out, so fewer funds are required to support receivables. Inventories are not replaced. Although the funds added to the business by earnings are reduced, the funds freed from the asset accounts also flow into cash. Cash may thus rise though business declines.

One company, whose management made an extensive study of how it could respond to business-cycle risk, found that its cash need was greatest in the two quarters following the peak of a business cycle. It took that long to figure out that a change in the cycle had occurred and to slow the production process. From then on through the trough of the cycle, the company became increasingly liquid as inventories were reduced and receivables collected. As sales recovered, the need to build up the current-assets created a significant drain on cash. This fund use tapered off once a new and higher level of operations had been established. The report underlined the importance of fast action to conserve funds at the start of a business cycle.

Growth and Debt Service

Minimax's changes in cash, which are mostly negative, suggest it will have difficulty paying back any debt, a common problem for a growing company. Many major corporations have net cash needs to support their activities. Over time, therefore, the company pays debt back but reborrows what it has repaid together with new funds. This process, as opposed to loans with no periodic amortization, protects both the borrower and the lender from becoming locked in permanently at the extremes of interest-rate cycles. The practice also simplifies a change of lending relationships should this become desirable.

To cite an example, in mid-2003, management of Minimax believed the business cycle was due to turn for its industry in 2004. It therefore considered investing $5 million in a major expansion. It would take three years to get to effective capacity, when the project was expected to earn $1.3 million before taxes. These profits would provide coverage of almost four times the $350,000 annual interest of the 7-percent, 15-year debt alternative management was considering, which seemed adequate.

Earnings of $694,444 would be required before 40 percent taxes to generate after-tax earnings (and funds) to pay the $416,666 annual repayment of principal (which would probably not begin until the third year). Total before-tax earnings requirements to cover both interest and principal were thus about $1 million. This amount perhaps presses the ability of this project to cover its financing by 100 percent debt over an entire business cycle.

An examination of a company's behavior during a severe cyclical downturn, such as the one Minimax experienced in 2000 and 2001, is more encouraging and points to effective management. In 2000, sales fell slightly, but cash dropped by $1 million to provide funds to operate the business (probably reflecting a runup in receivables and inventory). An additional $210,000 in after-tax interest plus $416,666 in debt repayment to service the debt could have caused considerable strain. Earnings remained at a reasonable level, however, providing good funds generation for the business. This would have encouraged the company's banks to extend additional short-term credit.

In 2001, when the earnings level dropped precipitously, Minimax generated some $2 million in cash. These funds, likely coming from a contraction of current assets, provided funds to prepay whatever short-term borrowing Minimax incurred in 2000 and also an adequate amount to service the new debt.

Minimax is thus a cash-hungry company that will probably have needs for net new financing in the future. Earnings from the new project will provide reasonable funds generation to service the new loan. Funds generated from the firm's present asset base provide a further cushion. In a financial pinch, expansion might have to be curtailed to free funds for debt service.

In periods of distress, Minimax does generate cash from its assets. Thus, in the future, more rapid response to the cycle would be helpful so a repetition of 2000 could be avoided. The cycle does not appear to be so long that the company's average earnings would fail to support the debt over a period of several years. Provided current interest was paid, a waiver of the principal repayment for a short period could probably be negotiated. A lender, after all, is reluctant to force a healthy company into financial difficulty when a one or two quarter deferral of a principal repayment is all that is required while the company restructures its assets.

The loan is thus not likely to threaten the solvency of the company. Until a higher level of earnings has been sustained over a period of years, however, the risk aspects suggest there may not be room for much more permanent debt than the $5 million under consideration.

> SMART FINANCIAL MANAGEMENT: In summary, you should consider how the company's cash flows respond to whatever the company's risk events are. If the business is going well, lenders are usually willing to

refinance debt so repayment is effectively deferred. **The problem arises when business is on the downward slope of the cycle, when operating cash flows are still negative. It is in this period when the lenders may be much more reluctant to refinance maturing debt. Thus, it is in this period that the cash flows provide the limit on the funds available for debt service. These funds, in turn, put a cap on the amount of debt the company can safely take on.**

Debt Service and the Dividend

A smaller growing company usually does not pay dividends. All the funds it generates are required to support the growth. As the growth slows, you and the other owners tend first to reward yourselves with higher salaries, taking your compensation in the most tax-efficient manner. With further maturity, however, some owners may retire. Limits on deductible compensation also exist for managers. In these circumstances, a company may begin to pay dividends.

For the smaller business, dividends are typically irregular in amount. Some companies pay a regular percent of profit after taxes in one payment after the yearly income statement is completed. Others may pay a regular, small dividend several times a year with one special dividend after yearend when it is clear what funds are available. These practices can create odd payout percentages for a company with volatile earnings.

The entrepreneur-owners of a private company are thus typically less concerned about maintaining the dividend level than the managers of a public company. You understand more clearly than an investor in a public company why dividends may have to be temporarily reduced so the company can service debt or complete an investment in assets. Lenders find it easier to gain cooperation from entrepreneurs in such decisions as curtailing the dividend than they do from professional managers of public companies.

> **WATCH THIS: The situation causing the greatest difficulty in smaller companies is a split among the owners. The tension is often between the previous generation or silent partners, who look to dividends as important income, and the current managers of the business. This latter group, whose members derive current income from their compensation and look to the future for reward, often wish to keep as much funds in the business as possible. The problem can be even worse if the current managers are professionals, vulnerable to discharge if the absentee owners become upset about dividends being curtailed.**

If maintaining the dividend is of strategic importance, in the sense that it avoids debilitating conflict among shareholders, you must allow for these cash flows in planning the maximum debt level for the firm. Having used the analysis described in the previous section to identify a cap on the amount of debt that can be handled in a risk situation, the flows available to lenders must be cut by the amount of the unavoidable dividends. This reduction results in a proportionate reduction in the maximum borrowing capacity.

> **KEY POINT:** This analysis must be explained carefully to the lenders. They will thus know in advance of the company's situation and not be surprised if the company maintains dividend payments through a risk event. Lenders will also be reassured about the quality of management's planning.

FLEXIBILITY

A firm's financial *flexibility* is its ability quickly to raise new funds to meet a major fund need created by a crisis.

Flexibility aspects of the capital structure decision are very similar to risk problems and are analyzed in the same way. In contrast with a risk problem, a flexibility crisis is one of the large number of improbable but possible events that threaten the basic earning power of the business. These are events with which the firm and its management have little historic experience and therefore have no real knowledge of its ability to respond. It is a thing that goes bump in the night, in the words of the *Scottish Book of Common Prayer*.

> **KEY POINT:** Flexibility problems are not usually solved by converting assets into cash because the event will typically have damaged the value of the company's assets and earning power. The resolution usually requires new external financing to purchase new assets, tangible or intangible. Occasionally, a firm faced with a flexibility crisis will have assets unrelated to its core business. These may be sold to generate funds to deal with the flexibility problem.

The differences between risk events and flexibility problems are of degree, however. One firm's crisis may be a normal recurring risk problem for another. Risk and flexibility questions can be clearly distinguished at the extremes, but toward the middle of the spectrum they blend. A normal business cycle can usually be analyzed as a risk. A major depression is more likely to present a flexibility situation.

Typical of memorable flexibility problems was the bankruptcy of Rolls Royce, which created a flexibility crisis for Lockheed because Lockheed had been counting on using new Rolls Royce engines in the 1011 jet airliner. Several unfortunate food companies have experienced flexibility crises when a product was found to be contaminated. Pharmaceutical companies have had flexibility crises created by sabotage. Weaker companies depending on the commercial paper markets experienced flexibility problems when Enron failed. Others have been severely threatened by governmental controls suddenly introduced or by sudden changes in foreign-exchange rates. Scarcity of raw materials or other commodities can present unexpected and difficult problems. A rapid decline in prices also can cause problems, especially for those with unhedged inventory positions. These are all sudden unforeseen events striking at the core of the business.

Odds are that events of this type will occur from time to time for most companies. It is impossible economically and perhaps absolutely to get insurance or other forms of protection against all possible flexibility problems. Nevertheless, as with an individual's financial program, some level of insurance is justified. The precise level depends on the size of the risks, the cost of the insurance, and the willingness of the entrepreneurs and the management to bear the risks. These considerations require careful analysis.

Analyzing the Flexibility Position

First, you must try to identify as specifically as possible the nature of potential flexibility events. Are they product-life problems, such as are found in high-technology business? Price-erosion threats? Receivables-collection or inventory problems? Loss of a major customer? Prolonged labor unrest? Are there dangers in transfer of payments or international monetary disorders that might confront a company with significant international business? Is the company possibly subject to pollution regulations for which compliance will require substantial funds?

> **SMART FINANCIAL MANAGEMENT:** Once the more likely flexibility problems have been identified (and you must be continually alert to changes in prospective flexibility problems), you must do your best to estimate the effect of these problems on the financial circumstances of the company. The more vulnerable the company is to one of these events and the more difficult it is for the company to rearrange its internal financial operations to generate funds to solve the problem, the more important it is for the firm to maintain easy access to outside funds. These can include debt capacity, new equity, or cash balances set aside for emergency, extraordinary purposes.

Case in Point: Although the case involved a sizeable company, the analytical approach would be the same for the smaller business. The management of an automotive-parts producer identified events it thought constituted the major flexibility problems the company could face. These included the obsolescence of a major product line, substantial price cuts by competition attempting to buy market share, major additional requirements for research and development, major additional requirements for capital investment to attain the level of sales and profits expected, and failure of the company's foreign affiliates to perform effectively.

Close examination showed that the most serious financial problems probably would be caused by product obsolescence, price problems, and cash drains of foreign operations. The other problems, in the judgment of management, would not cause a flexibility crisis.

The serious problems were explored in detail. Using the best information available about what might happen (but never had), management tried to judge the company's ability to marshal its internal resources to provide the funds necessary to survive these crises. Funds not available internally would have to be raised from the outside. Management found that $30 million in outside funds would likely be needed to combat either the obsolescence of a major product or a degenerating price situation. Foreign problems would require $20 million.

A sufficient reserve of debt to combat these problems plus a small reserve for odds and ends would absorb all the debt management believed the company could get from its financial sources. In fact, it might require that the small proportion of debt already on the books be refinanced with equity to create a full flexibility reserve. It certainly would force management to abandon plans to borrow additional debt to support prospective growth. But these actions were unattractive because issuing additional stock would dilute earnings and threaten the control enjoyed by the major shareholders group.

Management concluded the likelihood of one flexibility crises arising was strong enough to justify keeping some insurance in the form of debt capacity. The chance of two major simultaneous crises was so much less that full insurance was not required. The chance of more than two occurring simultaneously was so small that it did not justify, in management's opinion, any further sacrifice of current benefits. Thus, in balancing the possible dangers of lack of resources against the immediate sacrifice of income, management decided the company should keep sufficient flexibility in the form of debt reserves to protect against one $30-million problem. Additional debt reserves should be kept to go toward another major problem or a combination of minor problems. Therefore, the debt reserve was set at $45 million.

Reviewing the Minimax Situation

Although sufficient information has not been presented about The Minimax Company to allow a deep analysis of its flexibility situation, a brief comment on its general situation is a useful illustration. In the risk discussion above, it appeared that Minimax could barely service the proposed debt requirements in severe cyclical conditions. In addition, the basic nature of Minimax's growth suggests the company should place a premium on maintaining an easy access to outside funds. Growth requirements will probably exceed internal-funds generation and require additional external financing. An issue of common stock in a time of poor earnings or in a poor stock market could result in a significant erosion of the owners' control and perhaps require sale of the company to a larger firm.

It is thus unlikely that Minimax would have much room to maneuver if a flexibility crisis arose. The situation would be even more severe if the flexibility crisis coincided with a risk problem. Management must think carefully, therefore, whether the gain in ROE from using debt is sufficient to justify the commitment of most of the company's flexibility reserves. The alternative is to raise equity in some manner or to trim the investment project, perhaps stretching it out for several years.

> **KEY POINT: Flexibility aspects of a capital-structure decision are not easy ones to evaluate. The factors that must be considered vary substantially from case to case. The approach, in all cases, is the one outlined above, evaluating whether the tradeoff in additional ROE is worth the loss of ability to raise funds in a flexibility crisis. The extra "eating" must be measured against the extra "sleeping."**

TIMING

Timing decisions, as discussed in this chapter, include two major capital structure questions. One is the decision about the sequence in which the debt and equity issues should be arranged. The other, which involves only the debt decision, is the sequencing of debt issues: Should long-term debt be raised immediately or delayed by using short-term, interim financing? Will a more favorable long-term-debt market appear? The timing decision, in either context, does *not* refer to the speed with which an issue can be placed, which counts as an "other" consideration.

Unlike the income aspects, which usually favor debt, and the risk and flexibility considerations, which usually favor conservative financing (even additional equity), the timing decision does not inherently favor either debt or equity. The usual problem results from waiting to issue all long-term forms of financing until later: Interest rates will fall; they have never been so high! Earnings will rise, the price-earnings ratio will also rise, and the value will soar!

The temptation is frequently to extemporize by issuing short-term debt to defer the long-term decision or action. This section will show how this temptation can be analyzed.

Sequencing Issues of Debt and Equity

The tendency to delay equity issues is particularly strong. Often where new asset investments are being made, a strong increase in earnings is expected in a year or two. A short delay in raising equity would usually not be long enough to allow the issue's price to reflect the full benefits of the new investment's contribution to increased earnings.

> **SMART FINANCIAL MANAGEMENT: The longer the company can wait to sell itself or to sell equity, therefore, the higher the price should be if the price-earnings multiple remains fixed. Furthermore, the optimist will argue, as the earnings pick up strongly, the price-earning ratio may also increase. By waiting, the company could enjoy a price enhanced by both an increase in earnings and an increase in the multiple, a double-whammy that would significantly reduce dilution.**

After a couple of years have passed, in which you have used high leverage, the argument for further delaying an equity issue will run along different lines. Because the issue's purpose will merely be to "roll over" existing short-term debt, investors in new equity issues will not be enthusiastic about buying the issue. Rather than promising additional earnings, all the issue offers is stability. Therefore, debt financing should be continued until the company can go to the market with a good story to tell about prospective earnings from new investment plans. Equity never seems attractive.

> **IMPORTANT: When you are contemplating a sequence of debt and equity issues, which is often the case when equity is under consideration for a growing enterprise, you must recognize that you are not considering *whether* to issue equity but rather *when* to issue equity. The company's risk posture and flexibility position call for equity. That decision has been made. The question is whether a delay is likely to save enough dilution and to enhance the market value of the present owners sufficiently to justify their being asked to take the risk of a delay.**

Prices and price multiples go down as well as up. Market conditions deteriorate as well as improve. Unexpected problems arise in delivering earnings expectations. The judgment is whether the extra potential benefits in price justify the potential risk and flexibility problems of delaying an equity issue.

It is important, in evaluating the timing aspects of a set of alternate sequences, that the ending capital-structure proportions are as nearly the same as possible for the alternatives being explored. That is, the company should be at the target capital structure at the end of each sequence.

Otherwise, different income levels would be expected, and different risks from the capital structure would have to be analyzed. These questions are related to but separate from the timing question.

Without going into the mechanical details, in the Minimax situation, management had to decide whether a 4.5 percent improvement in earnings per share (and whatever benefit this might have on the market price in 2006) is worth the loss of flexibility associated with issuing debt rather than equity in 2003. Is the reward great enough to justify waiting for a better price and issuing 30 percent fewer new shares? Or, is the present market favorable and the stock price's historic high unlikely to be equaled soon—in which case, the difference in earnings and ROE would have disappeared.

Term Structure of Debt

Analyzing the term structure of a company's debt, deciding when to go long and when to temporize with a short-term issue in the hope that long-term rates will fall, is simpler than the debt-equity sequence decision. There are some aspects of risk and flexibility involved, of course. Lenders might find themselves in a credit pinch and be reluctant to renew a short-term credit. The company's financial position might degenerate, making the conversion to long-term debt impossible. But, compared to the basic debt-or-equity question, the problem is primarily one of cost with only a mild seasoning of risk exposure.

The cost of a poor term-structure decision is more than it might appear because of two factors. First, the differential cost of a mistake in issuing long-term debt is more than just the interest differential between the actual issue and the lower-cost opportunity that was missed. On a $1 million loan, for example, the difference between 6 percent and 7 percent is $10,000 a year before taxes and $6,000 after 40-percent taxes. The total difference is $120,000 if the loan is for 20 years with no sinking fund. The $120,000 also must be financed to keep the resources available to the company at the equivalent level under both options. Interest (and other costs) on this additional financing brings the total to over $180,000.

Second, to keep the debt-capital ratio the same, some proportion of these extra costs must be financed with equity. A $180,000 direct-interest-cost differential will require a company capitalized at 70 percent equity to issue (or retain) an additional $126,000 of equity to finance the equity part of the shortfall. (This figure would have to be adjusted for any differential between the interest assumption and dividends on the common stock.) Great care in considering the future of interest rates is thus clearly required for the decision when to issue long-term debt.

CONTROL

The *control* aspects of a financial decision generally favor issuing debt. Even in those rare situations when equity dilutes the ROE less than debt, an equity issue to new investors always dilutes the voting control of the existing shareholders. The importance of voting control varies widely, however. It is particularly important in a few easy-to-identify circumstances.

Control factors are not apt to be important in a large company whose shareholder group is widely spread and does not contain significant voting blocks. In the more common control case, where a significant proportion of ownership is in the hands of an individual, a family, or a business group, control questions are particularly sensitive at three points:

1. When the company is completely owned by the group, and a stock issue would admit outsiders for the first time
2. When the financing decision would lower the controlling group's ownership to less than 50 percent
3. When the proportion held would be reduced to some vulnerable level, often thought of as 20 percent to 25 percent of the ownership

Admitting Outsiders

The reluctance of those controlling the entire equity of a company to admit outsiders is not hard to understand. It means exposing the affairs of the company to the world, incurring greater costs for legal and professional fees, being concerned with the corporate entity as separate from the personal activities of the controlling group, and perhaps having to follow more complex security regulations.

This last problem is particularly difficult for the single entrepreneur to accept. Often, you have run the business with minimal concern for its separation from your own financial needs, estate planning, and tax circumstances. Often, in the early stages of the company's growth, legitimate actions are taken to reduce your total tax burden so maximum equity funds will be available for the company. Little concern, likewise, is given to potential conflicts of interest between your various ventures. Whichever alternative most enhances total value is appropriate.

Once outsiders are involved, however, it is necessary to look at the entity separately from yourself. Actions must be justified as best for the shareholders of that entity without considering other relationships owners may have with the firm. Otherwise, the management and the directors may expose themselves to suits from stockholders seeking to recover damages for the company.

> **IMPORTANT: The value added by the new equity thus must often be overwhelming if the owners of a 100-percent-controlled company are to sell part of the company to the public.**

Sometimes, the additional income from new investments is sufficient reward to cause the sale to be made. Other reasons for admitting outsiders include establishing a market value for the stock (which may be required for estate purposes) and creating liquidity for the owner's portfolio. It is possible that the level of debt makes you uncomfortable. But, the decision to admit outsiders is generally a painful one that requires more than the ordinary level of returns before it will be accepted.

Loss of a Majority Position

Once you have sold part of the company, you often find that dealing with outside interests is not as difficult as feared. The new and old shareholders usually have the same goal, enhancing the company's worth. If the new shareholders are not happy, or lose their optimism, they will probably sell their shares rather than start a fight—especially if the controlling group holds 50 percent or more of the stock. The existence of outside holders and a market for the shares creates considerable financial flexibility for both you and the corporation. This may compensate handsomely for the extra problems presented by more formal reporting requirements and arms-length dealings.

When a financing decision would reduce your controlling-ownership position to less than 50 percent, the control question again becomes a particularly prominent issue. Ownership of a majority of the shares in the company is absolute protection against a shareholder revolt. On critical issues, such as mergers or changes in the company regulations, 50 percent may be enough to carry the decisions. If it is not, the necessary two-thirds is not that difficult to get. It is certain that no one else can carry questions requiring a majority vote. A reduction to less than 50 percent eliminates that certainty, and again the benefits of an equity issue are carefully assessed.

> **KEY POINT: Perhaps the benefits should always be carefully assessed: The reduction from 80 percent to 70 percent is as much of a step in the direction of loss of control as the step from 60 percent to 50 percent. It is consistent with the flexibility analysis to point out that the loss of control, like the loss of flexibility, does not happen suddenly. Yet, you should be forewarned that the control question is given the most consideration and weight in coming to a capital-structure decision at the critical control points.**

Maintaining Effective Control

Finally, once a controlling group has lost absolute voting control, there is considerable room for further dilution without again forcefully raising the control question. The tendency of shareholders to vote their proxies for management's candidates for directorships and to follow management's recommendations is a well-documented phenomenon and a source of frustration to many who propose corporate reforms. The attitude of even most professional and institutional investors generally is either to support management or to sell. A fight for control of the corporation is likely to be expensive and may damage equity values, at least in the short term. Because short-term appreciation is a major component in measuring fiduciaries' performance, a hint of problems usually sends institutional investors into the market on the selling side. (This attitude may be changing and could be significantly different in the future.)

This flight may play into the hands of a group that wishes to challenge management or the existing dominant owners. The price of the stock is forced down as the institutions bail out, making it less expensive to accumulate a strong ownership position. If the management group owns 25 percent, however, it need only get the votes of one-third of the public stock to win. A challenger needs to buy or win the votes of two-thirds of the nonmanagement shares. This is such a significant disadvantage that fights for control are not often undertaken. The outsiders seldom win even if insiders hold as little as 20 to 25 percent of the voting power.

That "seldom," however, is often enough that the control question again becomes a strong concern when the ownership level drops below 25 to 30 percent. At this point, if there is any threat of danger from an unfriendly source, management and the controlling group will be most strongly opposed to further dilution of the equity. An exception to this generality occurs if the new shares will be placed in friendly hands. This can sometimes be arranged by a merger paid for with equity.

> **IMPORTANT: In the circumstances likely to raise control questions, your company's investment bankers can often provide ways of reassuring you or other anxious managers. By careful structure of the underwriting activity, which might increase the cost of the issue slightly, the shares can be spread over a wide geographic area. Limits can be put on the amount made available to any one purchaser. These techniques provide considerable short-term protection. They can provide longer-term protection, too, because a widespread holding of small amounts is expensive to combine into a control position.**

Control by Senior-Security Holders

It is erroneous to think that senior-security owners, such as long-term lenders, do not exert control on the company because they have no equity vote. It also would be an error to think that banks holding unsecured short-term debt with a minimum of formal covenants are not in virtually as strong a control position as a long-term lender who has negotiated a complex set of covenants.

The controls senior-security holders can exercise are normally spelled out at the time a security issue is made. The contract with preferred shareholders, a favorite form of venture financing, will specify the extent of their claims on the company and those issues and circumstances in which they will have a vote.

Debt indentures are usually much more detailed. An agreement may run to hundreds of pages, listing the actions management promises to take and avoid to protect the debt position. These provisions usually specify the circumstances in which the debt may be declared immediately payable. When one of these circumstances occurs, the lender or the trustee of the issue has considerable bargaining power.

In such circumstances, the debt owners may exercise their influence to have changes in management made. They may demand acceptance of onerous restrictions on management's actions until the default is corrected, the company's financial position is restored to some acceptable and agreed level, or the debt is repaid. As an alternative to bankruptcy, you may have to agree to extreme terms.

Short-term loans are frequently arranged with a minimum of complex formalities and agreements. The short-term lender's advantage is the ability to exert influence, if the circumstances require it, at each renewal date. The frequency of review gives the short-term lender considerable control potential much earlier than the long-term lender would get it without a covenant violation. The covenants of the long-term debt are, in fact, an early-warning arrangement for the lender. They give the lender an ability to move from a passive to an active stance when danger begins to develop.

Other Considerations in Capital Structure Decisions

The previous discussion outlined the major considerations involved in planning an enterprise's capital structure. Emphasis was placed first on analyzing the impact of these decisions on your income. Other conditions being equal, the higher the ROE the company enjoys, the better off you should be. The discussion then turned to the "other conditions" that might not be equal. The most important of these are the company's ability to survive in risk circumstances and whether it has kept sufficient flexibility to parry major threats. The higher-income debt route often increases a firm's risk and flexibility exposure. The impact of these dangers to your value must be thus evaluated to figure out whether it is increased or diminished.

The questions of timing an issue, within the context of a capital-structure policy, were also illustrated. Timing does not inherently favor either the debt or the equity policy. It may dictate temporary departures from a policy to take advantage of conditions in the capital markets. Finally, the nature of the control problem was discussed.

Most companies are faced with a host of other aspects relevant to the decision, any of which may be important enough to tip the balance if the scales are otherwise evenly weighted. It is not possible to list all significant miscellaneous considerations, but a few of the most common ones are:

➤ The *speed and certainty* with which new money is required. This situation may incline a company to issue debt privately rather than equity. As a subcategory of the timing problems, an unsettled market may cause you to take a route that can be privately negotiated with a minimum of documentation. The company should probably use short-term financing until the markets stabilize.

➤ Your desire as the owner of a private company *to create a market for its stock.* Though the firm's financial needs might be adequately fulfilled by debt issues, a stock issue will probably be more favorably received if the proceeds are to be used for the company's benefit.

➤ Your desire *to broaden the market for the stock.* The amount of stock held by the public is so small there is not enough investor interest to create a reasonable pool of willing buyers and sellers. If the number of publicly traded shares is below 200,000 to 400,000 shares, as a rule of thumb, then even regional brokerage houses will not have sufficient motivation to make a market in the security. Analysts will not take the time to follow the stock because there will not be enough shares for their clients to buy. If this situation prevails, the stock will probably trade at a lower price than it would with a more active market.

❯ KEY POINT: A sound analytical approach is a necessary ingredient for a wise capital structure plan. It is not sufficient, however. Neither is the necessary careful assessment of a company's record and future prospects. The final necessary element, which with the other items is sufficient, is the judgment of whether the rewards justify the risks. Two managements might be in total agreement on the first two steps. Because one was more sensitive to risk than the other, the final decision of the two managements might be entirely different. One would eat well, the other would sleep well.

PART III

FUNDING GROWTH

CHAPTER 9

NONEQUITY FINANCING FOR THE COMPANY

Financing the business is one of the greatest challenges you will ever face. This is a particularly serious challenge for the growing company, which seldom generates enough internal funds to meet its needs. Chapters 1 and 8 lay out the FRICTO framework, which you can use to determine whether to seek debt or equity to fund the business. The advantages and disadvantages of both are discussed. In the day-to-day world of the small business owner, however, implementing the result of the analysis is not always easy.

After reviewing the economic dimensions of funding smaller businesses, this chapter outlines common sources of noninstitutional and institutional nonequity funding. Chapter 10 discusses sources of equity.

The Entrepreneurial Funding Problem

The demand for small-business financing is greater than the supply, particularly for early stage businesses. Almost half of new firms begin with less than $5,000 in capital, less than 20 percent of the capital considered necessary. It is usually provided by the owner, family members, and friends. Consequently, most new businesses are undercapitalized from the beginning. They stay that way for most of their early lives.

> **KEY POINT:** Equity is always hard to find for the small business, regardless of the price the company is willing to pay. Debt is also hard to find. Banks, the principal source of debt financing for small enterprises, prefer not to lend to a business that is less than three years old.

Many professional investors use five categories to define the various stages of a company's financial development: startup, development stage or second round, expansion stage or third round, growth stage or fourth round, and public offering. The first four stages are equivalent to the first three life-cycle stages described in Chapter 1. A public offering can occur anytime after late life-cycle stage three.

Until it has achieved revenue and moved to the developmental or growth stages, it is hard for a small business to get external financing of any type, debt or equity. Once established, small businesses, like larger businesses, use a variety of types of financing to meet their financing needs. The types of financing a small business uses vary with its development stage and its cash flow situation.

Most small firms use external financing only occasionally. Less than 50 percent of small firms borrow at least once during a year. In their early development, this external financing is usually some form of equity. Small firms in their early development usually lack the demonstrated success necessary to obtain credit from institutional lenders. Overall, small firms rely more on equity capital and short-term debt, and less on external debt capital and long-term debt, than larger firms do. For the smallest firms, mom-and-pop operations with or without hired employees, owner capital is the most important source of financing.

Small firms experiencing rapid growth or those with high volumes of receivables, however, require frequent use of external financing. A 1990 national survey of small firm financing* completed for the Federal Reserve revealed the following financing patterns in 1990:

> Of all small firms, 26 percent had lines of credit, 9 percent had financial leases, 6 percent had mortgage loans, 14 percent had equipment loans, and 24 percent had motor-vehicle loans.

> Of larger firms with 100 to 499 employees, 60 percent had lines of credit, 30 percent had financial leases, 19 percent had mortgage loans, 29 percent had equipment loans, and 26 percent had motor-vehicle loans.

Banks are the dominant suppliers of these types of financing. Thirty-seven percent of small firms obtained some financing from commercial banks. Other major suppliers include finance companies, leasing companies, and other nonfinancial institutions. The cost of borrowed funds is higher for small firms—interest rates on bank loans average two to three percentage points over the prime rate. Fixed-rate loans are usually more expensive than floating-rate loans, at least at the time the loan is negotiated.

Noninstitutional Funding Sources

When you are seeking to meet the firm's capital needs, you generally first use noninstitutional funding sources. The most popular are personal resources, including friends and family. When available personal funds and resources of friends and family have been exhausted, a small business turns

* Elliehausen, Gregory E., and John D. Wolken, *Banking Markets and the Use of Financial Services by Small and Medium-Sized Businesses.* Washington, DC: Board of Governors of the Federal Reserve System, 1990.

to alternatives that provide the benefits of institutional debt or private equity. These alternatives include supplier financing, seller financing, business incubators, franchising, joint ventures and co-branding, but the business may not yet be eligible for direct support from a financial institution.

PERSONAL RESOURCES, INCLUDING FRIENDS AND FAMILY

Most entrepreneurs found their business by investing their own resources, such as personal savings and the equity in their homes. This is often supplemented by "borrowing" from family members and friends or, alternatively, by giving them a stake in the business. You face two major issues when using your own funds. First, are those funds sufficient for the business's needs? Second, can you withstand their potential loss? When you borrow from family and friends, you also must consider whether the family members or friends can afford the potential loss and what the impact of the loss may be on the personal relationship. In addition, you must deal with the family members or friends who may want a say in the business as a condition of investing. This arrangement can be a welcome one, but it also can be potentially troublesome.

SUPPLIER FINANCING

Once your business is going, you can often use financing from your suppliers but seldom from your employees. Many suppliers will provide financing either through very generous payment terms or through direct loans.

> **KEY POINT: Supplier financing has the advantage over financing by family and friends because it is not tinged with emotion. It can be costly, however, unless payment is stretched well beyond the due date. You are usually wise to substitute institutional financing as soon as possible so supplier discounts can be taken.**

Suppliers want your business to succeed. They often can provide a range of nonfinancial assistance besides the financing itself. This nonfinancial assistance can range from providing informal management consulting to providing introduction to potential customers.

SELLER FINANCING

You can also often obtain financing from companies selling you equipment or from sellers of commercial real estate you purchase for the business. Equipment sellers will finance a sale by allowing payment over time and taking a lien on the equipment. Or, they may have a leasing alternative. Many equipment manufacturers have specialized subsidiaries to finance their customers' equipment purchases. (Equipment leasing is discussed in greater detail later in this chapter). Equipment vendors, like suppliers, want your business to succeed and often can provide a range of non-financial help as well as the financing. Commercial real-estate sales are frequently financed by sellers' providing first or second mortgage loans on the property. These sellers, however, will be unlikely to provide non-financial support.

Finally, if you buy an existing business, the seller will often provide term financing for part of the purchase price. In this circumstance, a major consideration may be the seller's tax situation, a topic much too complicated to explore here. The seller also may want to remain involved in the business for a period, usually as a paid consultant. The terms of this association also need to be carefully drawn.

BUSINESS INCUBATORS

For startup companies, particularly in technology areas, *business incubators* can be an attractive source of financial support. Business incubators typically provide physical space to small businesses at a nominal or no charge. They can also provide other services, such as secretarial support, telephones, and office machines. In addition, by placing several fledgling businesses together, the business incubator provides you with a forum of peers for joint problem solving, support from others facing similar problems, and exchange of information and discussion of common commercial interests. Established by universities or nonprofit organizations, business incubators are intended to help the growth of small, fledgling enterprises that lack cash to pay full price for office space and services. Information about business incubators can be obtained from the National Business Incubation Association, 20 East Circle Drive, Suite 190, Athens, OH, 45701 (telephone: 740-593-4331; Web site: www.nbia.org).

FRANCHISING

Franchising provides small, successful businesses with an attractive way to enter a new geographic market without having to raise large sums of capital. It is particularly attractive to retailing consumer nondurables and services. A small business can sell a franchise to an individual or organization that wants to market the product or service the small business owns in a geographic area the small business is not currently serving. In the typical franchise arrangement, for an initial payment, the small business sells the right to market its products or services in a specific geographic market. The franchise grantor (franchiser) thus does not have to raise the capital to support an expansion of its reach. This is the responsibility of the franchisee.

The franchiser will also often receive periodic payments from the franchisee for the rights to continue the franchise. The franchiser also may be paid for goods and services provided the franchisee. Franchisers, however, typically must provide support to their franchisees. This is usually advice about the product and the business. General marketing support is often required if the franchiser provides a brand that relies on advertising to draw customers to the franchisee.

JOINT VENTURES AND STRATEGIC ALLIANCES

Joint ventures and strategic alliances provide ways for successful small businesses to use the resources and skills of another company without merging with it. They also can allow a small business to share the risk associated with a new business initiative. There are several reasons a joint venture may make sense for a small company including:

- ➤ Developing a new market
- ➤ Developing a new product or technology
- ➤ Sharing complimentary technology
- ➤ Accessing a distribution network
- ➤ Sharing in the execution of a contract
- ➤ Accessing capital

In the typical joint venture, a partnership, newly formed LLC, or a corporation is set up to bring the parties together to achieve a specific objective. The relationship between the parties is spelled out in the ownership agreement for the legal entity. This arrangement is common in the pharmaceutical industry.

CO-BRANDING

Co-branding is a form of informal partnership between the owners of two brand names, such as a resort and an airline. They combine to add value to each brand through increased consumer name recognition and economies of scale in functions such as advertising. Co-branding can be arranged through a variety of legal entities. It can be particularly valuable for a small business if it can partner with a larger business that has a large advertising program, a broad product line, and a well-recognized brand name. The advantage for the larger company is to round out its product line without the expense of creating its own product or buying an established brand.

Nongovernmental Institutional Funding Sources

As you get established, you will increasingly turn to financial institutions to provide financing for your businesses. Institutional loan sources come in a variety of flavors, each having a particular niche in the marketplace. The most significant of these institutions, from your standpoint, are commercial banks, credit-card companies, thrifts, and commercial finance companies (including factoring companies). Institutional loan financing products include credit cards, short-term bank loans and lines of credit, long-term bank loans, real-estate loans, letters of credit, factoring, account-receivable loans, inventory loans, and equipment loans and leases. Although they differ in the types of loan financing they offer, institutional lenders are alike in evaluating the borrower's credit. This process helps figure out the risk and reward associated with the borrower. It also identifies the fit between the borrower's needs and the institution's financial products.

> **KEY POINT: A basic distinction between types of institutional lending is whether it is secured or unsecured. *Secured loans* are protected in default by some form of lien on the borrower's property. The lien allows the lender to seize the asset if the borrower defaults on the loan. The lender becomes a priority creditor in case of a bankruptcy. *Unsecured loans* are loans that have no lien on the borrower's property to protect the lender upon default or bankruptcy. Unsecured loans usually carry a higher rate of interest for a given credit quality to compensate for the greater risk undertaken by the lending institution. In practice, many lending institutions will only lend to small businesses on a secured basis because they believe the risk is too great to justify an unsecured loan.**

COMMERCIAL BANK FUNDING

Credit-Card Loans

For many entrepreneurs, the first financial institution financing they use is credit cards. This may range from the borrowing against personal credit cards to provide capital to start the business to credit cards issued to existing, established businesses. Banks and other credit-card issuing institutions provide financing to small business through this mechanism when they would not otherwise provide credit to the business. First, the interest rates are very high. Second, the lenders look, informally or formally, to the credit of individuals associated with the business for ultimate repayment. Lenders informally look to the credit of the individual when they (sometimes unknowingly) allow an individual to use personal credit cards to finance a business. They look formally to the owner if they provide a credit card to the business for which the owner of the business is also liable. In most of situations, credit-card loans are an unsecured but expensive form of debt.

Commercial Bank Loans

Almost every small business has a relationship with a commercial bank through a depository relationship. One of the first actions a new small business takes is to set up a checking account, which is usually opened at a commercial bank but sometimes at a thrift. Consequently, when you need funds for your businesses, it is natural for you to approach your commercial bank.

> **KEY POINT: Commercial-bank small-business loans are a major source of funding for small companies. Typically, however, these loans are only available to the well-established small company with a track record of good credit performance with other forms of loans.**

Commercial-bank loans come in a variety of forms including short-term loans, lines of credit, floor plan lines of credit, construction loan lines of credit, long-term loans, equipment loans, real-estate loans, and letters of credit. A business qualifying for bank credit may have more than one of these forms of bank loans, each being tailored in its terms and conditions to serve a specific purpose. The nature of each of these loans will be briefly described in the following sections.

Short-term loans are commercial loans of one year or less. They are used to finance the short-term seasonal working-capital needs of a business, such as a build up of inventory by a retailer before the Christmas season. Most short-term loans are structured with thirty-, sixty-, or ninety-day terms, with all principal and interest being due at maturity. They are paid off when the assets purchased with the loans have been sold and the business has recovered the cash invested in them. The lender may take a security interest in the current assets the short-term loan is financing. In many industries, the banks take security for the short-term loans only against the accounts receivable, leaving the inventory to reassure the trade credit.

Lines of credit are longer term arrangements. They allow a business periodically to borrow short term over a longer period than a year without formally getting a new loan each time it needs funds. In a line of credit, a bank agrees to the maximum amount it will let a customer borrow. The customer may then borrow and repay at will, up to that limit. The outstanding balance is due when the line-of-credit agreement expires, although these agreements frequently provide that the loan must be repaid completely for part of every year.

A bank line of credit is designed to help a business maintain a regular cash flow in its day-to-day operations even if the business has significant volatility. The lender will often take assignment of current assets as security. The amount that can be drawn on the line may be set as a proportion of those assets but with a fixed dollar maximum. The terms might provide, for instance, that the company can draw up to 85 percent of its accounts receivable but no more than $1 million. Many factors are used by the bank in setting the limit on the line including the client's financial strength, need for credit, and the quality of the collateral.

Floor plans are specialized lines of credit financing the purchase of specific items. They are typically available to businesses whose inventory is characterized by large, easily identified, expensive units, such as automobile dealerships. The floor plan allows the retailer to buy inventory from the manufacturer and repay the line when the unit is sold. The bank typically has a security interest in each specific unit, which is released when the dealer sells that unit to a retail customer and repays the loan. Retail stores selling large-ticket consumer items, including automobiles, home appliances, furniture, and boats, can use floor plans to finance their inventories. Sometimes, the manufacturer will provide the floor-plan financing.

Construction loans are short-term loans to finance the construction of new real estate, both residential and commercial. They are usually repaid either by the sale of the real estate when the construction is complete or when the borrower gets a long-term mortgage on the property. Real-estate developers and building contractors are the principal users of construction loans. These loans are almost always secured by a mortgage on the property the loans are used to construct.

Long-term loans are normally defined as loans that are repaid according to a defined schedule over a period greater than one year. Most long-term bank loans have a maximum maturity of five years. The term of a specific loan is usually shorter than the useful life of the asset purchased with the loan. For example, loans to buy delivery vehicles for a business would have maturities tied to the period the vehicles were expected to be in use.

Equipment loans are a specific type of long-term loan used to purchase equipment used in the business. Equipment loans finance a variety of equipment from computers to metal stamping equipment to construction equipment. Typically, an equipment loan's maturity is tied to the expected useful life of the equipment financed. Useful life is determined by when the equipment becomes obsolete or wears out, whichever comes first. These loans are normally secured by a lien on the equipment financed.

Real-estate loans are loans secured by a mortgage on an existing piece of residential or commercial real estate. A real-estate loan may be used to purchase real estate, although lenders typically will finance less than 100 percent of the price. Alternatively, the real estate may be used to secure a loan used for another business purpose such as buying inventory.

Letters of credit are liabilities of the banks that issue them. They allow the beneficiary, or recipient, of the letter of credit to present the letter to the issuing bank under defined circumstances and be paid an amount stipulated in the letter. Letters of credit are used in a variety of ways to finance trade and are most actively used in international trade. Because of the bank's unconditional agreement to pay if the beneficiary presents the required documents (thus the term "documentary" letter of credit), banks issue letters of credit only for their most creditworthy customers. As an alternative, the bank will want strong collateral such as cash in a blocked account.

FINDING THE RIGHT BANK FOR THE BUSINESS

Most entrepreneurs and small business owners turn to their primary bank when seeking a bank loan. This is not always the right course of action.

There are several different categories of banks, and some are more attuned to the credit needs of the small-business customer than others. Banking analysts divide banks into four major categories: money-center banks, superregional banks, regional banks, and community banks. *Money-center banks* and *super-regional banks* are the largest banks in the banking system. They have their headquarters in major financial centers, such as New York, Charlotte, North Carolina, and Chicago. They operate in multiple states. *Regional banks* typically operate in one or a few adjacent states. They are large but much smaller than the money-center or super-regional banks. *Community banks* operate in one city or town or a particular region of a state.

The customers of money-center and super-regional banks include major U.S. and multinational corporations and extremely wealthy individuals. These relationships run into many millions of dollars each. In addition, these banks serve the ordinary consumer with a range of consumer-banking products, such as credit cards, whose profitability depends on large-scale operations. The largest banks also may have small-business banking services. You may be familiar with a large bank because you have your personal banking relationship there.

Because of the large size and bureaucracy of a large bank, however, it may be difficult for the small business to have a satisfactory relationship with the large bank. This is particularly true if the small business seeks a loan. To get the advantages of scale, many large banks have a highly structured approach to small-business lending that makes it difficult for them to tailor arrangements to special situations. One solution they may offer is a business credit card, which is usually characterized by high rates.

Regional banks typically do not have the lead banking relationship with major corporations or the economies of scale for mass consumer banking. Regional banks therefore pay more attention to small-business customers. Many small businesses find that regional banks are an attractive solution to their banking needs. They can provide specialized services, such as cash management and international banking, but are small enough to offer you more personalized service.

The customers of community banks are primarily small businesses and consumers in the community. Therefore, community banks are a good source of small-business loans. Federal Reserve statistics show that community banks hold a disproportionate share of small business loans.

Though community banks only account for 15 percent of the banking system's assets and 19 percent of its deposits, they hold 23 percent of small-business loans and 36 percent of small-business loans under $100,000. The entrepreneur or small-business owner will frequently find the community bank is the best source of the personal attention they seek. Terms and conditions will be competitive. If the interest rate is slightly higher, it can be offset by the individual attention given to the business's requirements.

> **KEY POINT: Not all banks are equally comfortable with all prospective customers. Lending officers may have had good or bad experience with certain business segments in the past. They may be more familiar with certain types of businesses than with others. It is therefore wise for you to interview several banks to select the one that appears most responsive in dealing with your company's requirements.**

THE LOAN APPLICATION PROCESS

Once you decide your business requires institutional debt financing, you must prepare loan applications. Each institution will have its own application forms, which you may supplement with additional material information. Whatever the specific forms, a good loan request will explain the business's strategy and include identification of the borrower, identification of the loan requested and its timing, uses for the funds, other sources of funds, cash flow projections, and collateral offered. Chapter 4 illustrates how forecasts are prepared. A monthly forecast is necessary for a short-term loan request. For a longer-term request, annual figures are acceptable after the first year. It is unwise to include downturns in the projections until they are asked for by the lending officer, who may want to know how sensitive the business is to a drop in sales.

The section *identifying the borrower* specifies the legal entity doing the borrowing and with responsibility to repay the loan. The borrower may be an individual, partnership, LLC, or corporation. The section *identifying the loan request* specifies the purpose of the loan and indicates how much money is requested and the proposed terms and conditions. For example, this section may ask for $500,000 to buy an additional piece of production equipment, to be repaid in quarterly installments of $62,500 each over two years plus interest.

The *sources and uses of funds* section list all the sources of finance for the business including equity infusions, the proposed loan, and other loans. It also will show out how the capital will be used, such as building inventories and purchasing new capital equipment. The *cash flow projections* provide a monthly schedule of cash flowing into the business from sources such as sales and new investment and out of the business for operating expenses and cash expenditures such as equipment purchases and debt repayments. The section dealing with *collateral* provides a schedule of all the assets of the business (tangible and intangible), their original purchase prices, their current market values, and a list of all liens against them.

Once the lending institution has received the loan application, its officers will evaluate the credit of the borrower. All institutional lenders look at the following factors for the company, its owners, and its management: character, cash flow, capital, capacity, collateral, and credit history. Depending on the nature of the institution, the officers will put different weighting and emphasis on the individual components of the "Six Cs of Credit." You should understand these factors, how the lenders you are approaching will evaluate and weight them, and how your company measures against them before preparing the loan application. Entrepreneurs who understand a lender's concern and approaches will have a better opportunity to secure the debt financing they want.

> *Character* is the willingness of a borrower to repay a loan, the borrower's essential honesty (particularly in adversity). No institutional lender wants to lend to a dishonest borrower. Lenders know that bad character can result in loan-recovery problems regardless of the borrower's other qualifications.
> *Cash flow* is the business's direct receipt of cash, which is normally the basis for loan repayment.
> *Capital* is the amount of money already in the business and available to protect the loan if problems arise.
> *Capacity* is the ability of the business to be successful over time and generate profits.
> *Collateral* is assets of the business (including those of its owners) that might be pledged to secure the loan.
> *Credit history* is the business's record of meeting its obligations as agreed.

Each bank has its own approach to deciding whether to grant a loan request. Depending on the size of the loan requested and its nature, some banks use a credit-scoring system. Others use a loan-committee process. A third common approach is to delegate the decision to an individual officer or group of officers with specific credit authority. Whatever process is used, the bank will be seeking to maximize its efficiency while limiting its vulnerability to loss.

Unfortunately, many small businesses do a poor job making their case on the loan application. Thus, a high percentage of first-time applications is rejected. Among the more common reasons for rejecting loan applications are:

> Lack of a complete loan proposal
> Cash flow projections without adequate supporting documentation

- Little or no experience by the management in the particular field of business
- Cash flow projections that do not demonstrate an ability to repay the requested amount
- Overstated, unrealistic revenue projections
- Understated and unrealistic expense forecast
- Underestimated capital requirements
- Lack of adequate collateral

Although commercial bankers are seldom experts in the borrower's business, they are skilled at asking questions to determine if the borrower is. Therefore, a loan proposal that is complete and fully documented, whose numbers are reasonable and consistent, will increase the likelihood the loan will be approved.

AFTER APPROVAL OF THE LOAN APPLICATION

If the loan application is approved, the paperwork associated with the loan has just begun. You will now be involved with important documentation. These documents typically include at least:

- The commitment letter
- The loan agreement
- The promissory note
- The security agreement (if required)

Other documents will be required if you are pledging collateral, particularly income-producing collateral. The *commitment letter* spells out the detailed offer the bank is making. The other important documents are described in the following paragraphs.

The *loan agreement* is the central document in the lending process. It sets out in detail the terms of the loan. It covers, for example:

1. The amount and disbursement of the loan
2. Repayment schedule and procedures
3. Restrictive covenants
4. The company's representations and warranties
5. Special conditions to closing and special fees
6. Insurance requirements
7. Conditions of default
8. How a default can be fixed

> **WATCH THIS: A very important part of the loan agreement is the section on restrictive covenants. This section lays out the detailed rules the company must live by to be in good standing on the loan. Violation of**

Restrictive covenants come in two forms: affirmative and negative. *Affirmative covenants* list specific actions the company must take under the loan agreement. They include the requirement that the company provide the bank with audited financial statements at regular intervals, maintain all property in good condition, and pay all taxes. *Negative covenants* specify activities that the company can only undertake with the bank's permission. They require the bank's permission to put a mortgage on company property, pay stockholders a dividend, increase the owner's and manager's salaries, and to merge with another company. The loan agreement should be reviewed carefully by both you and the company's legal counsel before being signed. If there are terms that would prove harmful to the company's progress, revisions should be negotiated. Although lenders want terms that will protect their money, they do not want to harm the borrower.

The *promissory note* normally contains the key provisions of the loan agreement in summary form. A promissory note specifies the interest rate, the term of the loan, the repayment schedule, whether prepayment is possible without penalty, the conditions under which a lender may declare the borrower in default, and the lender's rights and remedies in case of a default.

The *security agreement* is used with a *financing statement*. A financing statement details the lender's interest in a specific piece of collateral. Its purpose is to put other creditors or potential creditors on notice that the asset has already been pledged. A financing statement is normally filed with the state and local governments. The particular office of record can depend on the nature of the collateral (personal property, such as equipment, or real estate).

Other Nongovernmental Institutional Funding

THRIFTS

When the laws governing thrifts (savings and loans and savings banks) were changed in the early 1990s to give them a broader range of banking powers, many thrifts opened commercial-banking departments. These departments generally offer the same types of services to small businesses as commercial banks, including depository relationships and commercial loans. Thrifts can be an attractive alternative to commercial banks because of their effort to develop this new business. Thrifts will often give better service, better pricing, or more relaxed credit requirements than a regular commercial bank. More recently, however, regulators have encouraged thrifts to return to their historical role as real-estate lenders. They may therefore be most useful as a financial source for mortgages.

ASSET BASED LOANS

If a bank decides the business is too risky to justify a loan, another major source of institutional loans is commercial finance companies' asset-based loans. Commercial finance companies purchase time-sales obligations and offer direct leases and secured direct loans including asset-based loans. In 2001, asset-based loans totaled $314 billion and had enjoyed a compound growth rate of over 14 percent during the ten years from 1991 to 2001.

❯ KEY POINT: Asset-based lending uses a company's assets to secure its debt. In the broadest sense, all secured loans are asset-based loans. Asset-based lending, however, includes only those loans in which the lender looks primarily to collateral, rather than cash flow, for repayment. This collateral may be accounts receivable, inventory, machinery and equipment, or real estate, either alone or packaged in various combinations (for example, receivables and inventory or receivables and machinery).

The commercial finance company is willing to take greater risk than the commercial bank and thrift because it maintains greater supervision of the borrower's collateral and charges higher interest rates. The commercial finance company carefully monitors the borrower to ensure the collateral exists, its value, and its integrity. From the time the loan is made until it is repaid, the commercial finance lender is an active participant in its management. Collections, for example, are often sent directly to the lender and credited to the loan. Banks rarely police a loan as thoroughly.

❯ WATCH THIS: This monitoring and the constant collateral appraisal process distinguish asset-based loans from other secured commercial loans. It also explains why asset-based loans are an expensive form of borrowing. Asset-based loans are generally priced at prime plus three to four (or more) percent to cover cost of supervision and help given to customers.

To learn more about commercial finance or to obtain a list of commercial finance companies that might be appropriate to help the business, you should contact the Commercial Finance Association at 225 West 34 Street, Suite 1815, New York, NY 10122 (telephone: 212-594-3490; Web site: www.cfa.com).

FACTORING

A factor is a specialized financial institution that buys the receivables of its customers at a discount and then collects those receivables directly. Factors typically specialize in one or more types of businesses so they can efficiently gather and use credit information about those industries.

> **KEY POINT: Selling its receivables to a factor provides the small business with immediate cash, reducing its need for financing. The factor also may take on the credit risk associated with the receivables if the receivables are purchased on a nonrecourse basis.**

In a *recourse agreement,* the factor's customer agrees to repurchase or pay for any receivables the factor purchased and cannot collect. With a *nonrecourse agreement,* the factor purchases the receivable outright from the company and owns it regardless of whether it can be collected. Because a nonrecourse agreement presents greater risk to the factor, these agreements contain provisions allowing the factor to refuse to purchase receivables at its discretion. They also give the factor the option to purchase any of the business's receivables, protecting the factor from being offered only the most doubtful ones. Nonrecourse factoring costs more than recourse agreements.

Factoring has many advantages for a small business, particularly one that is short of cash:

- ➤ It can accelerate the cash flow into a company from its sales.
- ➤ It can be utilized whatever the credit quality of the company using factoring because the factor looks to the credit quality of the company's customers who generate the receivables and not to the credit quality of the company itself.
- ➤ The company avoids having to take on debt on its balance sheet, although the low level of accounts receivable will suggest that factoring is being used.
- ➤ A factoring arrangement can reduce the staff of the company by shifting the administration of receivables to the factor.

> **WATCH THIS: Despite its advantages, factoring can be expensive. Some customers may find the factor's credit checks intrusive. In some industries, use of a factor is considered a sign of financial weakness.**

You can learn more about factoring or find a factoring company through the Commercial Finance Association at 225 West 34 Street, Suite 1815, New York, NY 10122 (telephone: 212-594-3490; Web site: www.cfa.com).

EQUIPMENT LEASING

Leasing equipment provides a flexible, creative alternative to buying as a way of obtaining the necessary equipment to run a cash-short business. Leasing is used for a wide variety of equipment ranging from airplanes to vehicles to kitchen equipment for a restaurant to computers. In the typical equipment-leasing arrangement, an equipment-leasing company (the lessor) buys equipment or other fixed assets. It then executes a contract with the entity (the lessee) that will use the asset. In return for the use of the asset, the lessee makes fixed payments to the lessor for a specified period.

The two basic types of leases are operating and finance. Most small value equipment, such as office machines, are leased with an operating lease. In an *operating lease,* the lessee can typically return the equipment to the lessor any time after proper notice. The lease payments are treated as operating expenses, deducted immediately from operating revenues for accounting and tax purposes. In contrast, a lessee cannot cancel a *finance lease* (often called full-payout or closed-end lease). The lease payments recover most of the equipment cost for the lessor together with interest on the investment. Financial leases must be capitalized as a liability on the lessee's balance sheet. The value of the related equipment is capitalized as an asset and depreciated over the term of the lease. Financial and tax accounting for a financial lease is complicated and not necessarily the same. Qualified advice, such as a CPA with experience in accounting for leases, should be consulted before a financial lease is signed.

> **KEY POINT: Leasing is almost always more expensive than borrowing and buying. However, it provides other advantages that may justify its use. You don't have to raise the cash through a loan or an equity offering to purchase needed equipment. And your company's taxes are typically reduced more in the short run than if the equipment was purchased and depreciated over time.**

To learn more about equipment leasing or to obtain a list of vendors that might lease equipment to their business, you should contact the Equipment Leasing Association of America at 4301 North Fairfax Drive, Suite 550, Arlington, VA 22203 (telephone: 703-527-8655; Web site: www. elaonline.com).

Government Financing Programs

Besides institutional and noninstitutional sources of capital, you have access to a wide array of government financing programs designed to help small businesses. Because small businesses play a central role in creating new jobs, federal, state, and local governments offer a variety of financing programs. Most of these programs are sponsored by the federal government's Small Business Administration (SBA). State and local governments also offer financial incentives to new businesses that will create local employment. For the entrepreneur and small business owners, these programs can be a very attractive source of low cost financing for their business.

SMALL BUSINESS ADMINISTRATION LOAN PROGRAMS

The SBA offers a variety of loan-financing options for small businesses. These options primarily use guarantees of loans through private-sector lenders, including commercial banks and commercial finance companies. The SBA has three categories of lenders: regular, certified, and preferred.

With *regular lenders,* the SBA holds full authority for approving guaranteed loans. The SBA may qualify its most active and expert lenders under the SBA's Certified and Preferred Lenders Program. Under this program, the SBA delegates partial or full authority to approve loans, which results in faster service. *Preferred lenders* are chosen from among the SBA's best lenders and enjoy full delegation of lending authority. *Certified lenders* are those that have been heavily involved in regular SBA loan-guarantee processing and have met certain other requirements. Certified lenders account for 10 percent of the dollar volume of all SBA loan guarantees.

The SBA-guarantee program offers both short-term and long-term loans. Short-term loans usually mature in one year or less. These include working-capital loans, accounts-receivable loans, and lines of credit. Long-term loans are used for major business expenditures, such as purchasing real estate and facilities, construction, durable equipment, furniture and fixtures, and vehicles. The SBA loan-guarantee programs cover a wide range of loan types. The 7(a) Loan Guarantee Program includes general short- and long-term 7(a) loans and several specialized loan programs. The 7(m) MicroLoan Program makes very small loans to small businesses. The 504 Certified Development Company Program enables lenders to make larger, longer-term loans to small businesses with SBA-guaranteed debentures. In addition, the Surety Bond Program guarantees bonds for small contractors.

The 7(a) Loan Program

In the 7(a) Loan Guarantee Program, the SBA's primary loan program, the SBA guarantees major portions of loans made to small businesses by financial institutions.

KEY POINT: An SBA guarantee reduces the lender's risk. It thus allows the lender to provide financing on reasonable terms to businesses to which it otherwise would not lend.

The borrower may use a 7(a) loan for a variety of purposes, including expanding or renovating facilities; purchasing machinery, equipment, fixtures, and household improvements; financing receivables and augmenting working capital; constructing commercial buildings; and purchasing land and buildings. In certain circumstances, a 7(a) loan also may be used to refinance existing debt. The maximum loan available under the 7(a) program is $2 million, with a maximum SBA guarantee of $1 million.

The process begins when a small business submits its loan application to a lender for review. Bank documentation requirements vary from bank to bank, but they are generally similar to the loan application requirements discussed earlier for regular commercial loans. A prospective borrower must provide a description of the purpose of the loan, the history of the business, personal resumes of the owners and management, three years of financial statements, a schedule of term debt, and an aging of accounts receivable and payable. New businesses submit a projected opening day balance sheet, lease details, the amount of the owner's investment in the business, projections of income, expenses, and cash flow, and the owner's signed personal financial statements. The lender reviews the application and decides if the applicant merits a loan on its own or if it requires the additional support of an SBA guarantee.

If the lender approves the loan subject to an SBA guarantee, the lender sends a copy of the application and a credit analysis to the nearest SBA office. The SBA then decides whether to guarantee the loan to the lender. In guaranteeing the loan, the SBA assures the lender that the government will reimburse the lending institution for its loss up to the amount of the guarantee if the borrower does not repay the loan. The SBA charges the lender a small fee to provide the guarantee, a cost the lender may pass on to the borrower.

▶ **IMPORTANT: To qualify for an SBA guarantee, a small business must meet the 7(a) criteria *and* the lender must certify it could not provide funding on reasonable terms without an SBA guarantee. The criteria the SBA looks for in guaranteeing a loan include:**

➤ Good character, management expertise, and the personal commitment necessary for success
➤ Sufficient funds, including the SBA-guaranteed loan, to operate the business on a sound financial basis (for new businesses, this includes the resources to withstand start-up expenses and the initial operating phase)
➤ Feasible business plan
➤ Adequate equity or investment in the business
➤ Sufficient collateral

➤ Ability to repay the loan on time from the projected operating cash flow

Besides meeting these criteria, the borrower must pledge sufficient assets (to the extent that they are reasonably available) to secure the loan adequately. Personal guarantees are required from all the principal owners of the business, and liens on personal assets of the principals also may be required. However, the SBA might not reject the application because of lack of collateral if the other approval criteria are met. After the SBA approves the guarantee, the lender closes the loan and disburses the funds. The borrower must then make monthly loan payments directly to the lender. As with any loan, the borrower is responsible for repaying the full amount of the loan. The time allowed for repayment of the loan varies depending on the nature of the loan. Similarly, the interest rate may be fixed or variable, depending on the loan.

Special 7(a) Loan Programs

There are four special loan programs under the general 7(a) loan category:

1. The CAPLines program
2. The Export Working Capital program
3. The International Trade Loan program
4. The DELTA program

➤ QUICK OVERVIEW: (1) The CAPLines program is designed to help small businesses meet short-term and seasonal working-capital needs. (2) The Export Working Capital Program serves the working-capital needs of small-business exporters. (3) The International Trade Loan can be used by small businesses that either are preparing to engage or are engaged in international trade or have been adversely affected by competition from imports. (4) The DELTA (Defense Loan and Technical Assistance) program provides financial and technical assistance to small-business defense contractors adversely affected by defense cuts to help them diversify into commercial markets.

---

1. Of the special 7(a) loan programs, the CAPLines program has the broadest applicability across the range of small businesses. The five types of available loans are seasonal lines, contract lines, builder's lines, standard asset-based lines, and small asset-based lines. A *seasonal line* is a revolving or nonrevolving line of credit that advances funds against inventory and receivables to balance seasonal sales fluctuations. A *contract line* is a revolving or nonrevolving line of credit that funds the direct labor and material costs involved in performing assignable contracts. A *builder's line* is a

revolving or nonrevolving line of credit that funds the direct labor and material costs associated with constructing or renovating commercial or residential buildings with the building project normally serving as collateral for the loan.

The *standard asset-based line* is generally used by businesses that provide credit to other businesses. These businesses continually draw on the asset-based revolving line based on their existing assets (such as accounts receivable) and repay the asset-based lender as these assets are converted into cash. The standard asset-based line normally requires continual monitoring and servicing of the collateral (usually accounts receivable of the business).

Under all of the four CAPLine programs described above, a borrower may borrow up to $1 million with the SBA guaranteeing 75 percent. The fifth CAPLine program, the *small asset-based line,* operates like the standard asset-based line except that some servicing requirements are waived, but the maximum loan is $200,000. All five types of CAPLines can have a maturity of up to five years and an interest rate up to 2.25 percent over prime. The actual maturity and interest rate are negotiated with the lender. The collateral is usually the asset being financed.

2. Under the Export Working Capital Program (EWCP), a small-business exporter may borrow up to $1 million to fund short-term working-capital needs, with the SBA guaranteeing 90 percent. EWCP loan maturities typically either match a single transaction cycle or support a line of credit for 12 months. The EWCP uses a one-page application form and streamlined documentation. Turnaround is usually within ten days. Interest rates and fees are fully negotiable between the lender and the borrower.

3. Small businesses involved in international trade or adversely affected by imports can get an SBA guarantee for as much as $1.25 million in a combined working-capital and fixed-asset loan under the International Trade Loan Program. Loans for working capital may be made for up to three years. Loans for facilities and equipment, to purchase land and buildings, building new facilities, renovating, improving, and expanding existing facilities, and purchasing and reconditioning machinery, equipment, and fixtures, may be made for up to 25 years. The facilities and equipment must be located in the United States, its territories, and possessions.

4. The DELTA program applies only to a few firms that meet the 7(a) eligibility requirements. To qualify for the DELTA program, the small business must have derived at least 25 percent of its total revenues from Department of Defense contracts, defense-related contracts with the Department of Energy, or subcontracts in support of defense-

related prime contracts. In addition, it must meet at least one of three criteria:

1. Be adversely affected by reduced defense spending and use the loan to retain jobs of defense workers.
2. Be located in an adversely impacted community and create new economic activity and jobs.
3. Use the loan to diversify operations while remaining available as a defense contractor.

The principal benefit of the DELTA program is that the maximum 7(a) loan is increased to $1.25 million.

The SBA MicroLoan Program

Under the SBA's MicroLoan Program, the SBA lends money to qualified locally based nonprofit organizations, which use the SBA funds to make loans to new and existing small businesses. A small business can borrow up to $35,000 from the nonprofit intermediary, which also provides management and technical help to the small business. The average loan under the MicroLoan program is $10,500. Interest rates on MicroLoans vary depending on the lending intermediary, but they are usually competitive with other interest rates. MicroLoan proceeds may be used for working capital and to purchase inventory, supplies, furniture, fixtures, machinery, and equipment.

> **KEY POINT: Almost any type of small business is eligible for the Micro-Loan Program. The business must meet the SBA size standards for a small business at the time of application, but the form of business (sole proprietorship, partnership, or corporation) is seldom an eligibility factor.**

The MicroLoan applicant must normally meet the credit requirements of their nonprofit intermediary lender. The intermediary also sets the loan's collateral requirements. Loans are at least partially collateralized by equipment, contracts, inventory, and other property. Sometimes, the intermediary lender also may require a personal guarantee from the borrower.

The 504 Certified Development Company Program

The 504 Certified Development Company Program helps small, growing businesses create and retain jobs by helping them get long-term, fixed-rate financing for major fixed assets, such as land and buildings.

The program is administered through special-purpose finance companies called certified development companies (CDCs). A CDC is a non-profit corporation set up to contribute to the economic development of its community or region. CDCs work with the SBA and private-sector lenders to provide financing to small businesses.

> **KEY POINT: Section 504 loans must be used for fixed-asset projects such as purchasing land and improvements (including existing buildings), grading, street improvements, utilities, parking lots, and landscaping; construction of new facilities or modernizing, renovating, and converting existing facilities; and purchasing machinery or equipment.**

Typically, 504-project financing includes:

➤ A loan from a private-sector lender secured by a senior lien, providing up to 50 percent of the project cost

➤ An SBA-100-percent-guaranteed debenture from the CDC secured by a junior lien, providing up to 40 percent of the project cost to a maximum of $1.3 million

➤ A contribution of at least 10 percent equity by the borrower

As a rule, no collateral is required except the assets of the 504 project being financed.

STATE AND LOCAL GOVERNMENT PROGRAMS

Besides the special small-business financing programs of the federal government, there are many special financing programs offered by the 50 states and local city and county governments.

These programs are intended to simulate the growth of small businesses and the jobs they create in the sponsor's jurisdiction. State and local governments know that a vibrant small business sector is essential to maintaining the economic health of their economy and the tax base that supports the government.

State and local programs cover a wide range of needs. They include subsidized loan programs, direct equity investment, tax credits and deductions, and direct grants. The particular program may be targeted at a specific industry, a specific asset class such as manufacturing plants, or may be available to a full spectrum of small business. Most states have some form of economic development agency or finance authority that makes loans or guarantees loans to small business. In addition, many state commerce departments have direct or participating loan programs that may be even more attractive than the SBA-guarantee program. Furthermore, there are often specialized programs designed to help women and minorities.

Case in Point—Virginia: Because of the large number of programs across the 50 states, this Case in Point will review the programs available in Virginia, as an example of the programs available at the state and local level. The Virginia Capital Resources Directory, published by the Virginia Department of Business Assistance, lists more than 70 federal, state, and local government programs available to support Virginia's small businesses. Other states have similar directories.

Virginia is typical of most states in having both programs that provide direct aid to the small business owner and that try to leverage existing federal programs. It is also typical that Virginia uses the existing financial system, particularly commercial banks, to deliver its programs. And, Virginia is also characteristic in its program of funding nonprofit organizations that in turn help small business.

Most of Virginia's small-business financing aid programs are delivered through the Virginia Small Business Financing Authority (VSBFA), an agency of the Commonwealth of Virginia's Department of Business Assistance. The major small-business financing programs supported and managed by the Virginia Small Business Financing Authority include:

➤ The Industrial Development Bond Program
➤ The Loan Guarantee Program
➤ The Economic Development Loan Fund
➤ The Virginia Capital Access Program

The Industrial Development Bond Program arranges for the issuance of tax-exempt industrial development bonds to fund construction of manufacturing facilities for small businesses. A business may raise up to $10,000,000 for a specific facility under this program. The bonds are issued by either the Virginia Small Business Financing Authority or a local industrial development authority within Virginia. The bonds are issued for a specific company, which receives the proceeds of the bonds and is obligated to repay the bonds. The VSBFA or the local industrial development authority guarantees the bonds.

The Loan Guarantee Program guarantees part of a loan or line of credit from a bank to a qualified small Virginia business. Under the program, the guarantee is no more than 75 percent of the loan or line of credit to a maximum of $300,000. The business applies to the bank for the loan, which in turn requests the guarantee from the VSBFA if the small business would not qualify under the bank's normal credit criteria.

The Virginia Economic Development Loan Fund combines federal funding with state funding to help small businesses. The fund uses a combination of funds from the federal Economic Development Administration and the Commonwealth of Virginia. A company building a manufacturing facility in the state can receive up to $1 million and 40 percent of the project cost from the fund.

The Virginia Capital Access Program provides support for banks that lend to high-risk small companies. It insures a portfolio of these loans against loss. The program provides a higher than normal loss reserve for the portfolio, which is paid for by premiums charged to a combination of the borrowers and the VSBFA.

This list of Virginia's small-business financing programs is a sample of the programs available across the country. To find out about similar state and local government programs in your home state or local jurisdiction, you should contact your state's department of commerce or business, the local chamber of commerce, or the local economic development office. Alternatively, you could contact the local office of the Small Business Administration, which normally has information on state and local programs operating in its area.

Finding Financing

Although financing a small, growing company is a challenge, you should also explore many nonequity alternatives. Often the most efficient solution is a combination of sources. For example, because most governmental programs are delivered through private lenders, you should always ask a financial institution about the types of government programs it offers when discussing a financial need. Funds can be drawn from some financial sources with little formality, such as arranging extended trade payables. Others require more careful planning, such as a bank loan (with or without an SBA guarantee). For these sources, the more carefully you plan the presentation, the more likely the response will be a favorable one. In addition, developing a careful preparation is apt to help you learn more about the business.

CHAPTER 10

EQUITY FINANCING FOR THE COMPANY

During the late 1990s, entrepreneurs whose businesses required more growth capital than they could raise from nonequity sources enjoyed a bonanza of private-equity financing. Early successes in the telecommunications and Internet businesses, together with promising biotech developments, encouraged investors to make major commitments to venture-capital funds. Venture-capital investments rose 1500 percent, from $6.3 billion in 1995 to $89.8 billion in 2000. This, in turn, encouraged angel investors to fund early-stage companies because they had confidence the third- and fourth-round financing could be obtained.

The pop of the high-tech bubble in 2000, however, dramatically cut the volume of venture-capital investments. They fell to only $21.2 billion in 2002, still a respectable figure but far less than the peak period. This, in turn, made angel investors more cautious and selective. Nevertheless, because of the major reduction in venture-capital sources, angel financing is now the major source of private equity funds for the rapidly growing enterprise.

This chapter discusses the nature of angel financing, including an identification of the major categories of angels and the nature of their relationships with their investments. Venture capital will be briefly discussed, along with valuation and the types of return early-stage investors have to expect before they consider funding a company.

The Private Equity Capital Market

The distinction between the public and private capital markets in the United States is a legal fiction created by the Securities and Exchange Commission (SEC). As the law is written, virtually any financial transaction could be classified as a public issue and require arduous registration procedures. Because of the clear burden this would place on the flow of funds, the SEC has created a variety of classifications that allow transactions, such as bank loans and accounts receivable, to be considered private ones. (The rules related to private transactions are discussed in Chapter 2.)

> **KEY POINT: A *private company* is a company that has no publicly offered securities requiring full registration with the SEC. A *private offering* is the effort to sell a *security* that is not being publicly offered and therefore does not need to be registered with the SEC.**

The private capital market in the United States finances all the unregistered securities in the country. An overwhelming number of companies in the United States are private, and an overwhelming number of securities offerings are private offerings. This private capital market is heavily oriented toward smaller companies, which are the largest number of issuers.

Investors in the private capital markets can be divided into two groups: individual investors and institutional investors. Investing directly into companies by individuals is known as the *informal* venture-capital market. Investing through financial intermediaries is known as the *formal* venture-capital market. Individual investors invest both directly in companies and through financial intermediaries, with direct investing predominating. Institutional investors usually invest through financial intermediaries, primarily venture-capital limited partnerships, although they also directly invest in companies. Individual investors typically finance firms in their early stage, before they have significant sales. Formal venture capitalists typically finance later-stage firms, after their idea has been rewarded by the marketplace with orders.

ANGEL FINANCING: THE INFORMAL VENTURE-CAPITAL MARKET

Individual investors in the private capital market fall into two categories: angel investors and individual participants. The two categories are differentiated by the degree the investor participates in the company's affairs, the size of the minimum investment, and the number of investors involved in the company. An *angel investor* generally makes a substantial investment in an individual company, the company is closely held by a few owners, and the angel plays an active role in the management of the company. *Individual participants* in the informal private-equity market (as opposed to angels) tend to make smaller investments in several companies. They co-invest with other individuals and institutions to create more shareholders than is typical for an angel-funded company. They usually play no role in the management of the company. Individual participants are typically brought into the company by a licensed broker, who shops the company's securities on a best-efforts basis. The angel investor is the key type of individual investor for the entrepreneur and small business owner.

> **KEY POINT: Angel financing is the most significant form of financing for startup and early-stage companies—other than funds provided by the founders, friends, and families of the founders.**

There is no standard definition of an angel investor. The most widely accepted one is that angels are financially sophisticated, wealthy individuals, with net worths exceeding $1 million, who invest their funds on a part-time basis in startup or early-stage ventures. Surveys of angels have shown that they are middle-aged (average age of 47), experienced entrepreneurs with advanced education, whose wealth is partly derived from one or more successful entrepreneurial ventures.

The primary screening criterion for angel investments is whether the angel or an associate of the angel knows and trusts the entrepreneur. Angels typically invest in companies in an industry with which the angel is familiar and are located near the angel's home (one hour's driving time is the standard radius). The businesses appear to have high growth potential, proven management, and sufficient available information for the angel to assess the company's value. Because angel investment is private and not publicly reported, the total size of the angel market is not easy to find out. The Small Business Administration recently estimated that 250,000 individual private investors annually put $20 billion in early-stage companies.*

Besides money, angel investors often provide active assistance to the companies in which they invest. This can include technical and marketing help, advice on strategy, financing, and recruiting, and assistance with equity offerings and acquisitions. An angel also brings an extensive external contact network, including potential customers, vendors, and financing institutions. Because venture capitalists usually fund businesses a bit later in their development than angels, generally after one or more angels have invested in the business, angels play a critical role in screening the one million annual startups in the economy. Their participation is critical in determining which businesses will evolve to the more exclusive realm of formal venture capital.

Characteristics of Different Types of Angels

Angels fall into several broad classifications based on their experience and motivation in making investments. The four basic types of individual angel investors are value-oriented, deep-pocket investors, partner investors, barter investors, and socially responsible investors.

The basic types of angels vary in their degree of focus on return versus having fun and doing good. Value-oriented, deep-pocketed investors are the most focused on return. Socially responsible investors are least focused on return on investment. Rather, the socially responsible investor seeks the highest level of personal satisfaction and psychological rewards, which are least important to the value-oriented investor.

Value-oriented, deep-pocket investors are the most frequent and prominent type of angel investor, although most angels have a mixture of motivations that includes at least traces of all characteristics. Value-oriented investors seek attractive investments offering returns in the 50 percent

* Longe, Julian, Leleux, Benoît, and Bernard Surlemont. "Angel Networks for the 21st Century." *The Journal of Private Equity,* Spring 2003.

range. They usually bring both substantial capital and practical business experience to the investment process. The practical business experience often comes from successful careers as entrepreneurs who built and sold at least one company or from careers as investment bankers. These angels want to be involved in the business, to have fun in the business, but not to run the business because they often make investments in several companies. They are quite willing to have their equity diluted as necessary to finance rapid, profitable growth. They have little emotional hesitation about selling the company to capture their profits.

Partner investors are usually buyers in disguise. Partner investors would typically prefer to purchase a company but lack the financial resources to do so. Often partner investors are affluent senior executives or former business owners re-entering the workforce and buying their last job. Consequently, these investors usually have a very high need for control and often want to be president of the company in which they invest. These individuals will normally invest in only one company at a time and expect to be deeply involved in its operation. They will be willing to sell the company if the sale generates enough capital for them to buy another business. Partner angels may, however, become attached to the operation and be reluctant to give up their chief-executive position. They also may offer the entrepreneur a way to exit the business, as discussed in Chapters 11 and 12.

Barter investors provide their investment in kind rather than in cash, usually offering goods and services the company would otherwise purchase with cash. These individuals want to invest in early-stage ventures and to participate in the company and provide management assistance. A business incubator (discussed in Chapter 9), which provides office or other types of space and a variety of associated business services in return for equity in an early-stage investment, is the classic barter investor.

Socially responsible investors want to associate with individuals with high social and moral values in ventures addressing social needs. These investors seek a reasonable return, 10 to 15 percent, on an investment that supports their social values. They often enjoy inherited as opposed to earned wealth. They usually want to be involved in the venture but do not have the business experience and savvy that successful entrepreneurs provide. They are also likely to be distracted by many social obligations that make it difficult to devote extended periods to the investment's operation. They may, however, have an excellent network of contacts.

In addition to these types of angel investors, there is the family angel investor. The family pools its resources and selects an astute, trusted, skilled family member to coordinate the investment effort. A family angel investor is very common in the Asian-American community.

What Angels Look for in an Investment

Although angels invest early in a business's development, they look first and foremost to invest in a business, not an idea, and in a business with significant potential.

The typical angel invests between $25,000 and $250,000 in companies needing $50,000 to $1 million. The angel usually wants an expected return between 10 percent and 15 percent above the Standard & Poor's 500's return on equity. The typical holding period for an angel investment is five to seven years. Most angel investors make only one investment a year, although some may make four or more.

Angels also often want to have intangible rewards from their investment because they typically already have enough net worth to ensure their comfort. Thus, enjoyment of their involvement with the business and the investment process is often as important as the return on their money. Intangible rewards for angel investors—in different proportions depending on their type—include being active and involved in businesses they know and in which they are interested, being intellectually stimulated by new ideas and new technology, and being socially responsible.

This means that their evaluation of the business includes a determination of whether the business's product or service is something they can identify with and get excited about. Angels therefore might invest in a business developing a new cure for cancer even though the expected return may be far in the future. Angels, however, are unlikely to invest in nursing homes or funeral homes although these might promise handsome profits much sooner than the cancer investment.

At the same time, part of the fun for most angel investors comes from the satisfaction of making smart investments, so they critically analyze a company, looking for certain characteristics that suggest business success. These include:

1. A proprietary advantage in a unique technology that can act as a barrier to entry
2. Presence in a fast-growing market
3. Absence of entrenched players
4. A quality management team as shown by its competence and past track record, perseverance and desire to succeed, and financial commitment

Typically, angels fund the people, not the business plan. Thus, a lack of mutual respect, weak credentials, or a management team's limited track record can kill an angel's interest. Similarly, angel investors are unlikely to invest if they cannot understand the company's technology or its market. Finally, if the entrepreneur unrealistically overvalues the venture, the angel might reject the investment.

How Angel Financings Are Organized

Although formal introduction channels are growing, most angels appear to rely on informal networking through friends, family, other investors, and business associates to find potential deals. This practice limits typical angels to investments located near their homes, within reach of their informal networks. The limitation may be unfortunate when there is a regional mismatch between angels and opportunities, but it is consistent with the desire of many angels to have convenient investments in which they can be actively involved.

A recent development in angel financing has been the growth of *angel funds* or *structured angel investing*. These offer a way to overcome the individual angel's limits in generating deal flow, in monitoring and advising companies in which they invest, and in diversifying their investments over more companies. In angel funds, 10 to 75 individuals join forces to pool their capital in a common investment fund. The fund provides investment cash, and the angels provide advice to portfolio companies. The angel investors in the fund sit on the company boards, allocating their time to selected portfolio companies. This division of labor puts angels on all boards without every angel's having to serve on all of them.

Because they represent a larger fund than a single individual angel investor could deploy, angel funds find it much easier to attract a deal flow than a single investor does. Similarly, pooling the angels' expertise and focusing that expertise on selected portfolio companies where it will have the most impact improves the angels' monitoring and advising functions. Moreover, the arrangement makes it easy to call on nonboard members of the angel group if their particular specialty is needed. Finally, by pooling their funds, the angels can diversify their portfolios by having smaller investments in more individual companies.

Although they are a type of early-stage venture fund, angel funds differ in two ways from the usual early-stage fund. First, the partners in the angel fund are seldom full-time investors. Second, the partners are investing their own funds and not funds they have raised from institutional investors. The larger angel funds often have a full-time professional manager who handles administrative functions. The manager, however, does not make the investment decisions or monitor the portfolio companies.

Common Pitfalls of Angel Investing

From the investor's perspective, angel investing—that is, direct investment in a startup or early stage company—is fraught with a variety of risks not associated with an investment in a public company. Even experienced angel investors sometimes find themselves tripped up by pitfalls that only apply to early-stage, private companies.

The most common pitfall is being locked into a company with no attractive way out of the investment. An investment with this characteristic is called a member of the "living dead." From the investor's standpoint, this is a form of financial purgatory. The second most common pitfall is investing in a company whose management proves unable to handle the firm's growth, requiring the angel to save the company and the investment. This experience is often a painful one and sometimes costly as well.

To increase the likelihood of a liquidity event, experienced angel investors often insist on special provisions in their stock purchase agreement providing them with a variety of ways to exit the company. Because of the risk of failure by the company's management after the angel has invested, angel investors also seek provisions that allow them to change company management or takeover the company. (These provisions are reviewed in Chapter 2.)

From the company's standpoint, an angel investment can be a blessing or a curse. From a financial standpoint, an angel's equity investment has the pluses and minuses of equity generally. The pluses include the benefit of growth capital without the fixed expense of debt service, the maintenance of financial flexibility to allow borrowing for other opportunities, and access to capital earlier in the company's life cycle than would be otherwise possible. The minuses include a high cost of capital—the angel provides capital expecting a return greater than 30 percent—and the dilution of existing shareholders.

There also can be blessings or curses in the nonfinancial, personal relationship between the angel and the company. Much depends on the angel, the angel's background, and the angel's motivation. Besides cash, the blessings the angel can bestow on a company include valuable contacts and valuable advice, particularly if the angel is an experienced entrepreneur with a background in the company's industry. The angel's investment can be a curse if the angel's personality clashes with the company management's or if there are serious differences over the direction the company should take. This conflict can be particularly difficult if there are differences over such issues as bringing in additional investors or the potential sale of the company.

experiences. Partner investors have a very strong tendency to be micro-managers.

ORGANIZED PRIVATE EQUITY: THE FORMAL VENTURE-CAPITAL MARKET

The organized private-equity market includes the formal venture-capital market together with direct investment by institutional investors in private companies. The formal venture-capital industry consists of firms and organizations that professionally manage and invest in private small and emerging companies. Included in the industry are Small Business Investment Companies and private venture-capital firms.

Small Business Investment Companies

Licensed and regulated by the federal government's Small Business Administration (SBA), Small Business Investment Companies (SBICs) are private, for-profit investment firms. SBICs provide equity capital, long-term loans, and management assistance to qualifying small businesses. They make these venture-capital investments with their own funds plus funds obtained by borrowing at favorable rates with an SBA guarantee. There are two types of SBICs—original, or regular, SBICs and Specialized Small Business Investment Companies (SSBICs). SSBICs are specifically targeted toward the needs of entrepreneurs who have been denied the opportunity to own and operate a business because of social or economic disadvantage. With a few exceptions, the same rules and regulations apply to both "regular" SBICs and SSBICs. The principal difference between regular SBICs and SSBICs is that SSBICs receive additional help from the SBA to support their mission of financing entrepreneurs suffering from a social or economic disadvantage.

SBIC financing is specifically tailored to the needs of each small business. An SBIC can lend money to a small business, make an equity investment in it, or both. However, in making their investment decisions, SBICs strongly prefer equity investments and use the same analysis as purely private equity investors. They generally require the entrepreneur to provide a business plan, which they evaluate in the same way other venture capitalists do. An SBIC, however, is limited in how much of its funds it can invest in any one small business. Without written approval of the SBA, an SBIC cannot invest more than 20 percent of its private capital in securities, commitments, and guarantees of any one small business. (For SSBICs, the limit is 30 percent.) Moreover, under normal circumstances, an SBIC must hold less than half the equity in a company. Compared with other segments of the capital markets, the SBIC industry is small. Nevertheless, because of their focus on the equity needs of small and growing businesses, SBICs are an important segment of the financial service industry. The SBIC program fills the funding gap for younger and smaller new businesses, particularly those that are not high-technology based or are not located in the traditional venture-capital strongholds. Unlike other professional venture capitalists, SBIC investments are not concentrated in high-technology investment. Only one-quarter of the SBIC investments are in high-technology companies. Over half the SBIC-backed companies are located outside high-volume venture-capital areas such as "Silicon Valley" in California or the "Route 128 Circle" in Massachusetts. SBICs tend to make investments in the $300,000 to $5 million range. With an average investment size of slightly over $1 million and median investment size of closer to $700,000, SBICs provide critical smaller amounts of venture capital that their larger private-equity counterparts do not.

❯ KEY POINT: For many entrepreneurs and small business owners, SBICs present the best opportunity for getting a formal venture-capital investment in their company.

Banks play a very significant role in the SBIC program. Because banking regulations limited banks' ability to make equity investments except through an SBIC subsidiary, SBICs provide an attractive avenue for banks to make venture investments and to enhance the equity of firms to which they wished to lend. A bank can invest up to 5 percent of its capital and surplus in partially or wholly owned SBICs. Some banks have established and run their own SBICs; others have simply invested in SBICs with other private investors. Overall, bank-owned SBICs account for about half the SBIC capital and are the biggest source of capital for the SBIC program.

Private-Venture Capital

From the late 1950s, with the passage of the Small Business Investment Company Act of 1958, to the late 1970s, SBICs dominated the formal venture-capital industry in the United States. Then the passage of the Employee Retirement Income Security Act (ERISA) in 1974 changed the environment by allowing private pension plans to invest up to 10 percent of their assets in venture capital. This landmark legislation fueled the growth of the private venture-capital industry in the United States through the 1980s and 1990s.

Because they occupy the high ground of the private-capital investment process, venture-capital investments receive much attention from the press. This press coverage masks the reality that formal venture-capital investment occupies a very select niche in the panorama of private capital, both in the relative number of companies that receive venture-capital funding and in the specific industries for which formal venture-capital provides funds.

❯ KEY POINT: Formal venture capital is invested in about 2,500 companies annually in the United States. These companies are overwhelmingly

in high-technology industries, with information technology and medical technology (including biotechnology and drugs) being the primary industries receiving this investment.

Formal venture capitalists prefer to invest in small companies that are already established and in which others have already invested rather than in brand new business startups. Generally, less than 5 percent of annual venture capital investment goes to startups. The real role that formal venture capital plays is to fund a company as it begins to commercialize its innovation. Venture-capital money goes predominantly into the expenses (manufacturing, marketing, and sales) and assets (fixed assets and working capital) required to commercialize innovations and grow the business. Venture capital fills the void in a company's development between the time the R&D is completed and the company becomes eligible for institutional lenders and public-market equity financing.

Once they have invested, venture capitalists actively work with the company's management by contributing business experience and industry knowledge gained from helping other young companies. During the first few years, before significant revenues are generated, about two-thirds of the average venture-capital-backed company's total equity is supplied by venture financing. The average U.S. venture-backed company raises about $16 million of venture capital during its first five years.

From your standpoint, a venture-capital investment has both positive and negative aspects. Positive elements include substantial amounts of hard-to-get equity capital, credibility in the marketplace with other financing sources such as commercial banks, a broad range of helpful contacts, and professional advice and expertise on issues relating to your company's growth including advice about raising additional capital. On the negative side, the types of deals venture capitalists normally seek can have substantial adverse impact on the company's capital structure. You and the other existing owners may have to give up elements of control and future upside gains, sacrifices that are the normal result of an equity financing. In addition, the firm may lose some of its flexibility and increase its risk, the normal results of a debt financing.

Direct Investment

Direct investment is carried out by both nonfinancial corporations and financial institutions. Nonfinancial corporations typically invest in private capital through their own direct venture-capital programs. They normally invest in risky early-stage developmental ventures that fit their strategic objectives. Industries with the most active private-capital investment by nonfinancial corporations include the medical and health care, industrial products, chemicals, and electronics and communications industries.

The Search Process
for Equity Capital

The first step in the search process for equity capital is to develop a business plan that explains your company, its direction, and its financial needs to prospective investors (either angels or formal venture capital companies). Most standard business plans:

> ➤ Describe the company's products and technology
> ➤ Explain the company's markets including the competition
> ➤ Include financial statements and projections
> ➤ Detail the amount of capital being raised and explain how it will be spent
> ➤ Present the background of key managers and directors

Many elements of a standard business plan for financing purposes are the same as those required for a loan proposal discussed in Chapter 9. You can also find guidance in preparing a business plan in a variety of special books on this subject, such as the one by Joseph Mancuso listed in the Suggestions for Further Reading at the end of this book.

Sources of equity capital, however, are generally not as visible as banks. Thus, the next step in the process, finding an equity source to present the plan to, is often quite difficult. The difficulty has increased since the technology bubble burst.

FINDING VENTURE CAPITAL

Although you may be familiar with the major sources and characteristics of private equity and formal venture capital, actually finding real investors who will invest in the company is a difficult and time-consuming process. Normally, entrepreneurs and small business owners must themselves perform the search for angel investors or formal venture-capital investors. A risk is that this effort will distract you from the demands of managing the business. If it does, the consequences can be very serious. Angel investors lose interest quickly in a management that fails to perform.

> **KEY POINT: You may find an angel directly by contacting an individual angel you know either through past association or learn of by networking with friends and business associates.**

For many new angels, generating deal flow can be a significant problem. They therefore try to make themselves visible by offering to mentor local entrepreneurs, writing articles about venture investing for local publications, and by teaching evening courses on entrepreneurship. An angel also may be found through a formal introduction channel, such as angel clubs and funds, venture forums, venture fairs, broker-dealers specializing in these types of investments, private-investor networks, and online matching services. Bankers and local officers of the SBA are often familiar with these formal introduction channels and can direct the entrepreneur to them. In addition, links to regional angel networks can be found on the Web site of the Angel Organization Summit (www.angel-summit.org).

To find an SBIC that might be interested in investing in your company, consult your bank because many banks own or have invested in an SBIC. Even if the bank does not have its own SBIC, bank loan officers are often familiar with SBICs operating in their area. Alternatively, you may contact the National Association of Small Business Investment Companies (NASBIC) in Washington, DC. NASBIC publishes a directory of SBICs and can provide other information on the SBIC program. Its address is NASBIC, 666 11th Street NW, Suite 750, Washington, DC 20001 (telephone: 202-628-5055; Web site: www.nasbic.org). Information is also available at the SBA Web site (www.sba.gov).

Formal venture capitalists are listed in published directories of venture capitalists or can be located by contacting venture-capital associations, such as the Mid-Atlantic Venture Capital Association for the Washington-Baltimore region, the National Association of Seed Venture Funds for smaller venture funds, and the National Venture Capital Association for larger venture-capital organizations. In addition, many Web-search services include a heading for venture capital sources. The Mid-Atlantic Venture Capital Association may be contacted through its Web site (www.mava.org). The National Association of Seed Venture Funds is at 301 Northwest 63 Street, Suite 500, Oklahoma City, OK 73116 (telephone: 405-843-6550; Web site: www.nasvf.org). The National Venture Capital Association headquarters is at 1655 North Fort Myer Drive, Suite 850, Arlington, Virginia 22209-3114 (telephone: 703-524-2549; Web site: www.nvca.org). Entrepreneurs with early-stage companies will find it more productive to contact regional venture organizations or the NASVF.

❯ SMART MOVE: In the search for potential investors, small companies should explore the services offered by investment bankers. Investment bankers operating in the private-equity investment area provide two services for issuing companies. First, the investment banker identifies potential private-placement sources. Second, investment bankers represent client firms to potential investors and use their market knowledge to get better terms for their clients. If the smaller firm or early-stage firm is to get investment banking help, it must locate small, regional, boutique investment banking firms that have a practice in arranging venture-capital investments. (Major investment banks do not serve smaller companies because it is not profitable for them.) It is also important to check the

---

Structuring the Deal

A venture investment may be structured in a variety of ways, singly or in combination, including common stock, preferred stock, convertible-preferred stock, debt, convertible debt, and royalty payments. The investor's goal in structuring an investment is to control the investment's risk and to enhance the chances of recovering the value invested.

The investment contract that accompanies an equity investment in a small company by an angel investor or venture capitalist is typically lengthy, with many terms and conditions normally designed to protect the investor. The key documents involved are the *term sheet* or *investment memorandum,* the *stock-purchase contract,* and the *offering memorandum.* These documents create the foundation and structure of the typical venture-capital deal.

After a period of negotiation, you and potential venture capitalists must agree on certain basic principles of the deal if the transaction is to take place. The *letter of understanding* outlining these principles is called a *term sheet, investment memorandum,* or *letter of intent.* It is not legally binding, but it usually forms the framework for the definitive binding stock-purchase agreement. The term sheet defines:

- ➤ The parties involved
- ➤ The amount of financing
- ➤ The choice of a particular security type (such as convertible-preferred stock) and its special features (such as dividends, liquidation preference, and redemption rights)
- ➤ The price of the security
- ➤ The number of units of the security to be issued
- ➤ The closing date

➤ **KEY POINT: The issuance of a term sheet by the venture capitalist means the venture capitalist is highly likely to make an investment.**

Venture investors typically buy their stock from the company itself through a *stock-purchase agreement* or contract. As discussed in Chapter 2, this contract lists the terms under which the venture investors are purchasing the stock being offered by the company and the ongoing rights they will have after the purchase has been completed. These terms generally include:

- The amount and timing of the investment
- The terms of the convertible security such as conversion price (which can vary depending on the company's performance)
- Liquidation preference (including a description of the events that can trigger liquidation)
- Dividend rate
- Payment terms
- Voting rights

An *offering memorandum* is needed when one venture-capital company syndicates (that is, sells portions of) an investment to other venture-capital companies. An offering memorandum serves the same purpose as a prospectus in a public offering, but it is not subject to the same legal requirements. An offering memorandum provides potential additional venture-capital investors with information about the company and the investment being offered. The offering memorandum is more similar to a stock analyst's report than to a standard prospectus. It normally includes a description of the company and its prospects, including financial projections, industry trends, and production plans. Because the offering memorandum is normally prepared by sophisticated securities attorneys, they include a variety of disclaimers, particularly of the projections provided in the memorandum.

VENTURE INVESTORS AND THE CONTROL OF RISK

Every investment has risks. Early-stage companies have the same basic risks other investments have except these risks are magnified by the early-stage nature of the company. There are five basic risks that the investor must manage: management, product, market, operations, and financial.

Management risk revolves around the possibility that a cohesive management team cannot be formed. *Product risk* relates to the possibility that the product will not work. *Market risk* is the possibility that the market will not accept the product. *Operations risk* stems from the possibility that even if the market accepts the product, the company cannot produce the product in the volume and quality that the market requires. And, *financial risk* derives from the accuracy of the company's projected capital requirements and the chance that the amounts projected will not be sufficient for the company to survive.

Venture investors use a variety of techniques and strategies to manage the risk associated with their early-stage investments. These techniques and strategies fall into five categories:

1. Spreading risk by diversifying investments across a range of companies and sharing investment in an individual company with other investors
2. Screening and analyzing individual deals carefully before investing

3. Negotiating steep discounts from the company valuation offered by the entrepreneur
4. Negotiating terms and conditions coupled with a staged investment schedule to maintain an element of control after the investment is made
5. Monitoring the company continuously after the investment is made

Spreading Risk

Smart venture investors try to diversify investments by making small investments in several companies. According to Benjamin and Margulis, the experience of venture-capital investors with the survival of their portfolio companies has been that a third are a partial or total loss, a third are break even, 20 percent return two to five times the investment, and approximately 9 percent return between five and ten times the investment. Less than 7 percent return more than ten times.[1]

As this record shows, even companies that are carefully screened by full-time investment professional have a high risk of failure. Using a diversified investment approach increases the possibility of an attractive return on a venture investment, even allowing for the failures. Achieving the overall results of a venture-capital portfolio over a five-year period would provide a compound return of 15 to 20 percent on the portfolio. Consequently, most professional venture capitalists use diversification of their investments as their first method to control their risks.

Screening the Deal

While a diversified portfolio is the first line of defense against risk for a venture capitalist, careful screening of the deals being considered for investment is the second. Formal venture-capital firms receive thousands of individual business plans annually. On average, a firm will invest in only about 1 percent of the opportunities presented.

When reviewing business plans, venture capitalists assess the quality of the management team, the competitive position, and the financial prospects of the company. Typical reasons that venture capitalists turn down business plans include a belief that the business concept is not viable, the market is too small to provide a meaningful opportunity for an investor, or the management lacks the capability to execute the plan. You must persuade the potential investor that these conditions do not characterize the enterprise.

VALUING THE COMPANY

Valuation is the central task to be completed before a venture investor makes an investment. Because there is no active secondary market in the

---

1. Gerald A. Benjamin and Joel B. Margulis, *Angel Financing: How to Find and Invest in Private Equity* (New York: Wiley, 2000, p. 185).

stocks of early-stage companies, valuation is a major challenge for both the investor and you. Valuation of an early-stage business is extremely difficult because the company usually has no or a very limited operating history for revenues, expenses, and profits. Furthermore, early-stage businesses usually have limited assets, which put them in a different position than a well-established, existing business with physical assets whose value can be determined by well-defined formulas. Valuation of an early stage business is a highly subjective process with many elements. The assessment must include:

> The experience, track record, commitment, and reliability of your management team
> The size and growth rate of the business's market and the amount of market development required
> The nature of the business (manufacturing, service, or retail)
> The competitive position of the business's product or service
> The nature of additional financing requirements and other investors' responses
> The likelihood of an easy exit

Valuation is generally viewed very differently by you and the investor.

From the investor's standpoint, the lower the valuation, the lower the risk, and the greater the valuation, the higher the risk. Obviously, investors want the lowest valuation in making investments. On the other hand, from your standpoint, the greater the valuation of the company, the lower the company's cost of capital and the higher the total ultimate reward to you and your fellow owner/managers. Consequently, you want the highest valuation possible for the company when determining the share of equity the investor will receive. This difference in viewpoint and the subjective nature of valuation in early-stage investments can make achieving a satisfactory agreement on valuation very difficult.

> KEY POINT: Entrepreneurs typically put great weight on the "sweat" equity (unpaid time and effort) they have put into the business. This perspective focuses on past investment. Investors typically look to the future and the likelihood they can recover their investment and also receive an attractive financial return.

The reality of valuation in a venture investment, particularly for early-stage ventures, is that the investors' viewpoint wins because of the imbalance in the demand and supply of capital. In valuation, the perceived degree of risk is the critical variable. The greater the perceived risk, the higher the expected rate of return investors will demand to compensate for it. Because the rate of return is used to discount the venture's projected income stream, the higher the perceived risk, the lower the valuation, and vice versa. The valuation, in turn, translates into the percentage of the business that must be surrendered for a given sum of money. Therefore, the higher the perceived risk, the greater the percentage share of the business the entrepreneur must give up to get enough money.

The earlier the company's stage of development, the higher the perceived risk. A startup company is perceived as high risk, with investors requiring an expected return of 60 to 100 percent. A company with revenues and profits, but cash poor, is perceived as a medium risk, for which investors expect a return of between 30 and 50 percent. A rapidly growing company with revenues, profits, and adequate cash is considered a low-risk investment and will attract investors if it offers expected returns of 25 to 35 percent. (See Benjamin and Margulis, page 186.) These relationships suggest that negotiations about valuation will revolve around the projected future income of the company, the company's actual record, and the likely liquidation scenario for the company.

Reflecting the relationship between projected income streams and the discount rate applied and the relationship between estimated value and the percentage of a company that must be given up, three basic principals govern valuation. To raise a given amount of capital:

1. The greater the expected value of a venture in the future, the smaller the percentage of a company required to be given up
2. The longer the track record of a new venture, the lower the perceived investment risk and therefore the smaller the percentage of a company that must be given up
3. The shorter the expected period until liquidation, the lower the perceived risk and the smaller the percentage of a company that must be given up

There are several truisms in the valuation process:

➤ Investors usually do not share the enthusiasm for the enterprise the entrepreneur has and must be convinced of the merits of the opportunity.
➤ Investors are risk-adverse.
➤ Investors always discount projections when evaluating an investment proposal.
➤ Most exits from early-stage investments come from the sale of the company, not from an initial public offering.
➤ Computation of future valuation of the company is irrelevant if the company does not survive.

Consequently, in determining an acceptable valuation, rational investors always focus carefully on the likelihood of the venture's survival.

STAGED FINANCING
AND METHODS OF CONTROL

You want access to sufficient funds to carry the venture from one stage to the next without having to spend time raising money in frequent small amounts, as this is time consuming and therefore expensive. The venture capitalist, on the other hand, prefers to dole cash out only as needed. These diverging interests are often met by arranging for the venture capital to be provided in stages, when prespecified tasks have been accomplished.

For example, if a venture needs $9 million over two years to be ready for a second-stage financing, the venture capitalist might agree to provide the money in thirds. One-third would be paid immediately, one-third when the product has been tested, and one-third when certain sales levels have been reached. If the targets are not reached before the cash runs out, the venture capitalist can either refuse to fund the next stage or renegotiate the proportion of ownership the next cash infusion will receive. The venture capitalist will usually have negotiated the right to make all stages of the investment even if the venture turns out not to need all the funds to meet its objectives. A staged-financing provision often puts higher prices on the equity the company will give up in the later steps.

Along with their concern about investing all their cash up front, venture capitalists have several control concerns when investing in a company. The first is to ensure that investors maintain their ownership share as the company's growth requires bringing in additional investors. Several special features of convertible-preferred stock, including preemptive rights, rights of first refusal, and antidilution rights, are designed to provide this protection. Venture capitalists' second concern is to be sure they have adequate control over the company as it grows. They also want the necessary information to exercise that control effectively. Voting rights, information rights, and inspection rights are designed to meet these needs. Venture capitalists' third concern is to ensure management of the company is properly motivated to act in the venture capitalists' interests. Employment contracts and vesting agreements are used to motivate the desired behavior.

The fourth venture-capitalist concern is to be able to participate effectively in any public offering the company has, so the venture capitalists can get back their investment. Conversion rights, registration rights, co-sale rights, and go-along rights are all designed to meet this concern. The venture capitalists also have to be prepared to get their investment out with some form of return if the company is not successful or its stockholders choose not to take the company public or sell it. Dividend preferences, liquidation preferences, redemption rights, and put-and-call provisions are designed to address this concern.

ONGOING MONITORING AND EXIT

Once venture capitalists have completed an investment in a portfolio company, their attention turns to monitoring the investment to make sure that it performs and planning their eventual exit. Once an investment is made, it is difficult for investors to recover it, even if it is debt, unless the company is successful. Therefore, investors watch their investments so they can exert pressure on management to take timely action to remedy problems. Investors use a variety of approaches to monitor a company, including tracking financial progress through tight controls and strict financial reporting requirements, including monthly financial statements, regular meetings with management, and regular tracking and comparison of performance against business plan objectives.

The stock-purchase agreement's provisions normally anticipate these tasks by including specific details on such topics as board representation, rights to information about the company, voting rights, and registration rights. If the venture capitalists are unable to exit from the company by the usual mechanisms of sale or public offering, special clauses in the stock-purchase agreement often provide a third alternative. Under specific conditions, these terms require the portfolio company to buy out the investors by redeeming their investment according to a valuation formula established when the investment was initially made. Usually, the investors have the right (but not the requirement) to invoke this alternative when the specified conditions exist. Occasionally, the company has the option to buy out the investors under certain conditions.

To monitor their investments, venture capitalists often have representation on the boards of directors of their portfolio companies. A professional investor might serve on the boards of five portfolio companies, spending 100 hours a year on each company in addition to approximately 20 site visits annually and many telephone conversations. In the monitoring and assistance role, venture capitalists will help recruit key individuals and negotiate their compensation, play a major role in raising capital, and help structure mergers and acquisition. The venture capitalists are normally the main source of important contacts for the company, which can range from bankers and accountants to lawyers and technology experts and even to sources for more early-stage funding.

Of all the contacts that venture capitalists provide their portfolio company, the most important is often the introduction to investment bankers. Investment bankers usually provide the mechanism for both the entrepreneur and venture capitalists to make their investments more liquid and for the venture capitalist to exit the company. From a venture capitalist's perspective, there are normally two ways to exit—a sale of their portfolio company to a larger company or a public offering of a company's stock. Investment bankers can help develop both alternatives by identifying potential acquiring companies and by arranging to underwrite public offerings.

Although most venture capitalists exit their portfolio companies through the sale of the company to a larger (and usually public) company, or occasionally must use a forced redemption or put, the initial public offering is the most glamorous exit. It serves as the benchmark for all methods of exit. Investment bankers are indispensable for a public offering. They maintain constant contact between venture capitalists and the capital markets so their advice on the tenor of the market is critical to setting the terms of a successful public offering. Those terms, including a valuation, form the basis for evaluating other exit mechanisms.

> **SMART FINANCIAL MANAGEMENT: The private equity markets are extremely important to you as an entrepreneur and owner of a small, rapidly growing business. Though they are difficult markets for you to access because of the imbalance between supply and demand, accessing them is central to the long-term growth of many promising small businesses. An understanding of the different investors in the private-equity market, and what they look for, can be extremely valuable to you as a small business owner who wants your business to reach its full potential.**

PART IV
GETTING OUT

CHAPTER 11

EXITING THE UNSUCCESSFUL BUSINESS

Every entrepreneur and small business owner starting or taking over a business should realize they will ultimately exit it. Most business owners hope they will retire from their businesses, either by passing it on to a family member or by selling it. In practice, business owners exit their business in a variety of ways, from closing down the unsuccessful business to merging with a major public corporation. Each of the different ways of exiting has a significant financial impact on your personal financial well-being. All will be influenced by how well you use the principles and practices detailed in earlier chapters of this book in managing the day-to-day business.

> **KEY POINT: Exiting a business, whether it was successful or unsuccessful, can be as difficult as or even more difficult than starting the business. The financial decisions are more complicated because you are not starting with a clean slate. The implications of previous decisions, some of which might have been made 30 or 40 years earlier, may constrain your freedom to act. Getting the most value from the process requires advanced planning on many levels with guidance from skilled professionals.**

Part IV of this book deals with exiting your business, whatever the circumstances. This chapter describes how to exit a company that has failed; the following chapter gives you options for exiting a successful company.

In Case of Failure, Know Your Options

Every business starts with the expectation of success. Unfortunately, according to the Small Business Administration, 55 percent of all new businesses are closed within three years of their founding. As noted in Chapter 10, even professional venture capitalists—who select the businesses with the highest potential for their investments—expect a third of their portfolio companies to lose money.

Failure of a small business is not necessarily a reflection on the quality and capability of your management. Economic cycles, market change, technology change, regulatory change, and failure of major suppliers and major customers are all factors beyond your control. All can be the cause of a business's failing.

Consequently, even the most optimistic and capable entrepreneur and small business owner should be aware of the ways to exit an unsuccessful business. These include simply closing the doors and paying off the business obligations, selling the business or assets of the business to another company, or going through a formal bankruptcy process. The size and value of the business's customer base, the value of its tangible and intangible asset base, and the nature of its creditor situation will determine which route you choose.

CLOSING DOWN THE BUSINESS

Most small businesses that fail do not go through a bankruptcy process. A small business that operates on a cash basis, has no significant debts, or both, has no reason to consider using the bankruptcy process. Typically, a business in this category that was financed with equity will just close its doors. After paying its creditors, the residual value of the business will be distributed to the owners.

When a company has significant debt and is not able to meet its financial obligations, the owners or managers of the business will often try to gain a *voluntary arrangement* for a reduction in debt payments. This is an early step in simplifying, closing down the business, or selling it. The arrangement might include changing existing terms such as rescheduling payments to stretch them out (*an extension*), reducing the interest rates, and compromising creditor positions or amounts (*a composition*).

A voluntary settlement buys time for you to close down or sell the business in an orderly manner. The primary advantages you will gain from a voluntary settlement are limiting adverse publicity, allowing for continued business relationships, permitting great flexibility, and requiring lower administrative costs than a court-supervised bankruptcy. Because tax laws require companies to report forgiven debt as income unless they are in bankruptcy, arrangements must be made with an eye to the tax consequences as well as to how they might affect creditors in bankruptcy.

Voluntary restructurings can sometimes be treated as preferences, as defined later in this chapter, and voided if the company ultimately goes into bankruptcy. If a company declares bankruptcy within 90 days of a voluntary agreement, the court may conclude that the compromise was a preference and void it. Another potential problem is that if a group of creditors accepts a voluntary plan but the company later files a bankruptcy petition anyway, the creditors' original claim has been consensually reduced. The reduced amount becomes the basis for further reduction in the subsequent bankruptcy proceedings.

> **WATCH THIS: One creditor that should always be settled with before shutting down the business is the Internal Revenue Service. Although the IRS may negotiate about income taxes, it is particularly severe in recovering employee withholding taxes that were not paid. Because you, the financial officers, and the directors of the business may be personally liable for these taxes, it is always important to make sure that any withholding-tax issues are cleared up with the IRS before closing the doors.**

The five basic steps in a closedown are straightforward:

Step one is to convert as many of the assets of the business as possible into cash, using the cash to pay the liabilities. This is usually accomplished by letting the assets convert into cash in the normal course of the business while avoiding new liabilities. Receivables are collected, inventory sold, employees released, and new purchases avoided.

Step two is to set a formal date for closedown and to notify customers, suppliers, and various legal authorities—such as the IRS.

Step three is a final sale of the noncash, nonliquid assets of the business, such as the remaining inventory and equipment.

Step four is the final closure of the business on its last day, including returning the keys to the landlord if a lease is involved and cutting off the utilities.

Step five is the completion of final tax returns and other legal documents, such as the papers closing the corporation or LLC with appropriate state authorities and the surrender of business licenses to local government authorities.

SALE OF THE BUSINESS OR ITS ASSETS

The owners of a troubled business will often choose to sell it to another company that can take advantage of the troubled company's assets, particularly such intangibles as its customer base and goodwill. Such a sale may provide you more in return for your past sweat equity than a simple closedown. Key considerations in such a sale are the nature of the payment (cash or stock in the acquiring company), the timing of the payment (immediate or deferred), and any contingencies associated with the payment of the purchase price.

The type of payment is extremely important in determining whether sale is preferable to closedown. Cash obviously lets you exit cleanly, but it may subject the transaction to taxes. By accepting stock, you retain some residual risk depending on the strength of the company purchasing the business, the nature of the stock (public versus private company), and the valuation put on the stock versus the purchased business. The payment's timing is also critical. Payment deferred may be payment denied if the purchasing business itself fails later.

> **KEY POINT: In seeking to sell a troubled business as an alternative to closing it down, you should always clarify two key issues: Will the buyer assume the debts of the business? Will the buyer want the seller to finance the sale of the business? A buyer who is unwilling to assume the debts of the business or who wants seller financing does not allow the seller a clean exit. Similarly, if the purchaser requires you to accept payment contingent on the business's subsequent performance and the business is failing, the buyer is essentially asking you to give the business away.**

If a sale is undertaken as a way to close the business, the sale will involve the same considerations as those in the sale of a successful business, as discussed in Chapter 12.

FORMAL BANKRUPTCY: THE PROCESS

When closing down the troubled business or sale of the business are not practical alternatives, you should consider bankruptcy. Bankruptcy in the United States is governed by federal statute and is administered by a special part of the federal court system. The chapters included in the Bankruptcy Reform Act of 1978 that are most applicable to businesses are Chapters 7 (Liquidation) and 11 (Reorganization). If the business has many creditors, a formal bankruptcy process may be the most effective way to prepare the business for exit (through a reorganization under Chapter 11) or to close the business (through a liquidation under Chapter 7).

The bankruptcy process starts with a petition. Petitions for court protection can be either voluntary or involuntary in Chapters 7 and 11 proceedings. A voluntary petition is filed by the troubled company. If the company will not petition voluntarily and if there are 12 or more creditors, at least three creditors with unsecured claims totaling at least $5,000 must join to file an involuntary petition. When there are fewer than 12 creditors, a single creditor with unsecured claims greater than $5,000 is sufficient to file an involuntary petition. The only requirement is that either the debtor is in *equitable insolvency*—meaning that bills are not being paid as they come due—or that, within 90 days before the petition, a receiver, assignee, or custodian has taken possession of substantially all property. If, in the court's opinion, the required circumstances do not exist, the judge may grant judgment to the company for costs, attorney fees, damages, and even sentence the petitioner to jail. Thus, an error in filing an involuntary petition can be very severe.

Upon the filing of a petition, an *automatic stay* takes effect. The stay halts the efforts of creditors to collect funds due them, to obtain a lien or seize assets, or otherwise to gain any unfair advantage. It restricts secured creditors from taking further actions to collect claims or to enforce liens, but, unlike unsecured creditors, their interest continues to accumulate while the stay is in effect. Creditors are prohibited from sending dunning letters, using *setoffs,* or enforcing pre-petition judgments against the debtor. A secured creditor can gain relief from a stay only if the creditor can prove the debtor has no "equity interest" in the secured property, the property is not necessary for an effective reorganization, or the protection of the property value is insufficient. The court has broad latitude in providing *adequate protection* of a creditor's security in the property.

Covenants or clauses that place a debtor in automatic default are nullified by the automatic stay when a debtor files for bankruptcy. Also, a trustee may assume, reject, or assign executory contracts and unexpired leases even if prohibited by the contract or lease. These creditors, however, may file claims for proven damages, subject to certain limitations. Limitations are also placed on claims under employment contracts. Because many small businesses use secured forms of financing such as accounts receivable lines, the priority of secured creditors can have a major impact on a business in bankruptcy. Property pledged as security is not supposed to be taken for the benefit of any other party until the secured debts have been satisfied. Consequently, businesses in Chapter 11 bankruptcy reorganization usually seek to have secured creditors forgo foreclosing on their collateral while the business is in reorganization.

The law establishes classes of creditors (listed in their order on the priorities "ladder" on liquidation). They are secured creditors, administrative and priority claims, general creditors, and equity holders. The law, which is highly technical in this area, also creates subgroups in these major classifications, which are relevant in allocating distributions and in related negotiations.

The secured creditors are taken care of first with the proceeds of the assets they hold as security. Any portion of the secured debt unsatisfied by the secured assets becomes part of the company's unsecured-debt pool. Any value more than the debt remains with the company.

Then, the bankruptcy process turns to the unsecured creditors, working down the liquidation priority ladder. First on the priority ladder is the administrative classification. This group includes the administrative expenses of the bankruptcy proceeding itself, expenses of the trustee, and any legal fees. This priority group also includes:

- ➤ Creditors whose claims stem from activities occurring following the court's determining it has jurisdiction
- ➤ Creditors whose claims arose between the date of filing and this determination or the appointment of a trustee
- ➤ Wages, including vacation and severance pay, from 90 days before the petition was filed to the present time or from 90 days before the business ceased operations
- ➤ Liabilities to benefit plans incurred within 180 days of the petition filing

> Customer deposits

> Taxes

Distributions to the general creditors, including secured creditors' deficiency claims, come after distributions to the priority creditors. Equity holders rank last and are often wiped out.

REORGANIZING THE BUSINESS: CHAPTER 11

Chapter 11 covers reorganization proceedings rather than liquidation, although the Chapter does provide for a liquidation outcome. Chapter 11's intent is to provide for consensual plans, which are often encouraged by circumstances in which the creditors' claims will be more completely paid if the debtor continues to operate and generate cash flow. It makes provision for a creditors' committee, which performs the same oversight functions as a corporate board, and lists the rules for creditor acceptance of a plan.

After filing under Chapter 11, the court ordinarily appoints the seven largest unsecured creditors to serve as the *creditors' committee.* The committee, in essence, supersedes the corporate board. The debtor's existing management usually runs the company during the reorganization unless fraud or dishonest actions are exposed or the court decides that appointing a *trustee* is in the best interest of the creditors. The judge has the power to appoint similar committees to represent secured creditors and equity holders, if requested, and broad latitude to modify committee size and composition to ensure adequate representation and yet maintain a manageable group. The committee, which normally retains counsel and accounting support, can consult with the trustee or debtor on reorganization plans and can investigate a debtor's actions and financial condition.

In a Chapter 11 proceeding, an important early task for management is to arrange *debtor-in-possession* (DIP) financing to provide working-capital funding during the proceeding. The debtor is supposed to file a *plan for reorganization* during the first 120 days under court protection. The bankruptcy judge, however, can grant extensions if the circumstances require them.

The core of a Plan is your business plan forecasting the operations of the business for several years in the future. It focuses on the generation of free cash flow and the restoration of a positive capital base. The court reviews the Plan to ensure it meets the specific and complex content and disclosure requirements. Then, the business plan and its assumptions are reviewed by the Creditors Committee. If the Committee is convinced the Plan is a sound assessment of the firm's likely future performance, the Plan becomes the basis for determining the company's value and assigning that value to the creditor classes in order of priority. The terms of a Plan may alter the rights of any class of creditors, but *all* members within a class must be treated equally. The terms are free from security-registration requirements and from compliance with state law, which speeds up the process considerably.

A class of creditors accepts a Plan if more than one-half the class in number and two-thirds in dollar amount approve it. If the Plan is not approved by all impaired classes, then the court may *cram down* the Plan on the dissenting classes but must wipe out all claims junior to the dissenting class. For the court to have the cram-down option, at least one class senior to the dissenting class must have accepted the Plan.

Many companies in financial trouble use a Chapter 11 proceeding to validate legally a voluntary settlement in what is known as a *prepackaged bankruptcy* filing. Before the filing is made, the company and its major creditors negotiate a proposal and a Plan that most accept as an alternative to a potential bankruptcy. The company then files for bankruptcy, informing the court that a Plan has been negotiated and filing the Plan immediately. The relevant creditors accept it. The necessary restructuring takes place, and the company is discharged. This process can take as little as two weeks when all parties have agreed in advance.

Preferences

An issue that often arises in a Chapter 11 proceeding is the issue of preferences. As part of the effort to ensure that creditors are treated uniformly, the Code provisions address the question of payments made on *antecedent debt*—those obligations undertaken before the petition was filed. These rules are necessary because of concern that all creditors would not be equally familiar with the debtor's situation as its financial difficulties increased. Ways were therefore sought to protect the less familiar creditors and those with weaker bargaining positions from erosion of the debtor's value if the distressed firm tried to buy off trouble by making payments or concessions to in-the-know creditors.

These transfers of assets or security interests, known as *preferences*, are subject to recall or revocation by the courts. A transfer of property is considered a preference if it benefited one creditor, was made within 90 days before the bankruptcy petition, and was in satisfaction of an antecedent debt. Exceptions to the preference ruling include contemporaneous exchanges that create new value through the advance of funds, such as for the purchase of specific equipment. Another exception allows for payments made in the ordinary course of business. Similarly, payments to adequately collateralized creditors are *not* preference items because the payments free an equity interest for the troubled company in the collateral.

> **KEY POINT: Chapter 11's central benefit to the troubled small business is allowing the company to stave off its creditors while it reorganizes**

its affairs sufficiently to go out of business in an orderly way with the maximum benefits to all the creditors and to the owner. By converting to the liquidation alternative, a small business can go out of business by closing its doors or selling itself. Chapter 11 gives you the chance to straighten out relationships with creditors before closing the business and then to recover any residual value the business has.

LIQUIDATING THE BUSINESS: CHAPTER 7

When it seems unlikely that a troubled small business can be restored, it is less expensive to move directly for liquidation under Chapter 7 of the Bankruptcy Code. This procedure has the same impact as voluntarily closing the doors, but it gives you a legally mandated exit that usually will prevent any threats from creditors after the business is closed. Filing under Chapter 7 may be voluntary by the debtor or forced by the creditors. During a Chapter 7 liquidation proceeding, a trustee is appointed to collect all nonexempt property, sell it, and distribute the proceeds to creditors according to priority and position. The trustee receives compensation of 3 percent on asset realization.

CHAPTER 12

EXITING THE SUCCESSFUL BUSINESS

There are several reasons that you, as an entrepreneurial owner, would want to exit a successful business including:

➤ A general desire to harvest your efforts and do something else
➤ A general retirement
➤ Lack of a family member or other clear successor
➤ Estate planning and settlement issues

> **KEY POINT: Because you are the lifeblood of the business, exiting it and maintaining or extracting its value is a difficult challenge. You have many hurdles to overcome to ensure an exit without losing value.**

Considering the Options

The small business owner contemplating exit has a variety of options, including:

➤ Making an initial public offering
➤ Closing the doors and liquidating the assets of the business
➤ Retaining ownership of the business but hiring outside management
➤ Transferring the business to a family member
➤ Selling the business or merging with another business
➤ Establishing an Employee Stock Ownership Plan to buy some or all of the equity

In selecting and implementing a way to exit, you must consider many issues, including timing, form of consideration, types of buyers, management incentives and succession, indemnification and tail liability problems, valuation, taxes, certainty of closure, and process.

AN INITIAL PUBLIC OFFERING

An initial public offering (IPO) is a way for angel investors or formal venture capitalists to exit a company. It is a way for the entrepreneur/founder of a business to exit only if the owner's shares can be sold to the public as part of the IPO. Many successful IPOs, however, are predicated on the founder and management of the company staying with the business. Many investment banks limit the owners' ability to cash in their shares. Companies restrict the founders' ability to resign without incurring a substantial financial penalty. Consequently, in a majority of situations, an IPO is not a way for you to exit the business.

CLOSING THE DOORS

For many successful small businesses, the easiest way for the entrepreneur to exit is simply to close the doors, liquidate the assets of the business, pay the debts, and keep the remaining cash balance. The five-step close-down process, described in Chapter 11 for exiting an unsuccessful business, applies as well to closing a successful business. This allows you to retire to the location of your choice by investing the cash from the business in marketable securities and real estate. Knowledgeable legal advice can help reduce the impact of taxes on this alternative.

RETAINING OWNERSHIP AND HIRING OUTSIDE MANAGEMENT

If the business is highly profitable and its closure might have adverse tax consequences, you may choose to hire outside managers to run it while you retain ownership. This may be the simplest way to exit the business from a day-to-day management standpoint—other than closing the doors. It does not withdraw your capital, however, and can present problems of managerial motivation and the continued success of the business.

Outside managers drawing a salary are unlikely to have the same drive and interest in making the business succeed as you had. Lack of interest may be avoided by transferring the management of the business to a family member, such as a child, who has a vested interest in the firm's continued success.

>SMART MOVE: If you decide to go forward with hiring outside management, you might agree to allow the manager to buy out your interest over time. The arrangement can be structured to motivate the manager to high performance and still allow you a voice in the company even when your ownership falls below 50 percent.

TRANSFER TO ANOTHER FAMILY MEMBER

For many entrepreneurs and small business owners, the dream is not only to build up their own business (and wealth in the process), but to pass the business on to children. The transfer of a business to another family member can be a complicated process, with managerial, legal, and tax complications not present when the business is sold outright or merged. Because approximately 90 percent of businesses are classified as family owned, transfer to another family member is something that many small business owners will face.

The underlying issues include:

- ➤ Who can participate in the management and under what circumstances (including compensation)
- ➤ How to prepare the next generation to assume responsibility for the business
- ➤ How to help the founding entrepreneur let go of the business
- ➤ Liquidity
- ➤ Compensation and income for the older generation
- ➤ Estate taxes

Family members can have a variety of relationships to the business, including as an employee and owner, as an employee but not an owner, as an owner but not an employee, and as either an employee or owner. The particular relationships that family members have will color their outlooks on the question of transfer to other family members.

➤ **SMART FINANCIAL MANAGEMENT: Successfully transferring the business to another family member can take several years. To increase the likelihood of a successful transfer, you should undertake an extensive planning process including the development of a business strategic plan, a family strategic plan, a financial plan for retirement, an estate plan, and a succession plan. These plans should be communicated to family members involved in and affected by the transfer process so there is a clear understanding of what you are trying to accomplish.**

The transfer normally requires several phases including initiating and educating children or other family members in the business, determining who your successor will be, and developing a plan to transfer leadership. Announcing the chosen successor early can have several benefits including reassuring employees, suppliers, and customers, allowing siblings to make other career decisions, and allowing you to plan for retirement.

Key-Man Insurance

When business owners die suddenly without preparations for such a contingency, their businesses and their families are left in the lurch. Wise entrepreneurs plan for an orderly exit under this unfortunate circumstance. The essential element is for you or the company to carry enough key-man life insurance to provide the company or your heirs with sufficient cash to maintain the business during such a traumatic experience. Cash flows are likely to be diminished while the situation is being sorted out.

It is particularly important that the key-man insurance is sufficient to pay off the company's institutional debt, and many lending institutions require insurance as a condition of making a loan. Dealing with a debt-free company is much easier than struggling with one that has loans to renegotiate or repay when an executor is trying to settle an estate.

Legal Tools

Legal arrangements exist that may reduce the tax bite on both the transfer of ownership by you and on your estate. A *living trust,* for example, is a completely changeable agreement between the creator (donor) and a designated property manager (trustee) established for the benefit of a recipient (beneficiary), all of which can be the creator of the trust. The *marital deduction trust* is created in your will or living trust for the benefit of a spouse after your death. As of this writing, the federal tax code allows an *installment payment* of the estate tax due on a family business over a 14-year period if the family business is 35 percent or more of the estate. This provision is designed to avoid a forced sale of a family business to pay estate taxes. Skilled legal counsel and accounting support are essential for a successful transfer. Sophisticated planning is required for retirement funding, estate plan, and tax planning.

Additional legal tools are the transfer tax exclusion techniques including the unified credit/exemption equivalent trust, the dynastic trust, the annual exclusion gift, the unified credit/exemption equivalent gift, and the statutory grantor retained interest trust. The *unified credit/exemption equivalent trust* uses the normal estate-tax exclusion to allow transfer of the business without creating a taxable event. The *dynastic trust* allows passing the business to grandchildren without creating a taxable event. The *annual gift exclusion* allows avoidance of tax on gifts of $11,000 or less annually per recipient. The *statutory grantor retained interest* trust allows you to continue receiving income from the business after it is transferred. Because the tax regulations are in a state of flux, the rules and procedures are subject to change.

GENERAL SALE OF THE BUSINESS

Instead of closing the doors, hiring outside managers, or attempting to transfer the business to other family members, you may choose to sell the business to outsiders. This approach to exiting may be much simpler than the transfer of the business to family members, but it has its own difficulties and pitfalls. One of the greatest challenges is taxes. Another challenge is achieving a clean exit without ongoing responsibilities for the business.

After selling a business, most entrepreneurs want to be free of future responsibilities for it. The buyers, however, generally want to make sure the seller does not foist a lemon on them. Consequently, most purchase contracts for private companies provide for indemnification of the buyer by the seller if future problems arise as the result of acts that occurred before the sale. This requirement continues the seller's liability for a specified period.

Tax considerations are a major element in your approach to exiting the successful business. Having spent years building the value of the business, you want to extract that value when exiting. This invariably requires significant tax planning at both the personal and corporate levels. The particular method you adopt to exit can have significant tax consequences. If you receive cash for stock in the business, you have a taxable event. The profit on the transaction will be subject to long-term capital-gains taxes. Fortunately, capital-gains taxation of small business' capital gains receives special treatment.

Potential buyers of a company fall into the following categories: strategic, financial, strategic-financial, and competitors. Each has advantages and disadvantages. Because *strategic buyers* understand the industry they can do their due diligence more quickly, require fewer indemnities, and offer a higher purchase price because of synergies. *Financial buyers* will be more concerned with financing terms and indemnification and may expect the entrepreneur to stay with the business. *Strategic-financial buyers,* such as roll-up players, combine the attributes of both strategic and financial buyers. *Competitors* present problems of confidentiality and secrecy in auction efforts and busted deals.

What to Take for the Sale

Consideration for the sale of a business can take a variety of forms: cash, stock, seller paper, or a combination. Consideration can be deferred with the amount fixed or contingent, as in an "earn-out." The mix of consideration in a particular deal is negotiated and is influenced by tax considerations, the attractiveness of the buyer's stock (if that is part of the consideration), the estimated value of the company being sold, and special needs of the buyer and seller.

Cash. The sale of a privately held business for cash to an outside buyer is an easy way to create liquidity for current shareholders. The transaction provides existing shareholders with complete liquidity for their investment. The selling shareholders, however, face capital-gains taxes on their investment, which they might want to avoid. There are other, complex, tax rules if a company sells its assets rather than its owners selling their stock.

Stock. A sale of a business in an exchange of stock avoids creating a taxable event. This type of consideration allows you as the seller ultimately to move the assets represented by the stock into an estate without paying any capital gains, just as if the business had not been sold. If you choose a stock-for-stock exchange to avoid capital gains taxes, you must be very careful about the quality of the stock received.

Mergers

Merging your business with another business is a common way to exit a business. If the company is sold in a stock-for-stock transaction, the amount of liquidity that current shareholders get depends on whether the stock of the acquiring company is readily marketable. If the merger is with a larger, public company, public-company stock gives you a liquidity option. It does not become a liquidity event (or taxable) until you choose to sell the stock. You thus can time the conversion of personal capital from the business into cash or other investments.

Although a merger with a private company similar in size to your own may get you out of the day-to-day management, it will not always liquefy your equity in the business. In a merger of two private companies, the entrepreneur will typically receive stock in the merged company—still a private company. If the merged company quickly has an IPO, as sometimes happens, the current shareholders will have a more liquid investment. If the acquiring company remains privately held, however, you will be in the same position as before the merger. A further disadvantage will be less leverage with management because you will own a smaller position in the new company than in the original one unless special terms were negotiated, as suggested in Chapters 2 and 10. The stock-for-stock sale avoids the capital gains liability until current shareholders sell the stock they got.

Leveraged Management Buyout

The sale of a privately held business to management in a leveraged management buyout (MBO) can create liquidity for current shareholders who are not members of the management group. These selling shareholders receive cash for their shares. As in the sale for cash to an outside buyer, the sellers face capital gains taxes on their profits. Private companies, with stable cash flows, substantial excess cash, and additional borrowing capacity which management can tap make good MBO candidates. An MBO does have the disadvantage of potentially saddling the company with a heavy debt burden, which could be financially dangerous for the company in case of a business downturn or if it must finance an expansion. Arranging an MBO also must address the issue of how the company would be valued in an arms-length transaction.

When you are seeking to sell a business or an ownership interest in a business, you normally want to understand its valuation before putting it on the market. As explained in Chapter 7 of this book, there are several ways a business can be valued, including market capitalization (for a public company), a multiple of earnings or P-E ratio based on P-E ratios of comparable companies, a multiple of sales (for a private company), book value of the equity, replacement cost of the business's assets, liquidation value of the business, and discounted cash flow.

Each method has its advantages and disadvantages. The book value method, replacement cost, and liquidation value all focus on the business at a point in time rather than as an ongoing enterprise. The P-E ratio methods are quick, easy, and widely understood but are normally based on one period's earnings. Selecting the proper P-E ratio to use is judgmental, and finding comparable companies is often not easy. The discounted cash flow is the most rigorous. It is based on multiple-period earnings. It does not escape the need for many judgments about future performance (such as growth in sales and margins), which are not guaranteed.

> **IMPORTANT: Management succession and incentives are a major issue in any sale of any business. Enthusiastic and capable management creates value. Financial buyers, in particular, need some managers to remain and usually want them to invest in the deal. They also want bench strength. Frequently "deal bonuses" are paid to managers who stay with the company after sale. Some buyers, as discussed in the "angel" section of Chapter 10, plan to take over management of the company themselves. It helps the transition if this is understood before the sale is agreed to.**

One issue with the sale of any business is the certainty of closing the sale. Arranging a sale of a business takes time, effort, and money. The due-diligence agreement may preclude exploration of other sale options. A high degree of certainty about closing is thus a very desirable characteristic of the deal. To ensure a deal closes, a good sales contract provides significant penalties for failure to close the transaction.

AN EMPLOYEE STOCK OWNERSHIP PLAN

An alternative to selling the company to outside investors or to another company is to sell the company to its employees. This can be done through the creation of an Employee Stock Ownership Plan (ESOP) and the sale of the company to it. ESOPs are a specialized version of a profit-sharing or stock-bonus plan that can be used for corporate finance purposes with tax advantages. ESOPs are a special feature of the Federal Tax Code, designed to give companies tax benefits for providing employees significant ownership of their employer. Under the Federal Tax Code, company contributions to an ESOP are tax deductible as a form of employee benefit. Participants avoid taxation on their interest in the ESOP until after their retirement. As with all retirement plans, ESOPs have to qualify under section 401(a) for employer contributions to be tax deductible. There are also the customary complicated employee-benefit regulations that must be satisfied.

The vast majority of ESOPs are created by closely held companies, although many large public companies also have established them. One reason closely held companies use ESOPs is that their shareholders can sell shares tax-free to an ESOP if certain tests are met. This sale avoids, at least temporarily, recognition of the gain for tax purposes. To gain this tax advantage, the proceeds of the sale must be reinvested, within 12 months after the sale to the ESOP, in the securities of domestic operating corporations. The selling shareholders must have held the stock for at least a three-year period before the sale. The ESOP must own at least 30 percent of the company after the transaction and, more specifically, at least 30 percent of the total common equity on a controlling-interest basis. Alternatively, immediately after the transaction, the ESOP must own at least 30 percent of the total number of shares of each class of stock.

The three basic types of ESOPs are the leveraged ESOP, the nonleveraged cash-warehousing ESOP, and nonleveraged newly issued stock ESOP.

In a *leveraged ESOP,* the ESOP borrows money from a bank to buy a block of stock from selling shareholders. The ESOP also can buy newly issued shares from the company, which serves to raise new capital; usually, however, the ESOP buys stock from existing shareholders because of the major tax advantages this alternative offers.

Each year the company makes tax-deductible contributions to the ESOP of up to 25 percent of the company's payroll. The ESOP uses this cash to repay the loan. This arrangement makes both the interest and principal payments on the loan tax-deductible from the company's income. If the ESOP owns more than 50 percent of the company after the transaction, then the bank can exclude 50 percent of its interest earned from its taxable income. The bank can therefore offer the ESOP a lower than market interest rate for the debt.

In the *nonleveraged cash warehousing ESOP,* the company makes deductible cash contributions to the ESOP. After a period of years, the ESOP buys a block of stock using the cash accumulated, perhaps in combination with an ESOP loan. This approach is popular with companies required to make certain employee benefit or retirement contributions each year. The cash-warehousing approach is also popular with S-corporations that want to fund the sale of a block of stock but want to keep their S-corporation status as long as possible. An S-corporation cannot have an ESOP as a shareholder.

In the *nonleveraged newly issued stock ESOP,* the company contributes newly issued stock to the ESOP. The newly issued shares can be used to make discretionary contributions to an employee profit-sharing plan or to make the employer match in a 401(k). In either case, the dilution created by the new shares is usually small. The company's cash flow and net worth are improved versus what they would have been if the company had made cash contributions.

WHAT TO DO AFTER EXITING

Having cashed in on a business after many years of effort, successful entrepreneurs and small business owners must decide what to do with their lives. Do you want to be just another rich person, sitting on charitable boards and writing checks to charities? This decision can be more stressful than you imagined. Used to long days and a framework of business decision-making, many owners quickly miss the excitement of their previous business lives. One route many take is to become an angel investor, reinvesting some of your gains and helping other entrepreneurs. A variety of formal avenues exist for the successful entrepreneur to do this. Some of these were described in Chapter 10, such as an angel network or angel funds. Another alternative is working with local offices of the SBA, community college programs, and volunteer initiatives to advise budding entrepreneurs.

PART V
SUMMARY

CHAPTER 13

SUMMING UP: SMART FINANCIAL MANAGEMENT

You have now been given the basic financial management and legal insights you will need from the time your business is founded until you make your graceful exit. To manage your business between these events, you have been given guidelines about how to avoid the entrepreneur's nightmare—running out of cash. This is a serious problem for all businesses, but it is fatal for the smaller company whose sources of funds are limited. Therefore, many pages have been devoted to providing analytical approaches to help you plan and manage assets wisely and to plan and arrange funds before needing them.

Not all portions of this book are equally relevant to all business owners. Service businesses, for example, seldom have inventory concerns. However, managers of that firm will need to pay special attention to managing receivables and to fund planning, because a service business can seldom rely on accounts payable for funding.

Your company's financial management is an integral part of its business strategy that must be coordinated with your marketing and production strategy. For example, all first-time business owners realize that too few customers will be a major problem. Fewer realize that too many customers can cause serious financial difficulties as well. It is a serious strategic error to spend money selling products and services for which there are no funds to provide.

KEY POINT: Thus, one strategy does not fit all businesses. The basic financial management concepts, however, do. This book therefore presents the concepts and tools the small business owner needs to integrate the company's financial management into a successful business. This final chapter summarizes and reviews the key concepts.

Growth and the Company Life Cycle

Companies, like living organisms, have life cycles. To grow, a firm must go through the life cycle with its resulting financial implications. The main phases of a company's life cycle are start-up, initial growth, rapid growth, maturity, and decline. Each of these stages challenges the firm with significantly different financial requirements. Although companies progress through the stages at different speeds, it is important for you to know where your firm is and to plan the financial management accordingly.

During the *start-up* phase, the firm is often little more than an idea. You probably provide your own funding during this phase, along with others you can persuade to provide equity funds. The *initial growth* phase occurs after your company has begun to deliver its product or service. During this phase, the company absorbs funds to cover the money it is losing and to build the assets necessary to meet the growing demand of its customers. More challenging (and potentially more profitable for you and the other founders), but still easier than the initial growth phase, is a period of *rapid growth*. The company becomes profitable, marginally at first and then handsomely.

> **GROWTH RATE: A particular challenge faces you when sales are growing faster than equity because the situation may require external financing. At this stage, however, debt and/or additional equity may not be available or appropriate.**

A popular analytical tool to analyze this problem is the *sustainable growth rate* (SGR). This ratio shows the sales growth rate that can be sustained without recourse to external equity. A precise computation of the SGR can be complex. For many smaller companies, which do not pay dividends, the SGR is the same as the growth in equity (*Growth in Equity = (Profits – Dividends) ÷ Average Equity*).

If growth is expected to be higher than the SGR, you should plan financing as a sequence. This will allow an assessment of the complete picture of risks and rewards. A *fund-needs profile* should be prepared and a plan developed to finance these needs. A fund-needs profile is simply a balance-sheet projection, allowing for all existing financial sources, that shows a balancing "plug figure" on the right-hand side representing an additional need for funds.

The period of rapid growth will end when the consumers' demands have been fulfilled and the market enters its *mature* phase. In an ideal situation, the mature phase allows you to enjoy the fruits of your innovation. Cash flows will be positive and strong because funds are not required for new assets to support growth. The *decline* phase is a difficult one for a company, its management, and its external sources of capital. Profit margins gradually degenerate and ultimately turn into losses. The skill of getting out gracefully is an important characteristic for the management of a declining company.

Financial Management to Support Growth

As the company grows and goes through its life cycle, you should continually analyze the company's financial position and plan for future growth. In reviewing an enterprise's strategic position and financial situation, it is useful to identify the *capital position* in which the company is operating. The four positions or states are repaying net debt, maintaining the existing dollar amount of debt, increasing the dollar amount of debt but not the leverage ratio, and increasing the leverage ratio.

Which of these four states your company is in will be central in determining its capital requirements and the nature of those requirements—debt or equity. Knowing where your company is with respect to its capital requirements is important to your dealing with external financial sources. In making the analysis of an appropriate capital structure, six dimensions can be considered: **F**lexibility, **R**isk, **I**ncome, **C**ontrol, **T**iming, and **O**ther. These FRICTO components are mutually exclusive and collectively exhaustive.

Using the FRICTO factors to analyze the company's capital requirements leads to questions such as, What is the eat-well, sleep-well tradeoff? How well can the company meet its existing debt obligations? Does it have sufficient resources to handle potential adversity? How many flexibility challenges can it sustain at once without financial collapse? What is the amount of funds needed to resolve them? Has the company access to these funds? Can the company raise funds at a reasonable price, a cost the new assets can earn with room to spare? Or, will the company have to give away some existing owners' equity to survive? If so, how much?

> **SMART FINANCIAL MANAGEMENT:** Although the FRICTO factors are normally applied to the capital-structure decision, these factors are also appropriate for assessing capital-investment and dividend decisions. Thus, FRICTO offers a framework in which the effects of most financial decisions can be analyzed.

The Legal Aspects of Growth

As pointed out in the discussion of a company's life cycle, every business is born as a startup and goes through identifiable stages of development. During the development period, and particularly when the company seeks financing, you face many legal issues and questions involving corporate law, securities law, and contract law. Your decisions on these issues will usually influence potential financing. Typical entrepreneurs, working

20-hour days to build businesses and to realize dreams, do not want to be distracted by petty legal details as they seek financing.

Unfortunately, dreams can be destroyed if you ignore those details because they can come back to haunt you in many ways. Failure to maintain the corporation's legal basis through proper board activity, poorly thought-through legal capital structure, and securities laws violations can undermine the most promising developing business. Though dealing properly with the legal details of the corporation can be very time consuming for a company's senior management, it is an extremely important investment in the long-term success of the business.

> **KEY POINT: Because of their importance, you should give the same attention to the legal aspects of your business as you give to the marketing, financing, and operating aspects. They should not be left strictly to the discretion of the company's attorneys. Use of experienced attorneys is nevertheless essential. Attorneys lacking knowledge and experience in these highly technical areas may not guide the company effectively around dangerous pitfalls.**

Financial Statements and Financial Analysis for Growth

Reports, or statements, based upon financial data are prepared for a variety of users and uses. For most business organizations, the audience includes one or more of the following: management, creditors, stockholders, trade associations, employees, regulatory and other governmental agencies, and securities exchanges.

The usual statements prepared for both internal (management) and external (other users) purposes include the Balance Sheet, the Statement of Income (or of Earnings), and the Statement of Stockholders' Equity. In recent years, the Statement of Cash Flows has been added to the list of statements presented externally. The book explains these statements sufficiently that, even without an accounting background, you can use them to plan the company's funds needs.

> **KEY POINT: For the entrepreneur managing a business, financial statements and their interpretation are central to survival and success. Total fixation on the top line—sales—can lead to financial disaster. Financial statements let you know where the firm stands at a point in time.**

Analysis of the statements, particularly to identify trends, will help you spot problems ahead. In this analysis, ratios can be useful, especially for analysis of comparable periods (such as year-end to year-end) when underlying operating results are stable from period to period. Ratios can be extremely misleading, however, if some components are subject to major but routine fluctuations. The successful small business owner knows when and how to use ratio analysis, which offers an efficient way to forecast financial needs.

The analysis and interpretation of financial statements are also basic to the decision-making process of creditors, stockholders, and other external groups. The external analyst, such as a bank credit officer, must answer questions related to a company's earnings capacity, ability to meet interest and principal obligations, ability to pay dividends, and general financial strengths and weaknesses. A comprehensive analysis, presenting the data in meaningful terms, is a significant aid to understanding the profitability and financial strength of a company. When properly prepared, financial evaluations can be used in performance appraisal and to highlight similarities and differences among units of the same organization. Properly prepared forecasts are essential to obtaining loans and other external financing.

Management of Cash and Current Assets for Growth

The most important rule for the financial management of smaller enterprises is not to run out of cash. The rule holds true, of course, for all companies, but it is a more serious problem for the smaller enterprise that faces greater challenges in raising cash. You therefore must watch the cash balance more carefully than the profit figure. It is lack of cash, not lack of profits that forces firms into bankruptcy.

> **KEY POINT: Cash is an investment with characteristics similar to the investment in inventory, receivables, and property. Effective management of the cash position can increase the profitability of a company. Ineffective cash management can be costly and even threaten the company with insolvency.**

Cash management is closely connected to current asset management, particularly the management of accounts receivable and inventory. Proper management of these assets generates cash while improper management drains cash.

Effective management of accounts receivable includes not only evaluating and authorizing trade-credit extensions but also constantly supervising the credit customers' accounts to ensure collection. If you do not understand receivables evaluation and collection, your company can quickly get into deep financial trouble.

Inventory is one of the most difficult assets to manage because of the problems of controlling and valuing it. The natural tendency of a sales-oriented entrepreneur is to increase the level of inventory to avoid stockouts. On the other hand, return on investment can be increased by reducing funds tied up in inventories. Mismanaged inventories are the quickest way for a company to get into trouble. Volatility of demand, the seasonal nature of demand, and whether the business can build to order or must build inventory on speculation are the critical dimensions that determine the carrying cost of inventory. Although the change to the service economy has reduced the importance of inventory management to the economy as a whole, inventory is a critical asset for those who have it.

The preparation of funds budgets and forecasts is essential to the efficient use of cash and arranging financing for the additional cash needs or for investing cash surpluses. A budget is how you *hope* the enterprise will operate. A forecast is what you *think* will happen. Budgeting and forecasting mechanics are the same, but the budgeting process comes first. Forecasts are made later, when the outlines of the future are better defined. At that point, a comparison between budget and forecast may suggest actions need to be taken, adjustments made, to bring them closer together.

▶ **SMART FINANCIAL MANAGEMENT: A funds budget or forecast is constructed in the same way as a cash budget or forecast. Long-term cash and funds forecasts are important in highlighting major financing needs so you can do the proper planning for the best financing alternatives. Short-term forecasts are needed to manage the day-to-day cash position to make sure that cash is available for necessary disbursements and that the most appropriate investments are considered for excess cash.**

Managing Long-Term Assets for Growth

When funds are invested in a new asset, the asset usually appears on the balance sheet rather than being immediately charged against income as an expense. The asset is then charged against income through depreciation expense over its estimated useful life. Although the income statement provides some indication of the profitability of the business, it provides little indication of the true return on invested capital or whether a particular capital investment is worthwhile.

A project may provide a positive return, but the return can be too small to justify the investment. The return on capital invested must be measured on a cash-flow basis and take time into account. That is the purpose of capital investment analysis, also called capital budgeting.

Capital budgeting involves qualitative as well as quantitative analysis. From a qualitative standpoint, you must consider how well each project fits into the company's business strategy, how much management time it will absorb, whether forecasted returns justify assuming identified risks, and how that project might affect other projects under consideration. From a quantitative perspective, the key concepts are the time value of money, discounted cash flow analysis, and the following four methods for evaluating projects: net present value, internal rate of return, payback, and profitability index.

Discounted cash flow analysis is the quantitative base for capital budgeting. It is a method for identifying all of the cash outflows and inflows relevant to a project and adjusting them for both risk and the time value of money.

There are several ways to measure the discounted value of an investment. A project's *net present value* (NPV) is the sum of the present values of all its projected cash outflows and inflows, including all investments made and returns realized. A positive NPV suggests a financially attractive proposal. NPV is a particularly useful calculation for comparing investment opportunities that have different schedules of investments (cash outflows) and returns (cash inflows). This type of analysis is useful in ranking investment opportunities. A calculation related to NPV is the *internal rate of return* (IRR). This is the reinvestment or hurdle rate at which the NPV is zero.

A simple capital-budgeting measure, sometimes used alone but often used to supplement the NPV or IRR analysis, is the *payback*. This measure is simply the number of years required for the project's cash inflows to repay the capital investment. If two projects have about equal NPVs and IRRs, the one with the shorter payback probably has lower risk.

Summing
Up: Smart
Financial
Management

Managing the Capital Structure for Growth and Funding the Business

The capital-structure decision for the smaller company is both less complex and more critical than for the large corporation. It is simpler because there are fewer alternatives for nonequity financing. It is more critical because the smaller enterprise has much less room to maneuver if it meets financial-structure problems. The lenders, having little at stake, are less inclined to spend the time to work out the problem. Although the analytic approach to capital-structure decisions does not depend on the company's size, the relative weight placed on the decision's components may vary.

> **KEY POINT: A net increase in working capital and long-term assets (use of funds) can come from only two sources: an increase in long-term debt or an increase in equity (or a combination of the two).**

The increase in equity can be the result of an increase in preferred stock (not usually an alternative available to a smaller enterprise except to high-growth ventures) or an increase in the common shareholders' equity (or both). Common equity—ignoring preferred stock as a specialized financial instrument—can come only from two sources: retained earnings or the issue of new common stock (or both). Retained earnings are the result of profits earned on the assets after distributions to the government for income taxes, to senior-security holders for interest and preferred dividends, and to the common stockholders as dividends.

Generally, and particularly with the smaller enterprise, management makes the asset decisions first before looking at the capital-structure question. This is because the opportunity to invest often creates the need for capital that raises the capital-structure issue. Given projected operating earnings, a key decision of how to finance growth is how to divide the operating flows, the earnings before interest and taxes (EBIT), among the senior and junior sources of capital and the government (taxes). Additional significant miscellaneous considerations include:

➤ The *speed and certainty* with which new money is required
➤ Your desire, as the entrepreneur owner of a private company, *to create a market for the company's stock*
➤ Your desire *to broaden the market for the stock*

> **SMART FINANCIAL MANAGEMENT: A sound analytical approach is a necessary ingredient for a wise capital-structure plan. It is not sufficient, however. Neither is the necessary careful assessment of a company's record and future prospects. The final necessary element, which**

combined with the other items is sufficient, is your judgment of whether the rewards justify the risks.

Financing the enterprise is one of the greatest challenges you face as an entrepreneur. This is a particularly serious challenge for the growing company, which seldom generates enough internal funds to meet its needs. Although financing a small, growing enterprise is a challenge, there are many nonequity alternatives you should explore. Often the most efficient solution is not one or another source but a combination of sources. For example, most governmental programs are delivered through private lenders. Therefore, when discussing a financial need with an institution, you should always ask about the types of government programs the institution offers.

Funds can be drawn from some financial sources with little formality, such as arranging extended trade payables. Others require more careful planning, such as a bank loan (with or without a Small Business Administration guarantee). For these sources, the more carefully you plan your presentation, the more likely the response will be a favorable one. In addition, developing a careful preparation is apt to help you learn more about the business.

The private equity markets are extremely important to the entrepreneur and owner of a small, rapidly growing business. Though they are difficult markets for you to access because of the imbalance between supply and demand, accessing them is central to the long-term growth of many promising small businesses. An understanding of the different investors in the private-equity market, and what they look for, is extremely valuable if you want your business to reach its full potential.

Exiting the Business

Every entrepreneur or small business owner who starts a business or takes one over should recognize they will ultimately exit the business. Many business owners hope they will retire from the business by passing it on to a family member. In practice, business owners exit their businesses in a variety of ways, from closing down the unsuccessful business to merging with a major public corporation. The way you exit will have significant financial impact on your own personal fortune. That fortune will be affected by how well you use the principles and practices detailed in this book in the day-to-day financial management of the business and by the longer-range planning that is encouraged.

GLOSSARY

ACCREDITED INVESTORS Investors considered sufficiently knowledgeable about financial matters under the federal securities law that they do not need the full protection and information disclosure provided by a public offering registration. Unregistered securities offerings and sales may be made to this class of investors without violating Federal securities laws. The class includes financial institutions and individual investors who meet certain tests of financial worth.

ASSET TURNOVER The company's annual sales divided by its total assets. A measure of the efficiency with which a company uses its assets, as well as the asset intensity of the company.

BEST EFFORTS An arrangement by which a finder of funds agrees to make best efforts to raise a specified amount of money but does not guarantee or underwrite the issue. If the effort is unsuccessful, the funds raised are returned to the investors who contributed them. *See* Firm commitment underwriting.

BETA An indicator of the risk associated with a stock's return as compared to general market returns. A beta of 1.0 indicates the same risk as the general market; a beta of less than 1.0 indicates lower risk than the general market; a beta of more than 1.0 indicates more risk than the general market.

"BLUE SKY" LAWS State securities laws designed to protect residents against securities fraud. In addition to complying with federal laws, an issuer of securities must always follow the securities laws of the individual states in which it is offering and selling the securities.

BOND A long-term debt security issued by a borrower.

BOOK VALUE The difference between a firm's stated assets and stated liabilities.

BREAK-EVEN ANALYSIS An analytical method used to determine the sales volume needed for revenues to equal costs; the sales volume needed for a firm to begin generating profits.

BUDGET A key tool in the financial control of a business by which a business lays out its planned revenues and expenses for a specific time period.

BUFFER STOCKS Inventory in excess of normal needs that allows a company to continue production or sales despite such problems as a delay in delivery of raw materials or an unexpected sales increase.

BUY-BACK PROVISION A contract provision that provides a company with the right to repurchase shares owned by members of the management group if they leave the company's employ. *See* Vesting agreement.

CALL PROVISION A contract provision that defines the conditions under which a company has the right to repurchase a previously sold security at a predetermined price and time. Also known as a redemption provision.

CAPITAL BUDGETING A method for evaluating, comparing, and selecting projects for the best long-term financial return.

CASH CYCLE The number of days between payment for the purchase of raw materials and the receipt of sales proceeds for finished goods.

CASH TURNOVER The number of times a firm's cash is collected in a year, calculated as sales divided by cash.

CERTIFICATE OF INCORPORATION The basic legal document that creates a corporation.

COLLECTION PERIOD The usual amount of time it take a firm to collect the receivables from its monthly billings.

COMMON STOCK The most basic form of an equity security in a corporation. The owner of common stock is entitled to a proportionate share of the profits, assets, and voting power of the corporation not otherwise allocated to senior securities, such as debt and preferred stock.

COMPANY LIFE CYCLE The cycle of development and growth, and eventual decline that all businesses go through. The cycle begins with the startup phase and goes through five distinct phases, ending with decline.

CONVERSION RIGHT A contract provision that defines the conditions under which holders of convertible-preferred stock or convertible debt may convert their shares or bonds into common stock. Conversion rights may be optional (giving the holder discretion as to when and whether to convert) or automatic (triggered by the occurrence of specific events, such as the completion of a public offering).

CORPORATION A distinct legal entity organized under state (or, rarely, federal) law that usually has perpetual existence. It is managed by a board of directors elected by its stockholders. The distinctive characteristic of a corporation is its ability to insulate its stockholders and management from personal liability for the corporation's obligations in most circumstances.

CO-SALE PROVISION A contract provision that allows venture investors to sell their shares before a public offering if the founders are selling some of their shares.

CR/CD (cash received–cash disbursed forecasting) A financial analysis technique that focuses on cash deposits and cash disbursements to examine the disposition of funds in an enterprise.

CREDIT SCORING A mathematical approach to granting credit that uses the loan applicant's characteristics to calculate a score that represents the applicant's probability of default.

DISCOUNTED CASH FLOW ANALYSIS (DCF) A corporate valuation technique that discounts future cash flows of a company to arrive at a current value.

DIVIDEND PREFERENCE A contract provision that defines the conditions when dividends shall accrue to certain classes of shareholders rather than be paid or not accrued at all.

DSO (days sales outstanding) This ratio is calculated by dividing accounts receivable by total annual credit sales and multiplying the result by 365. (If the calculation is made using less than a full year of sales, the number of days used in the calculation must correspond to the number of days in the sales period.) Also known as the receivables collection period.

DUE DILIGENCE The process by which investors investigate and analyze a company to gain a full understanding of its business.

DUPONT RATIOS A form of ratio analysis, pioneered by the DuPont company, that displays the central financial relationships of a company's operations and financing, including its sustainable growth rate.

EBIT   Earnings before interest and taxes.

EBITDA   Earnings before interest, taxes, depreciation, and amortization.

ECONOMIC ORDER QUANTITY (EOQ)   The quantity of an item, when ordered regularly, that minimizes ordering and storage costs.

ECONOMIC VALUE ADDED   A measure of whether a business or investment is economically justified because its earnings will exceed its cost of capital.

EMPLOYMENT AGREEMENT   A special contract between a company and its key employees that details compensation, benefits, the conditions under which the contract can be terminated, and the consequences of termination.

ENTERPRISE VALUE   The value the external market places on an enterprise. For a public company, this value is the total market value of its interest-bearing debt and its stock. For a private company, this is the amount a purchaser would be willing to pay for the company, including the assumption of its liabilities.

EPS   Earnings per share.

EQUITY VALUE   The economic value of an enterprise's equity; the enterprise value less interest-bearing debt.

EXTERNAL SOURCES OF FUNDS   Funds raised outside of the business from current and long-term debt and sales of preferred and common stock.

FACTORING   The business of purchasing accounts receivable from an enterprise, usually at a discount and with no recourse to the seller should the buyer (the factor) fail to collect the receivables.

FCF (free cash flow)   The cash left from a business's operating income after taxes plus noncash charges and deductions for the reinvestment necessary to continue growing the business but before the payment of interest and dividends.

FINANCIAL RATIOS   Specific financial relationships between different key financial parameters of a company, such as sales and assets, which allow analysts to examine and compare the financial performance of companies. Several financial ratios are defined in this glossary. *See* Chapters 1, 3, and 4 for additional definitions.

FIRM-COMMITMENT UNDERWRITING   An underwriting effort in which the underwriters agree to purchase the securities of the company at a fixed price no matter whether the underwriters can resell them for as much as they paid the corporation. *See* Best efforts.

FORCED REDEMPTION PROVISION   *See* Put provision.

FORECAST   A financial projection of how the business is most likely to perform in the future.

FRICTO   A way of analyzing a company's appropriate capital structure that looks at six dimensions: flexibility, risk, income, control, timing, and other (all additional considerations).

FUTURE VALUE   The value of an initial investment after a specified period of time at a certain rate of interest.

FULL-RATCHET ANTIDILUTION PROVISION   A contract provision that prevents the percentage of the corporation owned by lead investors from being reduced by a subsequent sale of shares at a lower price than the lead investors paid. Normally, the lead investors are issued additional shares at no cost to maintain their percentage ownership.

GO-ALONG RIGHTS   A contract provision that allows venture-capitalist investors to sell their shares at the same times and on the same terms as key employees.

GROSS SPREAD The discount at which the investment bank (or syndicate of investment banks) underwriting a public offering buys stock from the company before reselling it to the public at its full offering price.

HIDDEN CAPITAL COSTS Adverse changes in the value of an entrepreneur's assets that result from the financing decisions.

INFORMATION RIGHTS A contract provision that requires a company to regularly send information to investors, including financial statements and budgets.

INSPECTION RIGHTS A contract provision that allows investors to examine and inspect the properties and records of the company, to make copies of the records, and to discuss the affairs of the company with officers, directors, and key employees.

IS/BS (income statement–balance sheet forecasting) A technique of financial analysis that provides comprehensive information about the future disposition of funds in a business. *See* Chapter 4 for more complete explanation.

INTERNALLY GENERATED FUNDS Funds that a firm generates from retained earnings and depreciation.

INTERNAL RATE OF RETURN (IRR) The discount rate that makes the net present value of a project equal to zero.

INVENTORY TURNOVER RATIO The cost of goods sold divided by the inventory. Normally, a faster turnover is better for the business.

LEVERAGE The use of debt to finance assets and investments. Also known as financial leverage.

LIQUIDATION PREFERENCE A contract provision that defines the priority claims that certain groups (usually creditors and preferred shareholders) have to the assets of the corporation over other investors in case of liquidation.

LINE OF CREDIT An agreement with a bank that allows a business to borrow a variable amount of money, up to a specific maximum, at any time during the duration of the agreement.

LIQUIDITY A measure of how easily a firm's assets can be converted into cash.

NPV Net present value or the present value of a project's future cash flow less the initial investment in the project.

PARTNERSHIP A distinct legal entity organized under state law in which control and profits are divided by agreement among the partners. A partnership terminates whenever a partner dies unless specified otherwise in a partnership agreement. The distinctive characteristic of a partnership is that *each* general partner is personally liable for *all* the debts of the partnership. Generally, no federal income tax is assessed on the profits of the partnership. Instead, each partner is taxed individually on that partner's share of partnership income.

PARTNERSHIP AGREEMENT The formal legal document that lays out the terms of the partnership. Typical provisions specify management control, partners' shares of the partnership profits, and whether the partnership will survive the death of a partner.

PREEMPTIVE RIGHTS A contract provision that allows existing shareholders to purchase new shares being issued to the extent necessary to assure that the investors' percentage ownership of a company's securities or value will be the same after the financing as it was before.

PREFERRED STOCK A form of equity that has preference to common stock as determined by the contract it has with the issuer. This may include preference for dividends and for recovery of principal in case of a corporation's liquidation.

PROSPECTUS The legal document containing detailed information about the business and the offering which is approved by the SEC and distributed by investment banks to potential buyers of a security in a public offering.

PUT PROVISION A contract provision that defines the circumstances allowing venture capitalists to force a company to purchase their shares (common or preferred) at a predetermined price. Also known as forced-redemption provision.

RATIOS *See* Financial ratios.

REDEMPTION PROVISION *See* Call provision.

REGISTRATION RIGHT A contractual right that defines the terms and conditions under which certain classes of investors (normally venture-capital investors) can force the company to register their securities under the Securities Act of 1933.

REGULATION A A regulation issued by the SEC under the authority granted by the Securities Act of 1933 allowing a company to make an offering of securities to the public, without completing the full public-offering registration process, if its offerings in total are less than $5 million over a 12-month period.

REGULATION D A regulation issued by the SEC in 1982 under the authority granted by the Securities Act of 1933. It defines the characteristics that qualify a company for a security issuance as a private placement and thus exempt it from registration with the SEC. Specific tests are more fully defined in Rules 504, 505, and 506, which clarify Regulation D.

RESTRICTED SECURITIES Securities issued under a private-offering exemption of the Securities Act of 1933 or held by a member of management or a principal equity owner that are subject to restrictions on sale until registered under the Securities Act of 1933.

RETURN ON EQUITY (ROE) Net profits after taxes divided by stockholder equity.

RETURN ON INVESTMENT (ROI) Net profits after taxes divided by assets. This ratio helps a business determine how effectively it generates profits from available assets.

RIGHT OF FIRST REFUSAL A contractual right that provides existing investors with the right to purchase all new shares being issued if they wish.

RULE 504 A specific rule clarifying the test for a private-placement exemption under Regulation D, exempting from registration offerings of less than a $1 million in a 12-month period.

RULE 505 A specific rule clarifying the test for a private-placement exemption under Regulation D, exempting offerings of less than $5 million in a 12-month period if they are made to accredited investors and to no more than 35 other persons.

RULE 506 A specific rule clarifying the test for a private placement exemption under Regulation D, exempting offerings of any amount that are made to accredited investors and to no more than 35 sophisticated investors.

SECTION 3(A)(11) A section of the Federal Securities Act of 1933 that allows a company to make an offering of a security within a single state without having to register the security with the SEC.

SECTION 4(2) A section of the Federal Securities Act of 1933 that allows a company to make an offering of a security without having to register it with the SEC if the offering meets certain tests to qualify as a private placement. The tests have been defined explicitly in SEC Regulation D and accompanying Rules 504, 505, and 506.

SECURITIES AND EXCHANGE COMMISSION (SEC) The federal agency charged with administering and enforcing federal securities laws.

SECURITIES LAWS The body of federal and state laws regulating the offering for sale of securities.

SECURITIES REGISTRATION The process by which an issuer of securities meets the legal requirement to disclose information about the company helpful to investors and receives federal and state approval to sell those securities.

SENIOR DEBT The low-risk debt of a company because it has highest priority on a company's unsecured assets on liquidation and a first claim on cash flows for the payment of interest.

SOPHISTICATED INVESTORS Legally, investors who routinely invest in early-stage and start-up ventures who attest they can assess and bear the risks involved.

STOCK PURCHASE AGREEMENT The central legal document in a private placement of stock. This document normally spells out in detail the terms and conditions under which the stock is being offered to and purchased by the private investors.

SUBORDINATED DEBT Debt whose claims in liquidation have been subordinated to one or more other holders of senior debt. It has pledged its proceeds in liquidation to make up any deficiency in the payments to the beneficiaries of the subordination. It also may have restrictions on its ability to enforce its claims on the company. Because of its higher risk, subordinated debt normally carries higher interest rates than senior debt.

TERM STRUCTURE The maturity structure of a company's debt that determines when it has to be repaid.

UNDERWRITING AGREEMENT A contract that defines the relationship between the company seeking to sell securities and the investment banking firms conducting the sale.

VESTING AGREEMENT A contract that defines how key employees of venture-backed companies actually receive title to their equity ownership in the company. *See* Buy-back provision.

VOTING RIGHTS A contract provision that determines the rights a particular class of stock has to vote for members of the board of directors and on certain key issues facing the corporation that require a shareholder vote of approval or disapproval.

WACC The weighted average cost of capital, a measure of a firm's overall cost of capital based on the percentage values of the securities comprising its financial structure.

WARRANT A security that can be converted into or exchanged for another security, such as a corporation's common stock.

SUGGESTIONS FOR FURTHER READING

If the reader wishes more in-depth information on subjects covered in this book, two basic corporate finance texts that are relatively non-numerical and approachable are:

Brealey, Richard A., and Stewart C. Myers. *Principles of Corporate Finance* (7th ed.). New York: McGraw-Hill Irwin, 2003.

Brigham, Eugene F., and Michael E. Ehrhardt. *Financial Management: Theory and Practice* (10th ed.). Cincinnati: South-Western College Publishing, 2001.

Two books presenting the basic mechanics of financial analysis are:

Helfert, Erich A. *Techniques of Financial Analysis* (11th ed.). New York: McGraw-Hill Irwin, 2003.

Higgins, Robert C. *Analysis for Financial Management* (7th ed.). New York: McGraw-Hill Irwin, 2004.

For more specialized topics, the following books are suggested:

Bagley, Constance, and Craig Dauchy. *The Entrepreneur's Guide to Business Law.* Cincinnati: South Western College Publishing, 1998.

Benjamin, Gerald A., and John Margulis. *Angel Financing: How to Find and Invest in Private Equity.* New York: John Wiley & Sons, 1999. (This is an update of their earlier book, *Finding Your Wings.*)

Bierman, Harold, and Seymour Smidt. *The Capital Budgeting Decision: Economic Analysis of Investment Projects* (8th ed.). Englewood Cliffs, NJ: Prentice-Hall, 1993.

Gladstone, David. *Venture Capital Handbook* (rev. ed.). Englewood Cliffs, NJ: Prentice Hall, 1988.

Mancuso, Joseph R. *How to Prepare and Present a Business Plan.* Englewood Cliffs, NJ: Prentice Hall, 1992.

May, John, and Cal Simmons. *Every Business Needs An Angel: Getting the Money You Need to Grow Your Business.* New York: Crown Books, 2001.

Sherman, Andrew. *Raising Capital: Get the Money You Need to Grow Your Business.* Washington, DC: Kiplinger Books, 2000.

Sisson, Robert. *Financing the Small Business.* Acton, MA: Adams Media Corporation, 2002.

Wasserstein, Bruce. *Corporate Finance Law: A Guide for the Executive.* New York: McGraw-Hill, 1975.

The following book provides information on budgeting techniques, oriented toward the company controller:

Burton, E. James, and Steven M. Bragg. *Accounting and Finance for Your Small Business.* New York: John Wiley & Sons, 2001.

Index